The *Zondervan Essential Companion to Christian Histo*[...] page a joy to behold. But what makes this book so s[...] tells the Christian story. Facts and stories about saints, martyrs, hereti[...], missionaries fill the pages. This is a history book that reads like an adventure novel.

Richard Beck, professor at Abilene Christian University, author of *Unclean* and *Stranger God*

This gathering together of snapshots from two thousand years of church history refreshingly lets each century tell its own part of the tale; and Stephan Backhouse is a brilliant guide through the bewildering twists and turns.

David Benjamin Blower, *Nomad Podcast,* writer and musician

Backhouse describes the history of official Christendom "from above," but crucially, he also tells the story of the numerous movements renewing Christianity "from below." No history of the church is complete that does not give time to these radical reforming men and women. A brilliant and beautiful book!

Pete Greig, founder of 24-7 Prayer International; senior pastor at Emmaus Rd, Guildford; author of *Dirty Glory*

This volume is an invaluable resource for anyone looking for a compact yet remarkably comprehensive summary of Christian history. It includes a welcome emphasis on a global perspective, as well as highlighting the role of women in relation to many of the key developments in the church. It comes highly recommended.

Lucy Peppiatt, principal of Westminster Theological Centre

Rich, concise, and built for our most dynamic leaders (who will never darken the door of a seminary), this short volume is Backhouse's latest masterpiece tool for the local church. If locally-deployed church planters knew their history, they would be far less likely to repeat its mistakes.

Graham Singh, executive director of Church Planting Canada, rector of St. Jax Montreal

This book is well-named. It is indeed an essential companion to those entering into the study of church history. It gives students an outstanding way of orienting themselves, putting the towering figures of history into their social and theological contexts. It is full of helpful detail without being overwhelming, and it is written in a clear and engaging style, which draws the student in, teaching without daunting them.

Jane Williams, assistant dean and tutor in theology, St. Mellitus College

ESSENTIAL

ZONDERVAN COMPANION TO
CHRISTIAN HISTORY

Also by Stephen Backhouse

Kierkegaard: A Single Life
Kierkegaard's Critique of Christian Nationalism

STEPHEN BACKHOUSE

ZONDERVAN ESSENTIAL COMPANION TO CHRISTIAN HISTORY

ZONDERVAN

Zondervan Essential Companion to Christian History
Copyright © 2019 by Stephen Backhouse

ISBN 978-0-310-59948-7 (softcover)

ISBN 978-0-310-59949-4 (ebook)

Requests for information should be addressed to:
Zondervan, *3900 Sparks Dr. SE, Grand Rapids, Michigan 49546*

Maps created by International Mapping. Copyright © by Zondervan. All rights reserved.

Cover design: RAM Creative
Cover photos: Photodisc; iStockphoto; Unsplash; Pexels; South African Tourism/Wikimedia Commons, CC BY 2.0;
  Ayasofya Muzesi/Wikimedia Commons, CC BY 3.0
Interior design: Kait Lamphere
Images in front matter and rear matter: © diak/Shutterstock, © Peter Zaharov/Shutterstock, © OSORIOartist/Shutterstock
Editorial: Katya Covrett, Elise Emmert, Robert Hudson

Printed in China

19 20 21 22 23 24 25 26 27 28 29 /WPC/ 20 19 18 17 16 15 14 13 12 11 10 9 8 7 6 5 4 3 2 1

To Francesca, Alexander, Rumi, Elijah,
Emilia, Sean, Evelyn, Keziah, Daniel,
Emmanuelle, Karyss, and Elena

CONTENTS

SERVANTS AND LEADERS: 1–100

Once upon a time in first-century Roman-occupied Palestine, an itinerant Jewish teacher began to attract attention for his surprising statements about God, his radical approach to religion and politics, and his healing care for the poor, lonely, and sick. His message offended the ruling authorities, and he was executed. Shortly thereafter, his followers began to claim that their leader was not dead but had been raised to life. What is more, they began to make startling claims about the divine nature of this man whose influence continued to animate their growing communities. It began to dawn on these people that this man Jesus was not only God's "Messiah" or "Christ"—a saviour awaited by the Jews who was expected to bring God's kingdom on earth—he was also, in some mysterious way, God himself in human form.

Jesus Christ's main message was that the kingdom of God was not only near, it was *here*. His followers taught that through Jesus, forgiveness of sin, reconciliation with God, and membership of this kingdom were open to all.

Citizenship in this kingdom came with its own set of freedoms, rights, and responsibilities: a new spiritual reality that had practical, social consequences. Belief in the God who became Man and belief in the values of his kingdom provided the twin drives for the new movement that came to be known as *Christianity*.

Christians have not always been true to their namesake, and the societies they produce have not always expressed the best of their values. Yet time and again Christianity has inspired heroic men and women to work against their own best interest, and against the common sense of their culture, in the service of others. Christendom's kings have started wars, and its merchants have traded in exploitation, while its peacemakers have brought down tyrannies and its scientists have cured diseases. Acts of deepest folly can be found alongside work of the highest wisdom: the same century that saw the first Crusades also saw the creation of the first universities and hospitals of the modern tradition. Christendom's thinkers provided the foundation for the philosophical ideas that continue to shape modern life. Its artists, writers, and musicians account for many of the world's cultural treasures. From the start, the various communities of Christ have displayed a vibrancy, originality, stubbornness, flexibility, ferocity, and gentleness unparalleled in history.

In the telling of this story, certain themes can be traced throughout the centuries. One recurring motif is that of martyrdom. Christianity began with a crucifixion, and persecution of Christ's followers remains a constant reality worldwide. Indeed, more people have been killed for their Christian faith in the modern age than at any other time in history. The reality of martyrdom is closely related to another common theme, that of the ambiguous relationship between Christians and their countries. From Constantine to Charlemagne, Kublai Khan to King Henry VIII, from Russian tsars to American presidents, the story of Christendom is, in many ways, the story of the state seeking to control, manage, or harness the power of Christianity. Another key theme is that of internal restoration. Wherever Christian institutions have become too much like the world around them, reform movements are never far behind. Historically, Christians have often proven to be the fiercest critics of Christendom.

Christianity is the most diffuse faith on earth. Its followers are widespread, its ideas profound, and its implications far-reaching. As a result, Christianity has provoked dissent as much as it has inspired emulation, and for this reason it is apparent that a history of Christianity is also, in many ways, a history of the modern world itself. The whole history of Christianity can never be told, as the full, real story lies in the day-to-day lives of men and women who lived

▲ The oldest known Christ Pantocrator, at St. Catherine's Monastery, sixth-seventh century AD

Z. Radovan/BibleLandPictures.com

the faith and transmitted it to others, keeping alive traditions and customs that would shape future generations. While not a total history, this book provides a guide through the whirlwind of extraordinary people, ideas, events of war, and pursuits of peace that have come to the attention of historians and that have shaped the major contours of Christian thought and practice throughout the world.

c. 40–44

- *Christians* (meaning "Christ's ones") first used in Antioch, probably as a pejorative term.
- Christianity develops as a contentious movement within Judaism. Stephen becomes the first Christian martyr. The apostle Peter is imprisoned and questioned by the Judean king, Herod Agrippa.
- Peter possibly in Rome.
- After his conversion experience, Saul of Tarsus adopts the name Paul and ceases persecuting the Christian sect.

c. 59–61

Paul in Rome.

c. 58

Paul writes his Epistle to the Romans to a church already well established in Rome.

30   40   50   60

c. 30

Crucifixion of Jesus, called by his Jewish disciples the *Christ* (meaning "Messiah" or "anointed one"). Shortly thereafter, the disciples begin to claim publicly that Jesus had risen to life and that this resurrection was a sign of the present reality and future hope of the kingdom of God. Their message is met with resistance in Jerusalem but also attracts many followers to the Way of Christ.

c. 47–57

- The apostle Paul active in Arabia, Tarsus, Cyprus, central Asia Minor, Macedonia, Corinth, Ephesus, and elsewhere, preaching primarily to non-Jewish gentiles.
- Jerusalem and Antioch are major bases for the movement. The word *church* (from the Greek meaning "assembled for a common purpose") is in common usage.

▲ The Crucifixion, altarpiece of San Martino

Gianni Dagli Orti/Shutterstock

▲ Paul Preaching at Athens, from the Sistine Chapel

Wikimedia Commons

📖 THE EARLIEST CHRISTIANS

Almost all the information that we have about the earliest Christians comes from their documents and letters collected together as the New Testament. Thus, the historical study of the first church is necessarily a matter for biblical scholars. The subject has attracted much attention and debate over the years, especially around the dating of the Gospels, with most scholars proposing dates ranging from before c. 70 to the late 90s.

▲ The interior of Karanlik Kilise in Goreme, Turkey, with fresco decorations   firdes sayilan/123RF.com

70   **80**   **90**   **100**

c. 70

Romans occupy Jerusalem and destroy the Jewish temple, creating a diaspora of Jews and Christians.

c. 96

Bishop Clement of Rome's *First Epistle* accepts Paul's letters as Scripture along with the Hebrew Old Testament.

c. 64

The term *Christian* is in common circulation by the time Emperor Nero (37–68) institutes the first official state persecution. According to tradition, Peter and Paul were among those martyred at this time. The fierceness of Nero's persecution and the behaviour of the Christians in the face of injustice are said to have provoked feelings of sympathy and admiration amongst the wider Roman population.

c. 81–96

The book of Revelation (the final book in the New Testament) most likely addresses churches under persecution by Emperor Domitian (c. 51–96).

LOVE AND COURAGE: 100–200

As the first generations of Christians passed away, the followers of Christ in the second century found themselves having to deal with the issue of legitimate authority. Who best preserved the message of Jesus and his apostles? As the new movement explored the depths of Christian thought, some groups radically diverged from the original teaching, spreading ideas that continue to divide Christianity to the present day. Christians also looked for ways to communicate the new theology to a world that was largely hostile: persecution and martyrdom form the backdrop to Christianity's development throughout this era.

Obstinate Atheists

By 100, Trajan (53–117) had been emperor of the Roman Empire for two years. In 111 he received the first of a series of letters from Pliny the Younger (c. 62–115), governor of Bithynia. Pliny was concerned about a new, "obstinate" religious group active in his region.

These people refused to incorporate local gods into their worship, he said, and they did not partake in the cult of the emperor. Although they were good citizens in other respects, their refusal to treat the emperor as a god was worrying. Since they did not worship any of the publicly available deities, these Christians were deemed to be atheists. And atheists are an unstable, subversive element to any society that requires displays of civic religion for the smooth running of that society. Trajan counselled that care should be taken over prosecution and that anonymous accusations of Christianity should not be accepted; however, he advised Pliny not to tolerate the obstinate religion.

The Way

But this subversive sect was growing. By the opening of the century, of the estimated 60 million of the known world's population, approximately 7,500 belonged to "the Way" of Christ. Their communities dotted the Roman

The long title of this work (which means "Teaching") is "The Teaching of the Lord, through the Twelve Apostles, to the Gentiles." The exact date is contested, but many scholars place it c. 100, making it the oldest Christian writing outside of the New Testament. The piece offers a window into earliest church culture, including instruction on the Way of Life and the Way of Death, early forms of the Lord's Prayer, and Eucharistic and baptismal liturgies. A Trinitarian formula is also present, as is instruction for the right way to deal with travelling prophets and residential teachers.

▲ In order to escape persecution, the early Christians often worshipped in rooms and tunnels carved from the underground, much like these catacombs at Kom al-Shuqafa, Alexandria.   Gianni Dagli Orti/Shutterstock

Empire and beyond. By 115 there were reports that Christianity had reached Edessa, outside of the empire's eastern border. The Christians met regularly in the houses of their richer members— textile merchants, Roman soldiers, and those in other professions. Organised under a network of deacons and bishops, they communicated with each other through travelling preachers and a robust exchange of letters, written instructions, and histories about their Jewish founder, Jesus Christ. Yet despite all this it was clear that not everyone agreed on what it meant to be "Christian."

Legitimate Authority

One of the most prominent church leaders of the early second century was Clement, bishop (or "pope") of Rome (active c. 96). The third man to hold this office after the apostle Peter, Clement wrote documents that offer a window

▲ Statue of Emperor Trajan in Rome

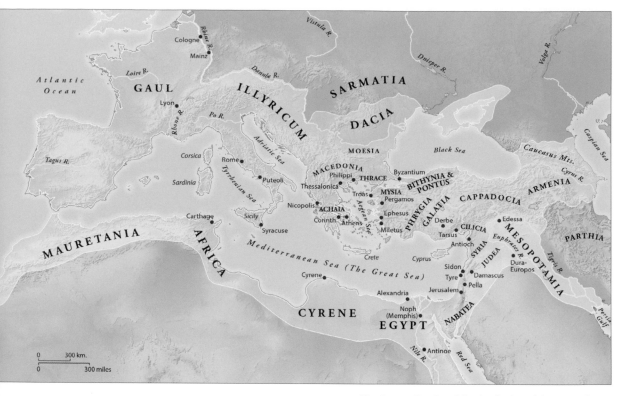

CLEMENS · I · PP · ROMANUS

into the issues faced by the Christian church of his day. His *First Epistle to the Corinthians* (written c. 96) addresses fierce inter-church factions, demands the reinstatement of deposed presbyters, and calls for a return to obedience of legitimate church authorities.

Legitimate authority was a key issue for the early church. For Ignatius, bishop of Antioch (c. 50–c. 98/117), unity under the care of proper authority was essential. It is probably from Ignatius that we first have the idea of a catholic ("universal") church. Ignatius insisted that without the action of the bishop, both marriage and the Eucharist were invalid. These practices were important because for Ignatius, bodies were important. Marriage affirms sex and birth,

▲ The Christian church in the first and second centuries

Legend:
- Extent of Christian Church, 1st century AD
- • Significant Christian community, 1st century AD
- Extent of Christian Church, 2nd century AD
- ◆ Significant Christian community, 2nd century AD
- ◆ Significant Chirstian community in both 1st and 2nd centuries

families, and hospitality. The Eucharist is a celebration of the life of Christ, who was both divine and human. With his affirmation of the physical and material, Ignatius joins the ranks of other church leaders concerned to counter the most potent of the contemporary rival claims to Christian authority and authenticity: Gnosticism.

Gnosticism

Flourishing in Alexandria and Egypt since the first decades of the second century, the various Gnostic groups claimed secret knowledge (or *gnosis*) handed down from the apostles. Apart from their claim to know more than what was

THE *SHEPHERD OF HERMAS*

A freed slave who later became a rich merchant before losing his fortune, Hermas was most likely a contemporary of Clement; however, some scholars date his work between 140 and 155. In any case, the *Shepherd* combines mystical visions with practical teaching, emphasising that even sins committed after baptism can be forgiven. The work was so popular and so influential that churches in the East considered it part of Scripture in the second and third centuries.

freely available in the Gospels and the Epistles, a further challenge came by way of the Gnostic distinction between the material and the spiritual worlds. Gnosticism demonizes matter by claiming that the world was created by an evil god (the Demiurge) and that the (secret) message of Christ is the only way to escape to the pure, spiritual realm. There are many bewildering Gnostic variations, but all tend to share two main features: the first is that because the Jews worship the Creator God, Gnostics seek to purge all Jewish influence from their own thought. The other main feature is that Gnostics are unwilling and unable to affirm the bodily incarnation of Jesus Christ. They argue instead for Docetism, the view that Jesus only appeared to be human.

▲ The Temple of Esna, a second-century shrine located on the banks of the Nile in Egypt.　　Public Domain

MARCION (C. 85–C. 160)

The Gnostic Marcion of Sinope was declared a heretic and excommunicated from the church in Rome in 144. Marcion denied that Christ was born of a woman or that his body was material. He rejected the Hebrew Scriptures as irrelevant to the new revelation of Christ, and he rejected the original apostles as being too Jewish to understand Jesus correctly. The debate with Marcion catalysed Christian thinking about the relationship between the Old and New Testaments and paved the way for the eventual formation of the Christian canon.

Apologetics

Christian claims were also a challenge to Roman and Greek philosophy. Aristides of Athens (?–c. 140) is thought to have written the first Christian *Apology*, reportedly presented to Emperor Hadrian in 125. Aristides helped set the pattern for much of Christian apologetics by attempting to prove the existence of God. He also addressed the limits of other worldviews, demonstrating how Christianity meets the moral and intellectual demands that other systems fail to meet.

Justin Martyr

Another early apologist, Justin (c. 100–c. 165) was the first writer to systematically combine the claims of faith and reason. Born into a pagan family, Justin converted to Christianity in 130, after which he embarked on a teaching career in Ephesus and started a school in Rome. His *First Apology* (c. 155) was written for Emperor Pius and argues that Christianity is the most rational philosophy. His *Second Apology* addresses the Roman Senate, again attempting to refute the rational objections to Christian life and thought.

▲ Justin Martyr taught the connection between philosophy and theology. He was killed for his faith.

Tupungato/Shutterstock

as the bishop of Smyrna, was Polycarp (c. 69–c. 156). A leading light of the second-century church, Polycarp is said to have been appointed bishop by the original apostles, and his *Epistle to the Philippians* (c. 116) provides insight into early Christian use of apostolic literature. But it was the *Martyrdom of Polycarp* (*Martyrium Polycarpi*), a book recounting Polycarp's trial and death by burning and stabbing in c. 156, that perhaps had the most lasting influence on the Christianity of the second and third centuries.

Cult of Martyrs

The story of Polycarp's last days became the standard for other martyr accounts, known as the *Acta* ("acts"). They emphasised both the graphic details of the martyr's execution and the holy, Christlike way in which the martyr went to his or her death. The common practice of venerating the martyr's bones began with Polycarp too, when his preserved remains formed the focus of an annual event celebrating the "birthday" of his martyrdom. This was the beginning of the era known as the "Cult of Martyrs," in which some Christians enthusiastically embraced persecution and many more revered the martyrs as attaining the heights of spiritual perfection.

Although his writings would later go on to be foundational works of Christian literature, they were not immediately successful in convincing pagan Rome, and Justin was martyred by beheading sometime around 165.

Martyrdom of Polycarp

Justin's fate at the hands of the state was not rare. Ignatius was martyred in Rome in 107. By 124, official persecutions had increased under Emperor Hadrian, leading to the execution of Telesphorus, bishop of Rome, in 137. Also sometimes active in Rome, but known primarily

Stoic Persecution

After Polycarp's death, a campaign of intense persecution of Christians took place under Emperor Marcus Aurelius. Since he was a Stoic philosopher, many Christians had hoped that Aurelius would give their religion a fair hearing, and apologists such as Justin addressed books to him. Yet Aurelius remained convinced that

▲ The remains of the Arch of Marcus Aurelius, Tripoli, Libya, dating from AD 163

Patrick Poendl/123RF.com

Christianity was an internal threat to Roman society. Rome at this time was troubled by wars, invasion by the Parthians (163–166), repeated attacks from northern Germanic tribes (166–180), a plague (166–167), and revolts in Syria and Egypt (175). In these times of unrest, superstitious populations were keen to find someone to blame, and often it was the "atheistic" Christians who drew their anger. Aurelius allowed his regional rulers to step up their attacks on local Christian groups.

Martyrs of Lyons

One such attack happened in Lyons in 177 when the governor executed all Christians who did not recant. The purge resulted in the capture and public execution of some forty-eight people, including the ninety-year-old Bishop Pothinus (c. 87–177) who was starved and then stoned to death.

BLANDINA (DATES UNKNOWN)

A slave girl, Blandina was one of the Martyrs of Lyons in 177. Although frail and weak after a period of starvation, she is said to have endured tortures that left even her tormentors tired and in need of a rest. When she was hung out on a pole as bait for wild animals, Blandina's fellow Christians took heart as they saw in her "him who was crucified for them." Finally, Blandina was scourged, burnt, tied up, and thrown into a ring where she was trampled to death by a bull. Her story is recounted in *The Letter of the Churches of Vienne and Lyons*, collected by Eusebius of Caesarea (c. 260–341).

MARCIA (DATES UNKNOWN)

Christians fared slightly better under Emperor Commodus (ruler from 180 to 192) than they did under his father, Aurelius. This was due in large part to the influence of Commodus's concubine, Marcia. She sought to benefit Christians and used her position at court to bring them favour. In one instance, Marcia ensured the release of Christians sentenced to penal slavery in Sardinia, including Callistus, a future pope.

◄ The Alexamenos graffito, one of the earliest depictions of Jesus's crucifixion, shows a man worshipping a donkey-headed figure. The graffiti reads, "Alexamenos worships his God," apparently mocking a Christian named Alexamenos.

Z. Radovan/BibleLandPictures.com

The First Catholic

The church was in disarray, leading to the election of Irenaeus (c. 130–c. 202) as the new bishop of Lyons in 178. Irenaeus is widely considered to be the first great Catholic writer and pastor. He mediated disputes between the Eastern and Western Churches and developed strong ties with Gaelic-speaking barbarian tribes. His rule of apostolic origin meant that it was bishops, not scholars or itinerant preachers, who had prime authority in the church, for their office was inherited from the original disciples. He upheld the Old Testament as Scripture and defended the four Gospels as canon. Irenaeus is primarily known for his battle with Gnosticism, and his most important work is called *Against Heresies* (*Adversus Haereses*, c. 185).

Carthage

Persecution was widespread, and not confined to the western reaches of the Roman Empire. One of the earliest African Christian documents is the *Acta of the Scillitan Martyrs*. Five women and seven men were executed at Scillium, near Carthage, in 180 on charges primarily related to the accusation that as Christians they owed allegiance to a Lord who was higher than emperors or kings. Accounts suggest that the martyrs enjoyed popular local support, and indeed, North Africa was a major centre of Christianity. Christians in Carthage were not allowed to own land in the city, but they had established a Christian graveyard outside the boundaries, and the Carthaginian Church was a leader in Christian life and thought. The African church father Tertullian (c. 160–c. 225) grew up in Carthage and joined the church there after his

THE MURATORIAN CANON

Named after the man who discovered the manuscript in 1740, the "Muratorian Fragment" is the oldest known list and overview of the canonical books in the New Testament. The original was probably written in Rome sometime between 180 and 200. The incomplete document describes twenty-two of the twenty-seven books in the New Testament and is an invaluable source for historians of the biblical canon. It provides a window into the writings used, and not used, by the early church.

conversion from paganism. Writing in Latin rather than the traditional Greek, Tertullian was a master of communication who aimed his writings at sophisticated Roman audiences.

Alexandria

In the Egyptian metropolis of Alexandria, Christianity seems to have emerged out of the strong Jewish community, perhaps at the instigation of Mark the Evangelist. Alexandria was known as a centre for religious ferment, and many cults jostled for attention. Much of Alexandrian Christian culture was strongly influenced by Gnosticism, and it is probable that the Gnostic texts *Epistle of Barnabas*, *The Gospel of the Egyptians*, and *The Gospel to the Hebrews*

▲ Patio of a Roman villa, Odeon Quarter, Carthage, Tunisia

Wikimedia Commons

▶ Tertullian, the premier North African theologian, is considered to be the father of Latin Christianity.

Historia/Shutterstock

all emerged from here. Orthodox Christianity also had a presence, represented most strongly by Clement of Alexandria (c. 150–c. 215).

The First Theologian

Said to come originally from Athens, Clement became head of the Catechetical School in the city in 190. The school taught Christianity as the true philosophy to advanced scholars but also trained new converts (*catechumens*) in preparation for full acceptance into the church. A flavour of their education can be seen in the trilogy of texts produced by Clement during his time as head of the school. *The Exhortation to the Greeks* (*Protreptikos*), *The Instructor* (*Paidagogos*), and *The Miscellanies* (*Stromateis*) engage with pagan Greek philosophy on one side and Gnostic Christian thought on the other. The books are not concerned simply with theory and often stress the moral discipline and duties that follow from Christian claims.

For this reason, Clement is sometimes regarded as the first self-conscious theologian and ethicist.

Clement was forced to flee his school, along with many other Christians in Alexandria and Carthage, because of a rash of local discrimination campaigns that flourished under the new African-born emperor Septimus Severus—a period of persecution that began at the close of the century in 199.

CHURCH FATHERS

Tertullian's *Apology* (c. 197) marks the high point of second-century writing and is considered to be the source of the Latin Christian literary tradition. Cyprian called Tertullian his "master," as did Augustine. Together, these three North Africans are considered to be the fathers of the Western churches.

EASTER

The early church was faced with a problem. Should Easter be celebrated according to the time of Passover in the lunar Jewish calendar, or was the solar, gentile "Julian" calendar more appropriate? The older traditions of Asia Minor celebrated the Christian *pascha* according to the Jewish date for Passover (called *Quartodeciman* because it fell on the fourteenth day after the spring full moon). The gentile Roman Christians held out for celebrating Easter on the Sunday following the spring equinox. The conflict mattered because it touched on the centrality of the resurrection of Jesus for Christian belief.

Furthermore, in addition to representing the division that had existed between Jewish and gentile Christians since the earliest days of Christianity (see, for example, Galatians 2:1–21), the conflict highlighted the emerging differences between East and West. Sensing a challenge to Roman authority, the African pope Victor I (presided 189–198) threatened to excommunicate the Quartodecimans, a move opposed by Irenaeus of Lyons. The search for a uniform method for establishing the calendar date of Easter was picked up again at the First Council of Nicaea in 325, but even today the date for Easter varies between Eastern and Western traditions.

3
MARTYRS AND HERETICS: 200–300

Persecutions continued throughout the third century, leading to the creation of both martyrs and apostates and to the question of their respective places in the hierarchy of church life. Further problems of order and authority were heightened by the rise of major heretical movements that would shape Christian thought for centuries to come. Despite these troubles, third-century Christianity witnessed the activity of some of its most prominent church fathers and expanded farther into the deserts and cities of the Roman Empire and beyond.

Authority of Martyrs

In a renewed effort to consolidate power throughout his empire, part of Emperor Septimus Severus's campaign was to ban conversion to Judaism and Christianity. Caught up in the wave of new persecutions in 203 was a group of catechumens in Carthage. *The Passion of Perpetua and Felicitas* describes the martyrdom of two women

📖 MONTANISM

Founded by Montanus (dates unknown, c. 170), the prophetic movement that took his name flourished in the early third century. Montanists were famous for their strict asceticism and their claim that they received direct revelations from God. Women held prominent leadership positions, the most famous being the prophets Maximilla and Priscilla (dates unknown). The Montanists do not seem to have been doctrinal heretics, but they clashed with Catholic Christianity over the Montanist belief that spiritual ecstasy overrode the prophet's own rational mind. Tertullian became a Montanist in 208.

▶ The Arch of Septimius Severus stands at the entrance of the Roman citadel of Leptis Magna in modern-day Libya. Severus was born here in 146.

Jan Hazevoet/Wikimedia Commons, CC BY 3.0

▲ Perpetua, noblewoman, church leader, and Christian martyr
Wikimedia Commons

in this group, the noble-born Perpetua and the slave girl Felicitas. The document is important because it provides first-hand accounts of prison life and also offers insight into the lives of Christian women in the third century, who, like Perpetua, often assumed leadership roles within the house-church communities.

The *Passion* also sheds light on internal church conflicts of the day. Questions of official authority, as well as debate over the role that the new martyrs were having in the shaping of Christian belief, are evident from the text—in one scene, the martyred Perpetua is depicted as resolving a dispute between a presbyter and his bishop. The unknown editor was a Montanist, and the book argues that through martyrs such as these, the work of the Holy Spirit was continuing in ways as significant as those recounted in the Scriptures.

Early Church Order

Different groups of Christians varied in the degree to which they accorded authority to martyrs, women, and wandering prophets, not to mention deacons, presbyters, and bishops. An example of early attempts to conserve church order and structure comes by way of the Greek bishop Hippolytus (?–c. 236) and his *Apostolic Tradition* (c. 220). Despite facing a large number of converts, Hippolytus opposed relaxing the penitential system, by which new catechumens were only allowed to participate in Communion after a rigorous time of teaching, confession, and discipline. The *Tradition* also reveals the strict hierarchy of ordinands and other ministers, and it details the standard rites of baptism, Eucharist, and other liturgical practices prevalent in the third-century Roman Church.

MANICHAEISM

Probably the most persistent of the heretical Gnostic movements, Manichaeism showed evidence in China in the tenth century, as well as continued influence into the medieval and modern eras. The teaching of Manes of Persia (c. 216–276) centred on belief in a primal conflict between Light and Darkness. Satan was supposed to have trapped particles of light within each human body, and it was the purpose of religion to release the pure spirit from its corrupt matter. Jesus, Buddha, the Prophets, and Manes were all helpers in this task.

▲ Origen, teacher and theologian, was the most prolific author in antiquity.　　Wikimedia Commons

Origen

It was in this church context of speculative thought and rigid structures that Origen (c. 185–251) lived and worked. His father, an Egyptian Christian named Leonidas, was executed under the persecutions of Septimus Severus in 201, and Origen was set to die alongside him until saved by his mother. Following his old teacher Clement, Origen served as head of the Catechetical School in Alexandria for twenty-eight years. A Greek father of the church, he was perhaps the most prolific writer of antiquity, with some reports attributing to him between 800 and 2,000 works. These include the first works of serious biblical textual commentary such as the *Hexapla* (c. 230), a parallel translation of the Old Testament written in six languages. Another essential work is *De Principiis*, one of the first systematic theologies in Christian history.

The Decian Persecution

Origen died in 251 after suffering imprisonment and torture as one of the final victims of the persecution of Decius. When Emperor Decius came to power in 249 he had intentionally adopted the name "Trajan Decius" in emulation of his successor's success at defending pagan Rome against the atheists. The Decian campaign was the first empire-wide persecution, and the bloodiest yet for Christians. When Decius was struck down in battle in 251, many Christians took this as a judgement from God and rejoiced. The persecution campaign may have been short-lived, but the consequences were far-reaching, for while the Decian persecution had produced many martyrs, it had created many more apostates.

DENYS

French martyr Denys (Dionysius) was the first bishop of Paris and is the patron saint of France. He was put to death at Montmartre (Martyr's Hill) in Paris in the second half of the third century

▲ Martyrdom of St. Denys, patron saint of France. Denys is seen receiving his last Holy Communion on the left, and on the right is being decapitated.

Wikimedia Commons

▼ The Basilica of Sacre Coeur built in the nineteenth century, Montmartre, Paris. It marks the place of the martyrdom of Denys (Dionysius), the first bishop of Paris, who was executed here c. 250.

Petr Kovalenkov/123RF.com

Lapsed Christians

After the period of intense persecution, by 251 the seat of the pope had been vacant for fourteen months. Cornelius was elected pope, and he served for two years before his death in 253. Cornelius was faced with the problem of what to do with all the members of his flock who had given in to persecution. For one thing, it was unclear what counted as a lapse. Did giving over Christian Scriptures and letters to the authorities count as apostasy? What about those who publicly renounced Christ but privately continued to worship? Were people who fled persecution equally as culpable as those who recanted their faith under pain of torture? Faced with such difficulties, Bishop Cornelius adopted a lenient position towards apostates, welcoming them back into the church.

Novatian

Cornelius was opposed by the presbyter and theologian Novatian (c. 200–258), who held a much more rigorist stance. Novatian did not allow for any concessions to be made to lapsed Christians. Eventually consecrated bishop as a direct rival to

NOVATIANISTS

The schismatic movement founded by Novatian continued well into the fifth century. Rigorous in their denunciation of compromising Christians, the group was doctrinally orthodox though they remained excommunicated from the Roman Church.

ON CATHOLIC UNITY

Written by Cyprian in 251, *On Catholic Unity* (*De Catholicae Ecclesiae Unitate*), a series of pastoral treatises and letters, provides a highly important resource for historians interested in early church life and structure. The book is practically minded, concerned more with administration and pastoral issues than with innovative theology. It affirms the system of apostolic succession for bishops over and against inauthentic schismatic churches.

LIBELLI PACIS

Some Christians obtained *Libelli Pacis* ("Letters of Peace") certificates in order to avoid persecution. The documents stated that the bearer had made the necessary sacrifices to the gods. Often no sacrifice had actually taken place, and the papers had merely been purchased from the civil authorities.

PLAGUE IN CARTHAGE

In 252 a severe plague struck the city of Carthage. The outbreak evoked widespread anti-Christian feeling, prompting church leaders to argue publicly that Christianity does not cause natural catastrophes. At the same time, Cyprian wrote a series of pastoral letters exhorting his fellow Christians to continue to help the dying and provide relief for those affected by the disaster.

Cornelius, Novatian established a separate church for those who refused to allow apostates back into the fold. He himself was martyred in 258 following the renewed campaign of Emperor Valerian.

Cyprian

The effects of apostasy were also being felt in North Africa. Cyprian (?–258) had been a pagan philosopher before converting to Christianity in c. 246 and became bishop of Carthage two years later. He fled the Decian persecution in 249 and only returned to his post after Decius's death in 251, a move that was seen with suspicion by his opponents, many of whom had stayed to face the persecution.

The Problem of Rebaptism

Cyprian was opposed to lenient treatment of the lapsed or those who had purchased their way out of persecution, but he did allow for them to return to the church after a period of penance. At the same time, the excommunication of the Novatianists had given rise to another, related problem: Were baptisms conducted by schismatics valid? Cyprian thought not, and in 255 demanded that anyone baptised by a schismatic or heretic be rebaptised in order to enjoy full communion with the true church. In turn, this drew criticism from Stephen I (?–257), who had been made pope of Rome in 254. Stephen held that as the sacraments drew their validation from God, their worth was not dependent on the standing of the priest who administered them. A series of significant letters between the two bishops followed, but the debate was cut short when Stephen died in 257 and Cyprian was martyred during the Valerian persecution a year later.

The First Toleration

Emperor of Rome from 253 to 260, Valerian ruled over an empire stricken by civil war and threats from Persia in the east and barbarian tribes in the north. To placate the Roman gods, Valerian issued edicts in 257 and 258 outlawing and executing Christian clergy, purging Christians from the upper classes of society, and banning Christian assemblies.

To help manage his unwieldy empire, Valerian set up his son Gallienus as his co-emperor, charging him with responsibility in the west. When Valerian was captured by Persian forces in 260, Gallienus assumed control of the entire empire. That same year he reversed his father's policy of persecution and issued the first Edict of Toleration of Christianity. The edict restored bishops to their churches, allowed burial in Christian cemeteries, and halted the practice of forcing Christians to publicly worship Roman civic deities. Christians interpreted Valerian's defeat and Gallienus's actions as God's protection of his followers. Although toleration was a welcome relief, Gallienus's edict was not due to conversion on his part. Instead, it was a pragmatic decision made to halt his father's failed empire-wide policy. Local persecutions continued to occur.

Desert Hermits

Sometime around 269 in Egypt, a wealthy Coptic man gave away all his possessions and withdrew to live in the desert. The long-lived Anthony (c. 251–356) was not the first hermit to pursue a life of religious solitude, but he was one of the first to do so for Christian reasons. A major figure in early Egyptian monasticism,

WEST AND EAST

Valerian's innovation of dividing the Roman Empire into western and eastern jurisdictions set a precedent that would have lasting consequences for the history of Christianity, with the eventual establishment of the Church of Rome in the West and the Church of Constantinople in the East.

DIONYSIUS (?–268)

Dionysius became pope in Rome in 260. One of the most important bishops of this era, Dionysius helped to restore church order after the decimations of the Valerian persecution. His letters reveal a pastoral concern for the bishops under his care.

SYNAXARIUM

Synaxarium is a list of saints and their dates of death used by the Oriental Orthodox churches. The large number of Diocletian martyrs commemorated in this list attests to the severity of the persecutions against the Coptic Church, a time known as the Era of Martyrs.

Anthony wrote little and spoke only Coptic. Nevertheless, his simple life and reputed wisdom attracted many followers. In 285 Anthony withdrew even further from society but was found again by others who wished to live as hermits.

▲ The desert hermits lived in structures similar to these rooms cut from the rock cliffs in Bilad el-Rum, Siwah Oasis, Egypt.   Nicholas J. Saunders/Shutterstock

These anchorite communities flourished in the deserts of Egypt and Syria, established monasticism as a viable Christian option, and helped lay the foundations for the future distinctive Coptic Church of the fourth and fifth centuries.

In later years, the Coptic Church would come to date their era as beginning in 284, for this was the year that Emperor Diocletian came to power. The instigator of the Great Persecution, in 303 Diocletian would unleash the most organised and extensive campaign against Christians yet seen in Roman civilisation.

VALENTINE

There are several martyrs called Valentine, but little is known of why their lives should be connected to the modern-day romantic celebration that bears the same name. Valentine of Rome was a priest, beaten and beheaded and buried on the *Via Flaminia* (the most important road northwards out of Rome) in c. 269. Also buried on the same road is Bishop Valentine of Terni, martyred sometime at the beginning of the century.

ESTABLISHMENT AND RESISTANCE: 300-400

Second only to the first century, the fourth century is arguably the most influential in the history of Christianity. This is when Christianity became the official religion of the Roman Empire, when the foundational creeds were formulated, the biblical canon finalised, major monastic movements established, and when the main strands of the Christian church shaped. The four doctors of the church were also active at this time.

The Era of Martyrs

In 303 and 304 Emperor Diocletian ordered that all churches be torn down, Bibles burnt, and clergy tortured. Diocletian abdicated in 305, but the persecutions continued until 312.

The Donatist Movement

In 311 Caecillian (?–c. 345) was made bishop of Carthage. The Great Persecution had hit North Africa hard, with many Christians exiled or killed and many more traditors ("the ones who handed over") forced to give up their writings and holy texts to be burnt by the authorities.

One such traditor had consecrated Caecillian. As a result, the rigorist church party claimed that Caecillian's position was invalid. Eventually, a bishop named Donatus Magnus (?–355) assumed the rival seat, lending the schismatic group its name.

▲ Emperor Diocletian is depicted along with three other rulers: Maximian, Galerius, and Constantius. A Roman Syrian work of the fourth century, the statue now adorns the Basilica of St. Marco in Venice. anshar/Shutterstock

The debate was not a new one for Christianity. What made the Donatist controversy singular is that it was the first to attract intervention from the new emperor.

Emperor Constantine

The son of Constantius Chlorus and Helena, Constantine (c. 273–337) was proclaimed emperor during a campaign in York in 306. However, it was not until 312 and the battle of Milvian Bridge that Constantine was able to secure the throne along with his co-emperor Licinius.

Before entering the fray, Constantine is reputed to have had a vision of the cross of Christ leading his soldiers into battle, and he consequently adopted the Labarum as his military standard. Constantine's victory soon led to toleration of the church, which in turn would lead to the favouring of Christianity as the pre-eminent religion of Rome.

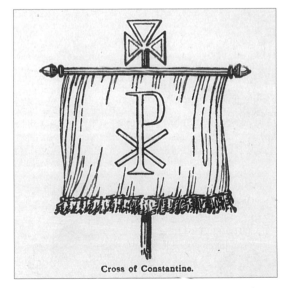

Cross of Constantine.

▲ The labarum—Constantine's symbol composed of a Christian monogram incorporating the Greek letters X and P, the first two letters of the Greek for "Christ" (ΧΡΙΣΤΟΣ)

Public Domain

 ALBAN (DATES UNKNOWN)

The first known British martyr, Alban is traditionally thought to have died c. 303 during the Great Persecution. A pagan who converted to Christianity when he offered shelter to a missionary, Alban volunteered to die in the priest's place.

 CATHERINE OF ALEXANDRIA (C. 285–C. 305)

According to tradition, Catherine was a scholar and virgin martyred in Alexandria c. 305. Celebrated in the East and West, Catherine was a popular object of devotion in the Middle Ages. Her symbol is a spiked wheel—the instrument of torture upon which she was killed.

▶ Catherine of Alexandria by Caravaggio   Planet Art

📖 *ECCLESIASTICAL HISTORY*

Bishop Eusebius of Caesarea (c. 265–c. 339) completed the first major work of Christian history in 325. His *History* is invaluable as it preserves documents and stories found nowhere else.

The Edict of Milan

In 313 Licinius and Constantine met at Milan and agreed upon a course of action that has since come to be called the Edict of Milan. The policy gave legal standing to Christian churches, granting toleration to all religions in the empire and bringing an end to the Great Persecution.

Although toleration at this time did not officially grant Christianity favoured status, it is clear that Constantine took a great interest in the Christian religion. Constantine's strategy

HELENA (C. 255–C. 330)

The mother of Emperor Constantine, Helena held a prominent position of authority in the Roman Empire. She was a passionate supporter of Christianity and led a significant excursion to the Holy Land in 326 where she founded major churches on the Mount of Olives and in Bethlehem. Helena is also known for collecting relicts and is fabled to have acquired pieces of the cross.

▲ Emperor Constantine is depicted alongside his celebrated mother, Helena.   Wikimedia Commons

CONSTANTINIAN BUILDING PROJECTS

313　Construction begins on the Church of St. John Lateran in Rome. Built on imperial property, it signalled Constantine's attitude towards Christianity.

320　Construction begins on the first Church of St. Peter's, the largest basilica in Rome.

325　Church of the Nativity founded in Bethlehem.

326　Building begins on the Church of the Holy Sepulchre in Jerusalem. The building would have a significant influence on later church architecture.

328　Byzantium given the new name *Constantinople* and made capital of the empire. A series of public, Christian building works ensues.

▲ The Church of the Holy Sepulchre
Nickolay Vinokurov/Shutterstock

of political consolidation was mirrored in his approach to Christianity, and he sought to bind the church to the state.

Council of Arles

Constantine's first opportunity came when the Donatists invited him to arbitrate in their dispute with Pope Miltiades (?–314) in 313. The following year, in partnership with Pope Sylvester (?–335), the emperor summoned the Council of Arles to deal with the problem. In 316 Constantine stood in opposition to the Donatists. A campaign of coercion against them lasted until 321, and thus for the first time in history the church and the state collaborated in the suppression of heresy.

Arianism—Christ Is Not God

Donatism revolved around the issue of leaders who had fallen short of the Christian ideal and asked questions about the nature of the church. While this controversy was raging, a debate about the person of Christ and the nature of God was also in full swing. Significantly, the problem of Arianism would also attract Constantinian intervention.

The Alexandrian priest Arius (c. 250–c. 336) preached that Christ was not God, but (following John 1:3) was made by God to be the instrument through whom the world was created. The teaching had consequences for Christian doctrines of the Trinity, of creation, and of Jesus's role in redemption, and it was condemned by the church in 320. Nevertheless, Arius continued to attract followers, causing dissention within the Christian community.

ARMENIA

In 314 King Tiridates III was converted by Gregory the Illuminator, making Armenia the first kingdom to officially adopt Christianity as its national religion. Gregory (c. 240–c. 328) was an Armenian by birth who returned from Caesarea to his native homeland as a missionary. After Tiridates's conversion, Gregory formed the Armenian Church, instituting a system of religious hierarchy following the Greek Church model. Armenia would become the base for missions to the neighbouring kingdoms of Georgia and Albania.

▲ Arius's heretical ideas prompted Constantine's intervention and led to the formulation of the Nicene Creed.

Wikimedia Commons

ATHANASIUS (C. 296–373)

The most prominent champion of orthodoxy against Arianism, Athanasius became bishop of Alexandria in 328. Because of its strong affirmation of the Incarnation and the Trinity, the fifth-century "Athanasian Creed" used by Anglicans, Catholics, and Protestants shares his name: "We worship one God in Trinity, and Trinity in unity; neither confounding the persons, nor dividing the substance."

▲ The Council of Nicaea as depicted in St. Sophia Cathedral
Wikimedia Commons

Nicene Creed

In an effort to quell the unrest, in 325 Constantine called the Council of Nicaea (modern-day Isnik in Persia). Over 300 bishops were present (mostly from the East), and the council settled on a formulation of orthodoxy. This first Nicene Creed affirmed the bodily Incarnation and stressed that the Son was "begotten, not made." At the advice of his bishops, Constantine also inserted the crucial term homoousios to describe the relation between the Son and the Father. A Greek technical phrase that means "same substance," it marks a significant development in Christian thought.

Desert Monks

While complex debates raged at the centre of Christendom, a life of Christian simplicity was flourishing at its edges.

There is evidence of early monasticism in Syria and the East. However, it was the *Life of St. Anthony* (written by Athanasius c. 357) that had the most effect on Christian monastic movements. In Egypt and North Africa, anchorite desert communities included Cellia, Wâdi'n Natrûn, and Scete (still a site for Coptic monasteries). It was in these three communities that the "Sayings of the Desert Fathers" were preserved. One Desert Father, Pachomius (292–346), created the coenobitic (or "communal") rule that would become the predominant pattern for most monastic movements. Another preeminent figure in

◄ Leading theologians and Christian leaders met at regular intervals in the early centuries of the Christian era to try to express New Testament teachings in a systematic and noncontradictory matter. These meetings are known as the "church councils," the most important of which were the councils of Nicaea and Chalcedon in 325 and 451.

Coptic Christianity was Shenoutte (334–450), a strict coenobite, Council theologian, and author.

Eastern Monks

Basil "the Great" was born in Pontus c. 329 and died in Caesarea in 379. He had lived for a time as a monk in Syria and Egypt and was able to put what he learned there to use when he founded a new Greek monastic order. Written 358–364, Basil's monastic rule emphasised *koinobios* (living in community) over and against the solitary life of the anchorite. This form of community life rejected harsh asceticism in favour of a life of prayer, liturgy, charity, and useful labour. It became the template for subsequent Slavonic and Greek monastic orders, and Basil is considered a doctor of the church.

Western Monks

The father of monasticism in Gaul, Martin of Tours (c. 335–c. 400), founded the first monastery in Legugé near Poitiers in 361. Martin wrote no rule, but his simple living attracted many people to the community. When Martin reluctantly became bishop of Tours in 327, the monastery relocated to Marmoutier.

THE CAPPADOCIAN FATHERS

Basil "the Great" (c. 329–379), his brother Gregory of Nyssa (332–395), and Gregory of Nazianzus (329–389) were churchmen connected to Cappadocia (in modern-day Turkey). Together, the three expounded on Trinitarian theology, Christology (theology of Christ), and Pneumatology (theology of the Holy Spirit). Their writings made extensive use of the Trinitarian definition, derived from Tertullian, that "God is one substance in three persons." It is their theology that largely underwrites the final form of the Nicene Creed, confirmed at the First Council of Constantinople in 381.

INDIA

There is much legend but little written evidence of early Indian Christian activity. Traditionally, the introduction of Christianity to India is attributed to the first-century missionary efforts of the apostle Thomas. The Persian *Chronicle of Seert* reports that Bishop David of Basra instituted a mission to India in c. 300. A Persian bishop "from India" attended the Council of Nicaea in 325. Contested reports say that the merchant Thomas of Cana and Joseph, bishop of Edessa, travelled to Malabar in c. 345 in aid of the native church there. Around this same time, Emperor Constantius is reported to have sent a missionary named Theophilus. The early documentary evidence of Malabar Christians (also called Syrian or Saint Thomas Christians) suggests Nestorian influence from the sixth century.

GOTH BISHOP

Bishop Ulfilas (c. 311–383) travelled to the Teutonic tribes in 341. Many converted to Christianity under his influence, and Ulfilas translated the entire Bible into Gothic. Ulfilas was a follower of Arius, and Arianism would remain a troublesome factor in Gothic relations with the Western Empire until the Catholic conversion of Clovis, King of the Franks, in 496.

Also significant was Jerome (c. 342–c. 420). After training in the Antioch desert, Jerome returned to his native Italy as a champion of monasticism. Women were especially attracted to his message of ascetic discipline, which offered an alternative way to live faithfully apart from the roles usually open to daughters, wives, and mothers. In c. 386 Jerome settled at a monastery in Bethlehem, one of four institutions founded by the matron Paula (347–404) and her daughter Eustochium.

The Biblical Canon

A doctor of the church, Jerome is primarily known for his work as a biblical scholar. Jerome argued that the church should follow the Hebrew canon and that it should exclude the Apocrypha.

The development of the Christian canon of Scriptures was a long-running process. By c. 130, Christian communities had largely agreed on the core texts of the Hebrew Scriptures and by c. 220 were treating the four Gospels and thirteen Pauline Epistles as their New Testament on par with the Old. Yet the issue was not concluded.

The first clear evidence of the complete New Testament canon, and indeed the earliest mention of the term "canonised" (*kanonizomena*), comes from Athanasius's list of the twenty-seven books of the NT in his "*Easter*" or "*Festal*" *Letter* of 367. Pope Damascus of Rome (c. 304–384) instituted a council in c. 382 that provided the complete list of Old and New Testament books known in the present age. Damascus's secretary during this council was Jerome, and it was here that he was charged with revising the biblical texts, a task he began in 386. Over his lifetime Jerome would translate most of the Bible into Latin—texts that would eventually be collected as the *Vulgate Bible* and become the most widely read Bible in Western Christendom.

AUGUSTINE (354–430)

Aurelius Augustinus is considered to be the greatest of the church doctors and the most influential thinker in the history of Western Christianity. Born into a North African Christian family, Augustine lived a dissolute life until joining the Manichaeists in 373. The influence of his mother Monica (?–387) and the preaching of Bishop Ambrose of Milan (c. 340–397) returned him to Christianity in 386. By popular acclaim Augustine was made bishop of Hippo (modern-day Annaba, Algeria) in 395. Augustine's most famous works include the autobiographical *Confessions* (387), *The Trinity* (399–419), and *City of God* (413–424).

ORIGINAL SIN

In response to the British monk Pelagius (active in Rome c. 383–410), Augustine refined his conception of "original sin." Pelagianism preached the possibility of sinlessness and spiritual perfection through the action of human free will. Against this, Augustine developed the idea of inherited guilt and taught that in order to obey God, humanity needs divine grace.

The Establishment of Christendom

Julian was emperor of Rome from 361 to 363. A pagan, Julian attempted to restore the old temples and rituals, exiled Christian clergy, and closed churches. Upon his death he became the last of the non-Christian Roman emperors.

JOHN CHRYSOSTOM (C. 344–407)

A celebrated preacher, John's epithet *Chrysostom* means "golden-mouthed." John was made patriarch of Constantinople in 398, but his zeal for church reform soon led him afoul of Empress Eudoxia and clergymen loyal to her. At the Synod of Oak in 403, John was condemned on trumped-up charges and banished. Even in exile, John remained enormously popular with the Eastern and Western Churches.

▲ Saint John Chrysostom and Empress Eudoxie by Jean-Paul Laurens   Wikimedia Commons

The last emperor of an undivided Roman Empire was Theodosius I (c. 346–395), who came to power in 379. Theodosius was a staunch supporter of orthodox Christianity, which until then had been the privileged—but not established—religion of the Roman Empire. In 380 Theodosius issued an edict that made Christianity official and deviation from Nicaea illegal. In 381 Theodosius called the first Council of Constantinople, which placed the bishop of Constantinople second in honour to the pope, outlawed Arian congregations, and confiscated property held by heretical groups. Many pagan temples were destroyed or forcibly converted into churches.

AMBROSE (C. 339–397)

One of the four doctors of the Western Church was Ambrose. Originally from Gaul, Ambrose became bishop of Milan in 374. He wrote *On the Duties of the Clergy*, a compendium of ethical teaching for priests. Ambrose's emphasis on emulating the Virgin Mary makes him one of the earliest supporters of Marian devotion.

of the church, demonstrating the strength of Ambrose's famous maxim: "The emperor indeed is within the church, not above the church."

Within Not Above

In 390 Theodosius killed over 7,000 Thessalonica citizens in retribution for a seditious riot. An outraged Bishop Ambrose castigated the emperor for his harshness. Theodosius publicly acknowledged his guilt and submitted to the penance. This marked the first time in history that an imperial power had bowed to the authority

East and West

Theodosius was the last emperor to rule over a united empire. Upon his death in 395 his eldest son Arcadius became emperor of the East; the other son Honorius took the West. The Roman world would never be united again, and the West would soon splinter further under barbarian pressure.

5 EAST AND WEST: 400–500

The story of Christianity in the fifth century sees the beginning of the long-standing historical division between Constantinople and Rome. The theological differences between East and West are exacerbated by the differing political fortunes of both empires, as Rome falls to barbarian invaders and Constantinople enjoys relative stability. In this era, investigation into the nature of the Trinity and the implications of the Incarnation leads to major statements of orthodox doctrine, the creation of influential heretical groups, and the start of significant church traditions that persist into the present age.

Eastern and Western Churches

By 395 the Roman Empire had been divided into East and West, with separate capital cities, ruling families, and even languages. As the fifth century opened there was still nominal unity in the church, but there was a marked drift between the Eastern and Western traditions.

The East, ruled from the city of Constan- tinople, enjoyed relative unity and stability. In the West the empire was soon to splinter into smaller fragments ruled by Germanic tribes from the north. Rome was growing increasingly untenable as a political capital, and in c. 404 the imperial residence was moved to Ravenna.

▲ In the fifth century, the city of Constantinople rose to become the centre of Christianity and politics for much of the world.

📖 **ARMENIAN LITERATURE**

In c. 400 the monk Mesrob Mashtots (or Maštoc', c. 361–440) invented the Armenian alphabet and continued the mission work of Gregory the Illuminator. Translations of liturgical books, theological texts, and the full Bible soon followed, as well as original native works.

The Falling Fortunes of Rome

The pope was now the most significant official left in the city, and the importance of the church grew in stature. The centrality of Christian Rome was assured under the leadership of popes such as Innocent I (?–417), Celestine I (?–c. 432), and especially Leo the Great (?–461), who was granted authority over the entire Western Church by Emperor Valentinian.

At the opening of the fifth century, hordes led by the Visigoth king Alaric were ravaging Greece and the Balkans. Alaric first advanced on Italy in 401. In 410 he sacked and occupied Rome for three days. The event shocked pagans and Christians alike, leading to much blame and recrimination on all sides. While Rome continued to be a centre for Christianity, its economic and political status fell further when it was sacked again by Vandals in 455.

▶ Alaric I, king of the Visigoths, was the first Teutonic ruler to successfully invade Rome.

Wikimedia Commons

📖 **INVENTION OF THE SECULAR**

Occasioned by Alaric's occupation of Rome, Augustine wrote *City of God* (begun 412, completed 426) in defence of Christianity against paganism on the one hand and Christian triumphalism on the other. *City of God* argues that the success of the Heavenly City is independent of the fortunes of the earthly City. The magisterial work encompasses history, politics, ethics, theology, and the philosophy of space and time. It is often considered to be second only to the Bible in terms of influence on the development of Christian civilisation. Its notion that all human institutions (including the church) occupy the "secular" sphere and that only God can determine membership of the "sacred" has been as influential as it has been misunderstood in the history of church and state relations.

The Rise of Constantinople

Apart from small-scale continuing warfare with the Zoroastrian Persian Empire, the Eastern Empire was comparatively stable. Constantinople was flourishing and the imperial government remained strong. Although also harried by Germanic invaders, Constantinople fared better than Rome, and Emperor Theodosius II (408–450) was able to appease Attila's Hunnic invaders with payments of gold.

▶ Attlia, the king of the Huns, threatened to overrun the Eastern empire.

Wikimedia Commons

The most important patriarch at this time was Cyril of Alexandria (?–444). Commissioned in 412, Cyril had a reputation for precise reasoning and an uncompromising style, and he presided over a number of controversies and key events in the development of Christianity.

Mary, Bearer of God

From the Greek *theos* (God) and *tikto* (to bear), the term *Theotokos* was a popular term for the Virgin Mary, mother of Jesus and "God-Bearer."

A favoured formulation of the Alexandrian school from Origen onwards, the term was important for preserving the Christology that emphasised the eternal and divine nature of the "Word become flesh." Cyril of Alexander was an enthusiastic champion of the term, and *Theotokos* was a central feature of popular Alexandrian piety.

Mary, Bearer of Man

Nestorius (c. 381–?) was made patriarch of Constantinople in 428. When he was a monk in Antioch, Nestorius had gained a reputation for his vehement style, and shortly after his consecration he caused offense when he preached against the title *Theotokos*. Instead of "God-Bearer," Nestorius recommended that Mary be referred to as *Anthropotokos* (Man-Bearer), or better, *Christotokos* (Christ-Bearer). The resulting major controversy had consequences that endure in the present age.

Nestorius came from the Antiochene school of theology, which was in tension with the Alexandrian tradition. Antioch Christology stressed the humanity of Jesus and emphasised that Christ's life involved growth, temptation, suffering, and love. These things were seen to be impossible in the face of an

▲ Cyril of Alexandria was one of the most important patriarchs of the early church. Among other doctrines, he promoted the idea that Mary, as mother of Jesus, was the *Theotokos* or "Bearer of God." Wikimedia Commons

◄ The Church of St. Mary in Ephesus Wikimedia Commons

Alexandrian Christology, which supposedly (in its extreme form) overemphasised the divine nature of Jesus Christ at the expense of the human.

Council of Ephesus

The ensuing controversy was thus as much about ecclesiastical politics as it was about doctrine. When Cyril of Alexandria defended *Theotokos* in his Paschal letter of 429, he was also defending the Alexandrian Church against infringement from Antioch. Cyril gained the support of Pope Celestine in Rome in 430, and in 431 Emperor Theodosius II convened the Council of Ephesus to settle the matter.

Cyril opened the council before the Syrian bishops or representatives from Rome had arrived. The council quickly found against Nestorian theology, and Nestorius was excommunicated (he died in exile sometime after 436). The result was a schism between Cyril's party (mainly Alexandria and Rome) and the Syrian

 MELANIA THE YOUNGER (C. 383–C. 439)

Due to Visigoth excursions in Italy, Melania fled Rome in 408 and lived the monastic life in a number of locations before finally settling in Jerusalem. In c. 431 she founded a convent for nuns on the Mount of Olives. A friend of Augustine and Jerome and influential in the conflict against Nestorianism, Melania was venerated early by the Greek Church but was relatively unknown in the West until the twentieth century.

NESTORIANISM

The Nestorian Church gradually formed from the Eastern bishops who refused to accept the Council of Ephesus and the compromise of 433. Its patriarchal centre was in Persia at Seleucia-Ctesiphon, with significant schools of Nestorian theology in Edessa and Nisibis. In the following centuries the Nestorians would be an active missionary church, with a significant presence in India, China, and Arabia. During Persian-Arab rule, the patriarchal see relocated to Baghdad. The Nestorian Church was decimated under Mongol rule in the fourteenth century, but remnant groups survive today.

▲ Sixteenth-century fresco from Galata, Cyprus depicting the Council of Ephesus, which condemned Nestorianism in 431.

Third Ecumenical Council, held at Ephesus, 431 AD, Axenti, Symeon/Church of St Sozomenos, Galata, Cyprus/ Sonia Halliday Photographs/Bridgeman Images

SCOTLAND

The first missionary to the Scottish Picts was Ninian (c. 360–c. 432). Little is known about Ninian's mission except that he was consecrated in Rome in 394 and based in Whithorn, Galloway, where he founded a church known as Candida Casa ("White House").

and Mesopotamian churches. Eventually an agreement between Cyril and John of Antioch (leader of the Syrian churches from 429 to 441) was reached in 433, but the Nestorian rift was widening.

Too Human or Too Divine

The clash between Cyril and Nestorius had opened wide much deeper discussion in the church about the nature of God, Christ, and the Incarnation. Nestorianism implied that there was a clear divide between the human and divine natures of Christ to the extent that its critics charged it with doing away with the divine nature altogether. The perceived implication of Nestorian theology was that Jesus was "too human" to allow for the reconciliation with the divine that is so important for Christian thought and practice. In turn, this led some theologians to react the other way. As a correction to Nestorianism, in 448 Eutyches (c. 378–454) formulated a view in which there was only one divine nature, with the implication that the life of Christ was "too divine" to be of much moral or spiritual relevance for normal humans.

IRELAND

The earliest introduction of Christianity to Ireland is obscure, but it probably occurred in the fourth century. Sometime c. 431 Pope Celestine I sent Palladius to be Ireland's first bishop. He was joined a few years later by Patrick, a British priest and former Irish slave. Patrick (probably c. 390–c. 460) founded churches in Meath, Ulster, Connaught, and elsewhere, and is celebrated as the patron saint of Ireland.

▲ St. Patrick   Florida Center for Instructional Technology

Council of Chalcedon

Both views had implications for philosophical matters of human and divine identity, as well as the Christian doctrines of creation and redemption. In 451 Emperor Marcian convoked the

MONOPHYSITES

The distinct movement known as Monophysitism came into being as a direct result of the Dyophysite ("Two-Nature") doctrine of Chalcedon. Regional, independent, and often isolated from the rest of Christendom, churches that were founded on anti-Chalcedon principles include the Syrian Orthodox Church (also called the Jacobites), the Egyptian Coptic Church, and the Ethiopian (or Abyssinian) Church.

Council of Chalcedon to deal with the issues. Most attending bishops were from the East, but after a two-year delay the Western Church accepted most of its decisions, including its definition of faith.

The council formally rejected the formulations of both Nestorius and Eutyches, denying that the humanity of Christ could be separate from his divine person and also that the two natures were fused into one. The Definition, or Creed, of Chalcedon set out the existence of one person in two natures and also affirmed *Theotokos*.

Fall of the West

In the West, the empire, ruled from Ravenna, was racked by constant revolutions and imperial intrigues. In 475 the young Romulus Augustus was put in place as a puppet emperor. In 476, taking advantage of the disarray, the Germanic mercenary general Odoacer launched a mutiny and was proclaimed king of Italy. This event marked the end of the Western Roman Empire.

▲ Theatre at Ephesus, Turkey built third century BC, and rebuilt during the Roman period to house 24,000 spectators.

© 2012 by Zondervan

GERMANIC PEOPLES

The Gothic tribes were divided into Ostrogoths (Eastern Goths) and Visigoths (Western Goths). Other tribes included the Vandals, Lombards, Alans, and Burgundians. Many of these tribes followed Arian Christianity, a source of further conflict as the Germanic peoples gained a foothold in the Catholic empire.

The First Schism

At this time there was also some political unrest in the East, contributing to the first significant schism between the Western and Eastern Churches.

In 475 the usurper Basiliscus forced the Eastern emperor Zeno to flee Constantinople. Basiliscus was a supporter of Monophysitism, a movement that had nationalist, anti-imperial undertones to accompany its theology. When Zeno reclaimed the throne twenty months later, he faced an empire divided on regional and religious grounds.

In partnership with Acacius (?–489), patriarch of Constantinople, Zeno drafted a

▲ The invasion of the western empire by Germanic peoples during the fifth century

document of union between the Monophysites and the Orthodox. Acacius and Zeno's *Henoticon* of 482 affirmed the Nicene Creed and condemned Nestorius and Eutyches. However, as a concession to the Monophysites, it deliberately did not mention the Definition of Chalcedon. The *Henoticon* compromise was accepted by the majority of bishops in the East, but it was completely rejected by Rome. In 482 Pope Felix III (?–492) excommunicated Acacius and was anathematised in turn. The schism between Rome and Constantinople would last until 518.

POPE GELASIUS I (?–496)

Gelasius became pope in 492 and was the first to assume the title "Vicar of Christ." He is one of the great architects of papal primacy: "There are two powers by which this world is chiefly ruled. . . . Of these that of the priests is the more weighty."

6 CENTRES AND MARGINS: 500–600

The first schism between East and West is temporarily healed at the beginning of the century, but the attempts to re-create the united Christian empire lead to deeper divisions when Rome objects to the emperor meddling in theological affairs. The sixth century also sees the growing political importance of the pope in the West and the ecumenical patriarch in the East. But the flourishing of the church in this era is not confined to these major centres of power, as Christianity spreads to India, Sri Lanka, and Scotland and thrives in Ethiopia, Armenia, and Ireland. Untouched by the barbarian wars in mainland Europe, sixth-century Celtic Christians are able to preserve literary, artistic, and monastic traditions that will irrevocably alter the future development of Christendom.

The First Healing

The first significant schism between the Eastern and Western Churches was not healed until the accession of Emperor Justin in Constantinople in 518.

BOETHIUS (C. 480–524)

The Greek-educated Boethius served the Ostrogothic court at Ravenna. Because he disagreed with Arianism, he was charged with treason and imprisoned in 522. It was there that Boethius wrote *The Consolations of Philosophy*, a reflection on identity, God, and morality that would become one of the most influential texts in medieval Europe. He was executed in 524.

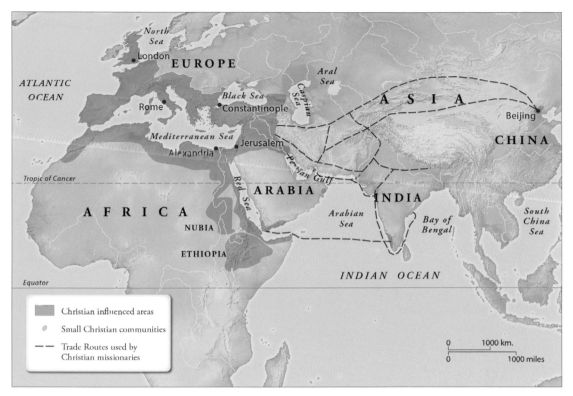

▲ The early Christian world, sixth century

▼ Emperor Justinian depicted in a mosaic from the Emilia Romanga Region, Italy.   The Met Museum, Fletcher Fund, 1925

◄ The sun rises over the Hagia Sophia in Instanbul (Constantinople). The structure stands on the site of the foundations of a church built by Justinian in 538. Converted into a mosque by the Ottomans in 1453, since 1934 it has been used as a museum.   givaga/123RF.com

Justin revoked the offending *Henoticon* compromise and brokered peace between the churches. In this, he was advised by his nephew Justinian (482–565), who took a keen educated interest in theological matters. When Justinian succeeded his uncle in 527, he sought to revive the universal Christian empire of old.

Emperor Justinian

Emperor Justinian I enjoyed much success in his efforts to restore the fortunes of Christianity. In 529 he closed the pagan philosophical schools in Athens and waged a campaign against the Montanists, the heretical group still lingering from the second century. Also in 529 Justinian updated and revised imperial statutes, producing a new code that would become the basis for civil and church law. Justinian commissioned a series of major building works, including Constantinople's most celebrated church, the Hagia Sophia ("Church of the Holy Wisdom," begun 532, completed 538). However, it was Justinian's continued efforts to solve the problem of Monophysitism that finally served to exacerbate, rather than calm, tensions within the church.

THEODORA (C. 500–C. 547)

Crowned co-empress in 527, Theodora was as active and interested in Christian theology as was her husband, Justinian. Theodora was sympathetic to Monophysitism and sponsored a Monophysite monastery in 531. Also by her patronage, Syrian Monophysites established themselves as a separate church under Bishop Jacob Baradaeus (?–578). A known moral reformer, Theodora used her influence to raise Vigilius to his position as pope of Rome, although she later would be disappointed when his support proved inconstant.

▲ Theodora's portrait mosaic in the Church of San Vitale in Ravenna

seraficus/iStock

The Three Chapters

In 543 Justinian interjected himself into church affairs when, in an attempt to placate the powerful Monophysite group, he issued an edict condemning the fifth-century writings (or chapters) of Theodore of Mopsuestia (c. 350–428), Ibas of Edessa (?–457), and the Syrian bishop of Cyrrhus, Theodoret (c. 393–c. 457), all of which held Nestorian or christological positions opposed to Monophysitism. The Eastern patriarchs assented to the edict, but the pope in Rome refused, declaring that the edict of the Three Chapters went against the Council of Chalcedon.

Council of Constantinople

Pope Vigilius (?–555) was forcibly brought to Constantinople and reluctantly agreed to uphold the Three Chapters in 548. The Western Church's reaction was fierce, and Vigilius returned to his original rejection of Justinian's conciliatory measures. At the Second Council of Constantinople in 553, Vigilius vacillated once again, this time allowing the council to confirm the edict and go against the Western bishops. Major sections of the Western Church, led by northern Italian clergy, refused to submit to Vigilius, causing a schism with Rome—a church that itself had uncertain relations with Constantinople.

The 553 council demonstrated plainly the distinctive nature of the early Byzantine Church in the East in contrast with the Western Roman Church. As well as moving closer to the Monophysite position, the council also added another title to Mary. Along with *Theotokos* (God-Bearer), the church also bestowed *Aeiparthenos* ("Ever-Virgin"), thus fixing the dogma of Mary's perpetual virginity.

The First Ecumenical Patriarch

The relationship between East and West was further troubled when the patriarch of Constantinople John the Faster (?–595) assumed the title "Ecumenical Patriarch" in 588. The title has been used by his successors in the Eastern tradition ever since. This claim to universal church primacy was challenged by Pope Pelagius II (?–590) and then Pope Gregory I (c. 540–604).

RECARED (?–601)

Recared was king of the Visigoths in Spain. In 586 Recared renounced his Arian creed and became Catholic. He suppressed Arianism amongst the Visigoths, and in 589 the Council of Toledo proclaimed Catholic Christianity the official religion of the Spanish kingdom.

FILIOQUE

Latin for "and the Son," the *Filioque* is associated with the Trinitarian doctrine of the "Double Procession of the Holy Spirit," the belief that the Spirit proceeds from the Father *and the Son*. The *Filioque* clause had been in steady use (especially in the West) from the time of the early church fathers but was not officially interpolated into the Nicaean Creed until the Council of Toledo in 589. At the time, the insertion passed without controversy, but Patriarch Photius (c. 820–893) would make the *Filioque* the basis for the Eastern attack on the church in Rome in 864.

Gregory the Great

Gregory (c. 540–604) became pope in 590. His objections to John the Faster stemmed from the conviction that Rome was the original see of Peter, and as such it was to Rome that the care of the universal church had been entrusted. As pope, Gregory extended the responsibilities of the papacy more than any of his predecessors.

▲ Pope Gregory did much to expand papal authority in religion and politics, earning his appellation "the Great."

The Metropolitan Museum, gift of J. Pierpont Morgan, 1917

In 592 he sent papal troops against the Lombards in an effort to stave off their impending invasion of Rome, achieving a temporary respite. When the Lombards did eventually invade in 598, it was Gregory, and not the civil authorities, who administered the peace settlements with the barbarians. This action paved the way for the eventual creation of the Papal States and the establishment of the pope as a temporal power.

AETHELBERT (?–616)

Aethelbert (or Ethelbert) became king of Kent c. 560 and was converted by Augustine of Canterbury in 597. Aethelbert's wife Bertha was a Frankish Christian, and it is because of her influence that the Roman missionary party was welcomed. Aethelbert and Bertha were enthusiastic supporters of the Roman Christian cause in England, although they failed to reach agreement with the Celtic British Church.

HIMYARITES

In the sixth century, Himyarite Christians lived in Zafār and Naǧrān in the southern Arabian peninsula (modern-day Yemen). The Persian king and Jewish convert Dū Nuwās persecuted the Himyarites harshly, decimating the population. In c. 523 King Kaleb sent soldiers to aid at the request of the emperor in Constantinople. The Himyarites' plight and Kaleb's success are well attested in early Syriac literature.

Gregory also consolidated papal power in church affairs. His *Pastoral Care* was an influential book detailing the duties of bishops and other clergy. Through his efforts, the independent Frankish Church was incorporated into Rome. Gregory welcomed the conversion of the Spanish Arian Visigoths and worked closely with Leander, bishop of Seville (c. 534–c. 600). Gregory also attempted to align the Celtic Church with Rome, and he established a major mission to England, instituting Augustine (?–c. 609) as first archbishop of Canterbury in 596.

Ethiopia

Native Christian culture flourished in other regions relatively independent of Constantinople

COSMAS INDICOPLEUSTES (MID-SIXTH CENTURY)

Cosmas was a merchant, geographer, and mapmaker. His *Christian Topography* contains many fantastical details but also provides useful information about the spread of Christianity throughout Sri Lanka, South India, and North Africa.

▲ Cosmas's map   Kharbine-Tapabor/Shutterstock

or Rome. After the Council of Chalcedon in 451, Christianity in Ethiopia became firmly identified with Monophysitism under the influence of Syrian and Egyptian missionary refugees. By the start of the sixth century, the explorer Cosmas Indicopleustes could describe Ethiopia as a "thoroughly Christian country." Between 514 and 542 Christianity thrived under the reign of King Kaleb (?–c. 540) in the northern Ethiopian kingdom of Axum. It was during this time that the Bible was translated into Ge'ez (Ethiopic), and a number of patristic writings were preserved (most notably the *Shepherd of Hermas* and texts attributed to Cyril of Alexandria called the *Qerellos*).

Armenia

Native Armenian Christian art and literature grew after the missionary Mesrob's scholarly innovations of the previous century. In 555 the Armenian Gregorian Church formally repudiated the Council of Chalcedon, aligning itself with the Monophysite movement, if not full theological Monophysitism. The schism (which remains in effect) was made largely for national, cultural, and political reasons in an effort to avoid Constantinople's dominance.

Ireland

Irish Christians wrote in Latin and adopted Latin forms of biblical commentary and hagiography. Yet the Christianity of the Celtic fringe in the sixth century was distinct from that of Europe. Following the strong influence of Patrick, Irish Christianity was a religion of powerful countryside monasteries rather than the urban church culture of Rome or Constantinople.

▲ The Celtic cross is a distinctive symbol of ancient Scottish and Irish Christianity. stroop/123RF.com

It is from this monastic, rural tradition that the great names of Irish Christianity emerge, including Finnian of Clonard (?–549), Brigid the nun (dates obscure), Brendan, the celebrated navigator and abbot of Clonfert (484–c. 580), and Comgall, abbot of Bangor (?–c. 600), whose skill as a monastic church founder was known in Europe.

Untouched by the Germanic barbarian invasions racking the Western Empire, Irish monasteries were free to foster learning and study, as well as preserve important texts. It was in Ireland that the earliest forms of the Latin Bible were recovered, as well as the writings of Pelagius, Gregory the Great, and other Latin theologians. From this base, Irish monks and scholars engaged in numerous missionary journeys, evangelising Scotland and northern England, and reintroducing or reinvigorating Christianity into France and Italy.

IONA

The monk and scholar Columba (521–597) founded churches and monasteries in his native Ireland before leaving the country in 563. Columba made the perilous journey to Scotland where he founded the monastic community of Iona. Iona soon became the catalyst for missionary activity to the northern Pictish tribes and the people of Northumbria. A major centre for Celtic Christianity, the Columban order survived until the Reformation. A new community was revived in the twentieth century.

▲ Iona Abbey   Luca Quadrio/Shutterstock

THE RULE OF BENEDICT

Drawn up c. 540, the *Rule* reformed previous monastic rules and provided guidance for the spiritual and administrative direction of monastic life. It became the template for virtually all monastic communities for men and women in Western Christendom.

▲ Benedict of Nursia   Nancy Bauer/Shutterstock

The Rise of Monastic Orders

The sixth century saw the formulation of monastic rules and the creation of important monastic orders. During the chaos following the collapse of the Western Roman Empire, these communities would play a crucial role in preserving scholarship, social organisation, art, liturgy, and Christian theology.

Benedict

Benedict of Nursia (c. 480–c. 550) and his sister Scholastica (?–c. 543) were foundational figures of Western monasticism. In c. 500, Benedict withdrew from Rome, a city he thought had grown hedonistic and corrupt. Although Benedict was not ordained, he became the focal point for other like-minded ascetics, and a monastic community thrived under Benedict's supervision. Sometime between 525 and 529 the community moved to Monte Cassino and became the principal monastery of what would become the Benedictine Order (Benedict did not found an order in his lifetime). Around this time, Scholastica also established the convent of Benedictine nuns at nearby Plombariola in Italy. Following attacks from the Lombards in c. 570, the Monte Cassino monastery was forced to relocate to Rome.

Columbanus

In the Middle Ages, Benedict's *Rule* would eventually supersede the rule of Columbanus, although for a long time the Irishman's more severe rule was also popular. Columbanus (c. 543–615) travelled to Burgundy c. 590 where he established a monastery at Luxeuil. Monasteries in Gall, Würzburg, Salzburg, and others soon followed. The monastery rule was strict and rigorous, and the monks were known for their adherence to Irish Christianity and outspoken attacks on the laxity of the local clergy and governing authorities. As a result, Columbanus was expelled from Burgundy in 610, after which he founded a notable monastery at Bobbio, Italy.

SOLDIERS AND MISSIONARIES: 600-700

Seventh-century Christianity sees the furthering of deep cultural divisions between East and West. It is here that the Eastern Empire becomes identifiably Greek and Byzantine, accompanied by the flowering of Constantinople as a major centre of church activity. In Persia, perpetual war between Zoroastrians and Christians—as well as infighting between the Christian groups themselves—paves the way for the dominance of the new, vigorous religion of the Prophet Muhammad. Elsewhere, Assyrian Christianity takes root in China and Central Asia. In northern Europe and Britain, the Roman Church is both challenged and invigorated by the infusion of Celtic Christianity.

The Bobbio Monastery

The Irish abbot Columbanus settled in the small northern Italian town of Bobbio in 612. The monastery there would soon become famed as a centre for scholarship, the collection of manuscripts, and the production of works such

▲ The Basilica of San Colombano in Bobbio

as Columbanus's *Penitential* and the influential *Monastic Rule*. However, as a standard pattern for monastic life and the right ordering of abbeys, this severe rule would eventually be superseded by the more lenient and inclusive rule of Benedict of Nursia.

Celtic Christianity

The outspoken rigorous Christianity preached by Columbanus that proved so unpalatable to much of Europe was a product of the Christianity of the Celtic fringe. British, Cornish, Irish, Scottish, and Welsh Christianity were not united under one church leadership; however, they did tend to share common characteristics that could be contrasted with other mainland traditions. The differences were largely cultural rather than doctrinal. Since the withdrawal of the Roman Empire in the fifth century, the Celtic peoples had operated independently of foreign control. One consequence for Celtic Christianity was that its energy was spent mostly on the creation of autonomous monasteries rather than on conformity to the structure and authority of a central church. The Celts followed their own calendar and celebrated Easter on a different day from the rest of Christendom. (The southern Irish Church was urged to conform over Easter c. 638 by Pope Honorius I [?–c. 638]. The northern churches, including Iona, held out until c. 768.) The Celts made different demands on their monks, with one example being the practice of tonsuring. In addition, Celtic Christianity was more rural than urban. Vernacular Christian poetry reveals an emphasis on the natural world, and Celtic saints were often portrayed as communing with animals and other representatives of the wild.

Anglo-Saxon Christianity

The Anglo-Saxons in seventh-century England operated under the influence of two Christian traditions.

In the south, Augustine and King Aethelbert founded Roman monasteries and churches in Canterbury and York in 597. In 601 Pope Gregory the Great sent Paulinus (?–c. 644) to aid the Augustine mission. By 625 Paulinus had converted King Edwin of Northumbria and become the first bishop of the cathedral at York. In 604 the priest Justus (?–c. 627) was appointed bishop of Rochester, and Mellitus (?–624) was made the first bishop of London. A succession of pagan Saxon kings hostile to Christianity forced Mellitus and Justus to flee to Gaul in c. 617, but they were soon invited back by the king of Kent.

The Lindisfarne Community

In the northern regions, the Irish missionary Aidan (?–651) established a monastery at Lindisfarne and was consecrated bishop there in 635.

▲ The Isle of Wight, the last pagan region in England, accepted Christianity sometime between 681 and 686.

laurencebaker/iStock

▲ The Irish monastery at Lindisfarne was an early and important base for the spread of Christianity among the Celts.
DouglasMcGilviray/iStock

THE FIRST ENCYCLOPAEDIA

Isidore (c. 560–636) became bishop of Seville c. 600 where he oversaw the enforced baptism of Jews in Spain and worked to strengthen relations between the Spanish Visigothic rulers and the church. A celebrated scholar, Isidore wrote the twenty-volume *Etymologiae*, the first compendium of knowledge to date, which earned him the title "Schoolmaster of the Middle Ages."

LINDISFARNE GOSPELS

The illustrated manuscript now known as the *Lindisfarne Gospels* was created at the namesake monastery sometime between 696 and 698. The book is an important indicator of the preservation of biblical translations throughout Christendom.

▲ Reproduction of the title page of John's Gospel, from the Lindisfarne Gospels   Wikimedia Commons

With Lindisfarne as their base, Aidan and his successor Finan (?–661) established Celtic Christian churches across modern-day Scotland and northern England. In 664 many of Lindisfarne's Celtic monks relocated to the Iona monastery. Their move was prompted by the increasing Romanisation of Christianity and their displeasure at being forced to conform to Roman discipline under the Synod of Whitby.

Synod of Whitby— Return to Rome

In 663 the problem of the two strands of Christianity came to a head when the Northumbrian king Oswy realised that as a Celtic Christian he would be celebrating Easter on a different date than his Kentish wife Queen Eanfleda, who followed the Roman rite. Oswy convened a synod

👤 HILDA (614–680)

Hilda was a Northumbrian princess who was baptised by Paulinus in 627. In 659 she founded a double monastery for men and women, located on the cliffs of Streanshalch (modern-day Whitby, Yorkshire). As abbess, Hilda defended the Celtic customs, but she accepted the decision of the Synod of Whitby in 664. Under her care, the abbey became a celebrated centre for scholarship, literature, and theology.

at Hilda's abbey in Whitby. Representatives from both traditions argued their case, and the king eventually ruled in favour of the Roman party. The decision to turn to Rome was unpopular with some members of the Celtic party, but it served to align Anglo-Saxon Christianity with mainstream Christendom and marked a turning point in the history of Christianity in England. The decision paved the way for significant structural reforms under the direction of Theodore of Tarsus (602–690), who, as archbishop of Canterbury, introduced strong church hierarchy and the Roman parish system.

Chinese Christianity

There are legendary accounts that the apostle Thomas travelled to China as well as India. The first historical evidence for the presence of Christianity in China comes from the Sian-Fu (or Hsi-an-fu) Stone. The monument was erected in 781 and recounts the arrival in 635 of a missionary named Alopen (A-lo-pên in Chinese characters, which may possibly be a version of the name Abraham [dates unknown]).

▲ Facimile of the Sian-Fu Stone

Plaster cast of Nestorian Stele from Chang'an, today Xi'an, China, Chinese Civilization/De Agostini Picture Library/J. E. Bulloz/Bridgeman Images

▲ Closeup of the top portion of the Sian-Fu Stone

Wikimedia Commons

Alopen came from the Church of the East (or Assyrian Church) and settled in the T'ang dynasty capital where he was welcomed and saw some missionary success. There was a Buddhist reaction against the mission c. 698, but Assyrian Chinese Christianity would remain in some form until the tenth century (some accounts suggest possibly as late as the fourteenth century). However, as the Chinese Church did not have a Bible or contact with the wider communion, the religion did not flourish and syncretism with Buddhism was inevitable.

Byzantine Christianity

While Rome and the Western regions were struggling to align their Christianity, Constantinople in the east was becoming a consolidated church power, even while it suffered multiple attacks from Visigoths in the west and Persians and Muslims in the south.

Emperor Heraclius

Heraclius (575–641) became emperor in 610 and ruled until his death. Although the empire was

📍 CHURCH OF THE EAST

The Assyrian Church does not follow the teachings of Nestorius, although it is opposed to the Definition of Chalcedon. Originally centred in Mesopotamia (modern-day Iraq), the "Church of the East" operated largely independently of the great councils of Rome and Constantinople. It emphasised monastic life and missionary activity and was active throughout Central and East Asia and India. Long persecuted by the Zoroastrian Persians, the Christians were treated better by the Muslim Arabs after the conquests of 651.

📍 CROATIA

Sometime in the middle of the century, the Croatian duke Porga applied to Emperor Heraclius for Christian teachers to be sent to him. Heraclius asked Pope John IV of Rome (?–642) to help, as John himself was originally Croatian. The Christianising mission to the Croats began in 641.

harassed by many invading armies during his time, Heraclius's reign marks an era of revival for the Eastern Church in which the culture became distinctly Greek and Byzantine.

During the period 620–629 the Visigoths gained complete control of Spain, removing Heraclius's armies. At the same time, the Byzantine army was gaining ground previously lost to the Persians who had seen successful advances in 611. In 627 Heraclius won back Nineveh,

▲ Detail of *Knights in Combat from the Battle of Heraclius Against Khosrow II* by Piero della Francesca

Wikimedia Commons

and Egypt was under Byzantine rule in 629, the same year that Heraclius regained control of Jerusalem and expelled the Jews living there.

The One Activity of Christ

In their territorial skirmishes with the Eastern Empire, the Persians were greatly assisted by the fact that the Christian populations of the contested regions were not themselves united.

From 624, in an effort to rally the Monophysites with the orthodox Chalcedonian Church of Constantinople, Heraclius attempted to create a christological formula acceptable to both sides. In 633, together with Sergius, patriarch of Constantinople (?–638), Heraclius promoted the nuanced teaching called *Monoenergism*, namely, that Christ had two natures but one mode of "activity"—that of the Divine Word. The solution was rejected as heretical by many churchmen, including Sophronius of Jerusalem (c. 560–638).

The One Will of Christ

In 634 Sergius wrote to Pope Honorius I in Rome seeking assistance in the defence of Monothelitism. Honorius's suggestion resulted in the *Ecthesis*, a statement of faith drawn up by Sergius that replaced mention of the "activity" of Christ with his one "will." Although the *Ecthesis* was initially accepted by Eastern Church councils in 638 and 639, it was repeatedly condemned by Pope Honorius's successors in the West, including Pope Martin I, who was exiled to Crimea for his refusal to adopt Monothelitism. When Martin died in 655, he became the last pope to be venerated as a martyr.

Two Natures

The Monothelite solution had the opposite of its intended effect of promoting good relations between the traditions. To keep the peace, Emperor Heraclius disowned the teaching, and it was finally pronounced a heresy at the Council of Constantinople in 681, making two natures and two wills in Christ a matter of orthodox faith.

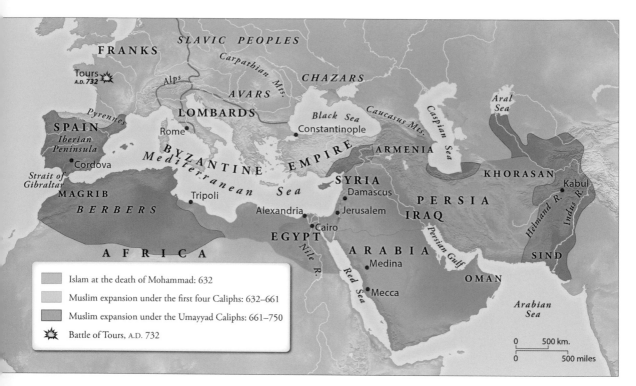

▲ The expansion of Islam

Map legend:
- Islam at the death of Mohammad: 632
- Muslim expansion under the first four Caliphs: 632–661
- Muslim expansion under the Umayyad Caliphs: 661–750
- Battle of Tours, A.D. 732

JOHN CLIMACUS (C. 570–649)

A hermit and abbot of the monastery at Mount Sinai, John "the Climber" wrote the mystical *Ladder of Paradise*, widely read by Orthodox Christian monks.

Muslim Advance

At the same time as doctrinal battles were being fought in the city churches, Byzantium's frontier war with the Persian Empire had weakened both sides, opening the way for the rapid expansion of the new Muslim Arab army. In 636 the Arabs won a significant victory over the Byzantine army at Yarmuk. By 638 Jerusalem was under Muslim control and some Jewish families were allowed to return.

As the Arabs advanced further, Constantinople lost Antioch (638), Edessa (641), and Alexandria (643), marking the end of Byzantine rule in Egypt. In 653, Muslim Arabs conquered Armenia, and between 673 and 678, Constantinople was forced to fend off a Muslim siege by land and sea. The event marked the high point of Arab threat to the capital city.

The Quinisext Council—Away from Rome

Arab conquests may have made the empire weaker, but the loss of Alexandria, Antioch, and other cities to the Muslims meant that the Church of Constantinople grew in stature and importance. In 692 the Eastern bishops met in

MAXIMUS "THE CONFESSOR" (C. 580–662)

Maximus was a Greek theologian who opposed Monothelitism and was eventually banished in 653 when he would not agree to the settlement. His prolific writings and influential teachings focused on the origin of evil by man's unreasonable sensuality, and the defeat of that evil through the Incarnation.

▶ The Greek theologian Maximus "the Confessor" is depicted preaching outside the city walls.

Universal History Archive/Universal Images Group/Shutterstock

synod to complete the work of the fifth (553) and sixth (680) General Councils. The Quinisext ("Fifth-Sixth") Council met in the palace of Emperor Justinian II, and its findings were strongly pro–Constantinople. Many of the 102 canons produced there were directed against the Roman Church, including the Western practice of clerical celibacy. Neither the pope nor any Western representative was present at the council, and they did not approve of its conclusions.

THE END OF BYZANTIUM

In 697 and 698 Carthage was under Muslim Arab control. The mass exodus of Greek and Roman populations from the city marked the end of Byzantium's rule in North Africa.

MONKS AND EMPERORS: 700-800

In the eighth century, the iconoclastic controversy over images and authority racks the East for the best part of the century and beyond, laying the groundwork for the final schism between Constantinople and Rome in the process. While the formerly culturally dominant Christians in North Africa and the Middle East adjust to new life under Muslim rule, the church in Rome asserts its political power with the formation of the Papal States. On the western frontier, Celtic Christians are threatened by Viking invaders while the dramatic conversion of Germanic pagan tribes continues apace. The century also witnesses the rise of the Frankish king Charlemagne and his Catholic cultural renaissance, a movement that will eventually usher in a new Holy Roman Empire.

East

Icons

The Jewish and Muslim religions strictly forbade the use of images in the worship of God.

▲ Eighth-century icon from Monastery of St. Catherine of Sinai, Egypt

Kharbine-Tapabor/Shutterstock

Manichaeism held that all matter was evil. Monophysites emphasised the divine nature of Christ at the expense of his human nature. In the face of other religions and heresies hostile to images and objects, much of the Christianity in this era strongly emphasised the veneration of icons.

The popular practice of veneration was challenged by Emperor Leo III (c. 675–741). Leo became emperor in 717 and earned his reputation for breaking the Muslim siege of Constantinople in 718. As well as noticing the often-excessive cult of devotion that had grown up around some icons, Leo also thought that icons formed the main obstacle in the conversion of Jews and Muslims and contributed to the hostility directed at Christendom. In 726 Leo issued an edict declaring that the veneration of icons was idolatrous, and he ordered all images to be destroyed in an iconoclastic purge.

Iconoclasm

The edict was not welcomed by many, and monks became the core group defending icons. The driving force of resistance to the iconoclastic movement was Patriarch Germanus (c. 640–c. 733), although he was aided by many Greek theologians, such as John of Damascus (c. 655–c. 750), who wrote three influential discourses in favour of icons. After Leo had Germanus deposed in 730, a systematic movement of persecution, seizure, and destruction followed throughout the Eastern Empire.

The culture of icons was not strong in Roman Christianity, but the popes were alarmed by the emperor's tendency to pronounce on matters of theology. They too opposed Leo from 727 onwards. When the Synod of Rome, led by Pope Gregory III, denounced the iconoclasts in 731, Leo retaliated by removing papal jurisdiction from its territories in southern Italy and seizing other Italian territories belonging to the papacy.

Synod of Hieria

When Leo's son Constantine V became emperor in 741, he had to put down a pro-icon rebellion before securing his power. In 754 he instituted the Synod of Hieria, which affirmed Leo's edicts that icon veneration was heretical and idolatrous. Many Orthodox clergy accepted the ruling, but many monks refused and were martyred when they resisted the suppression of their monasteries. As the synod had no representation from Antioch, Alexandria, Jerusalem, or Rome, its decrees were not considered to be representative of the wider church.

Empress Irene

Iconoclasm abated somewhat when Constantine's son Leo IV was emperor between 775 and 780. After Leo died, his wife, Empress Irene (c. 752–803), attempted to totally reverse the iconoclastic policy of her predecessors. Irene was the first woman to rule the Eastern Empire, and she was zealous in putting down challengers to her reign, including her own son. Irene's support of icons also drew violent opposition, as the army was governed by anti-icon forces.

CHINESE CHRISTIANITY

A monument to Assyrian missionary activity in China, the Sian-Fu Stone records that the church in the T'ang dynasty was at its height from 750 to 780.

▲ The Empress Irene was the first woman to rule the Eastern empire. She was deeply interested in theological matters.
Wikimedia Commons

CHRISTENDOM AND ISLAM

c. 700 Arabic control of Tunis ends Christian dominance in North Africa.

711 Beginning of Moorish era in Spain.

725–831 The Coptic Church had survived the Muslim domination of Egypt and North Africa begun a century earlier (c. 650). From the mid-eighth century onwards, unrest and internal divisions within Coptic Christianity aided the consolidation of Islam in the region.

732 Muslim advance into France halted at the Battle of Poitiers.

782 Muslim armies advance on the Bosporus. Peace is bought by a heavy tribute from Constantinople.

For Christianity, Irene's reign marks a time of conciliation between the pro-icon Eastern members of the Synod of Hieria and the wider church. Working together with Tarasius, patriarch of Constantinople (?–806), and Pope Hadrian I (?–795), Irene called the Second Council of Nicaea in 787.

Second Nicene Council

Over 300 bishops gathered at the council, including representatives from all the parties formerly absent at Hieria. Their first attempt at meeting was blocked by the iconoclastic army, but when the council convened a second time they reversed the decrees of Hieria. Veneration of icons was defined as a matter of respect and admiration that was not in itself idolatrous. Absolute adoration, on the other hand, was reserved only for God.

Nicaea is also important in that it passed a number of disciplinary measures intended to reform the church. Simony was condemned, as was the practice of priests living outside their diocese without permission. Clerics were encouraged to live a simple life. The foundation of new double monasteries (where men and women would live together in the same enclosure) was forbidden in order to preserve propriety.

Continued Antagonism

Although icons were officially restored throughout the empire, iconoclastic sentiments did not disappear and remained especially strong in the army. In 790 the Imperial Army rebelled and established Constantine VI as emperor. His reign until 797 was unpopular and short-lived, but it paved the way for the accession of Emperor Leo V "the Armenian" (775–820) and the Second Great Iconoclastic Controversy of the following century.

West

Papal States

Leo III's confiscation of papal land in the 730s highlights the source of much of the Western Church's power at this time. By the eighth century, the papacy controlled land throughout Italy, as well as in Sicily, Gaul, Illyria, Corsica, and Sardinia.

The emergence of the Western Church as a temporal power brought it into conflict with other powers seeking political and economic gain. In 754 Rome was besieged by the Lombard king Aistulf. Initially, Pope Stephen II (?–757) sought protection from Byzantium, but

this was not forthcoming. So Stephen turned to the Frankish king Pepin III (714–768) for assistance. In 756, after defeating the Lombards, Pepin donated significant regions of Venetia and Istria to the pope and firmly established Ravenna and Rome under church authority. The accumulation of secure lands free from the authority of the emperor in the East marks the creation of the Papal States.

Conversion of Germany

Meanwhile, concerted missionary projects to convert pagan Germanic tribes were also under way in the eighth century. The greatest figure during this time was Boniface, the "Apostle of Germany."

DONATION OF CONSTANTINE

Written towards the end of the eighth century, the *Donation* purports to record the gift of land and authority from Emperor Constantine I to the pope and his successors. Although the document's authenticity was suspected early on in its circulation, in the Middle Ages it was influential as a support for the claims of papal primacy. In the sixteenth century, the *Donation* was conclusively proven to be a forgery.

THE OAK OF THOR

Boniface cut down the sacred tree at Geismar (modern-day Fritzlar, Germany) in 723 in front of a hostile crowd. When they saw that Boniface was not struck by lightning, the crowd converted to Christianity and a chapel was built on the spot. The event represents a key turning point in the acceptance of Christianity in pagan Germany.

▲ The Oak of Thor   Historia/Shutterstock

Boniface (originally named Wynfrith, 675–754) was born in Wessex, England. After training as a scholar and monk, Boniface made his first journey to the Frisians in 716. The mission did not thrive and Boniface returned to Rome. In 719 Pope Gregory II instituted a new mission, returning Boniface to the Rhineland to work with the heathen Frisian and Hessian people. In 722 Boniface was made bishop of Germany. He did not have a fixed see but was charged with ministering to the whole Germanic frontier. Under Boniface's influence, parishes and monasteries were founded, including Salzburg, Ratisbon, Fritzlar, Kitzingen, and Fulda.

Charles Martel

The Franks were the most powerful of the Christianised Germanic people. Charles Martel (c. 690–741) was a Frankish ruler from 714 who enjoyed support from bishops and other influential Christian leaders. Under Martel, Christianity made further inroads as he waged campaigns against Bavarians, Saxons, and Frisians. The growth of Christianity was secured when Martel repelled the Muslim invaders at Poitiers in 732.

Martel considered himself a champion of Christianity; yet his support was often more opportunistic than constructive, and under his reign the Frankish Church fell somewhat into disrepair. High church offices were often sold to the highest bidder or given to court favourites for political purposes. Many priests held more than one position, making it impossible for them to devote their full attention to one parish. There had been no Frankish synod or church council for over eighty years, and many of the clergy were untrained and ill-disciplined.

▲ Charles Martel, king of the Franks. Christianity spread throughout the Germanic peoples under his reign; however, his leadership also brought the church into disarray.

f.86v Charles Martel looks after punishment and banishment of two men, from the Grandes Chroniques de France, 1375–79, French School/ Bibliotheque Municipale, Castres, France/Bridgeman Images

Teutonic Restoration

Martel had given Boniface protection and support. After Martel's death in 741, Boniface was freer to act as he saw fit to restore the church. A series of reforms quickly followed. The Synods of Germanicum (742) and Soissons (743) and a council of Frankish clergy in 747 did much to deal with errors and abuses within the Teutonic Church.

In 746 Boniface was made the first archbishop of Mainz. In 754 he was martyred in Frisia, where pagan violence continued until a final revolt in 784. Boniface's body was returned to the abbey he had helped found at Fulda. The site at Hesse Nassau soon became a popular pilgrimage destination, increasing the stature and reputation of the church in Germany. In the following century, Fulda would become one of the most important centres for Christianity, culture, and learning in all of Europe.

King Charlemagne

Charlemagne ("Charles the Great," 742–814) inherited the powerful Frankish kingdom of his father Pepin and grandfather Martel. When he became the sole king in 771, he set about expanding the empire over other Teutonic peoples, violently incorporating the Saxons under Frankish rule in 772 and defeating the Lombards by 774. Charlemagne fought the Spanish Moors in the southwest of his kingdom and also expanded eastwards, defeating the Asiatic Avar tribes and other pagan Slavic groups.

THECLA (?–C. 790)

In 749 Boniface sent a request back to England for Anglo-Saxon women to be sent in aid of the mission to the Teutons. One of these, Thecla, became abbess of the Benedictine convents of Ochsenfurt and later Kitzingen. Letters sent to her by Boniface reveal the extent to which he relied on her as a fellow labourer, especially in the education and conversion of hostile Teutonic women and their children. Thecla was martyred c. 790.

CHURCH HISTORY OF THE ENGLISH PEOPLE

Bede (c. 673–735) was a celebrated scholar and monk at Jarrow when he wrote his book (completed 731). His was the first ever work on English national and church history.

Carolingian Renaissance

Along with military expansion, Charlemagne sought to re-establish a common culture to the West. His revival of learning, language, administration, and theology became known as the Carolingian Renaissance. The campaign itself would collapse after the Norse invasions of the ninth century, but it still helped to preserve knowledge and paved the way for later medieval renaissances.

Charlemagne gathered Italian historians and grammarians, Spanish poets, and Irish theologians to his court. He founded academies in monasteries at Tours and Fulda, amongst others. Following the educational system of Boethius, Charlemagne's schools taught the seven liberal arts: arithmetic, astronomy, geometry, grammar, logic, music, and rhetoric.

▲ Charlemagne receives the scholar Alcuin, with whom he planned a "new Athens" of Christian civilization. Fresco by Victor Schnetz (1787–1870). Alfredo Dagli Orti/Shutterstock

69

VIKINGS

From 789, constant attacks from Norse Vikings brought chaos to the coastal regions of England and Scotland. Monasteries and churches were sacked for their wealth (including Lindisfarne in 793 and Jarrow in 794), and many people were displaced as a result of the raids. Norsemen would dominate Northern Europe in the following century.

▲ Vikings were considered "Kings of the Sea," as in this French engraving *Les rois de la mer en expédition*, after Albert Sebille (1874–1953).

Gianni Dagli Orti/Shutterstock

▲ Painting depicting the coronation of Emperor Charlemange by Pope Leo III at St. Peter's Rome.   Wikimedia Commons

Alcuin and the New Athens

For his campaign, Charlemagne intentionally followed the lead of the old Greco-Roman civilisation, although this time his focus was primarily on creating a literate, educated Christian clergy. In this his chief aid was the scholar Alcuin (c. 735–804), who wrote to him in a letter: "It may be that a new Athens will arise in Francia, and an Athens fairer than of old, for our Athens, ennobled by the teachings of Christ, will surpass the wisdom of the Academy."

Alcuin was invited from York to run the Carolingian palace school of Aix-la-Chapelle in 782. There he organised the literary and educational aspects of the renaissance and assisted Charlemagne's interventions in matters of church discipline and doctrine. Alcuin wrote biblical commentaries and led the scholarly reworking of the Vulgate Bible, fixing many corruptions of translation that had crept in. In 794 Alcuin took part in the Synod of Frankfort, which did much to align Spanish clergy with the Roman Church. He was appointed abbot of St. Martin's Abbey in Tours in 796.

Emperor Charlemagne

In Rome, on Christmas Day in the year 800, Pope Leo III (?–816) crowned Charlemagne as the emperor. The claim, which solidified Charlemagne's desire to restore the Western Empire, caused consternation in the Byzantine East. The action would also have ramifications for church unity in East and West and would eventually lead to the creation of the Holy Roman Empire of medieval Europe.

▲ Portrait of Emperor Charlemagne by Albrecht Durer

Wikimedia Commons

CAPITAL AND SMALL LETTERS

In an effort to make reading easier, Alcuin helped to develop "Carolingian miniscule": today's system of writing using Roman capitals with small letters.

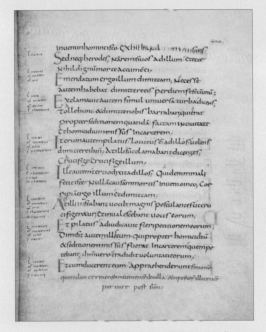

▲ Page of text (folio 160v) from a Carolingian Gospel Book (British Library, MS Add. 11848), written in Carolingian minuscule

Wikimedia Commons

CONVERSION AND CULTURE: 800-900

In the ninth century, old conflicts continue, yet the era also witnesses a revival of mission and conversion amongst new peoples. In the East the advent of the second iconoclastic movement, although initially bloody, will lead to renewed confidence in the Orthodox Church. The rejuvenation of Constantinople spreads to the nations on the eastern frontiers, leading to the conversion of Slavic and other pagan peoples. In the West, Charlemagne's renaissance flags in the face of the barbarian Norse onslaught affecting all of Northern Europe. Yet the potential for resurgence remains in the West. As Viking conquerors settle in Christian lands, they too begin to adopt Christianity for themselves, and missions to the Scandinavian tribes begin at this time.

▼ Instanbul (Constantinople)   Berkomaster/Shutterstock

East

Theodore of Stoudios

Between 797 and 799 the threat of Muslim raids led the Byzantine abbot Theodore (759–826) to move his monastery from Saccudion in Bithynia to the site of Stoudios (Latin *Studium*) in Constantinople. Under the energetic Theodore, the Studite monks thrived and the monastery became the principal centre for monastic life in the East. Theodore was prolific, writing many influential works and over 600 letters in defence of a strong, independent church.

Theodore's austerity and Christian idealism often brought him into conflict with morally lax emperors and the priests who supported them, and he was occasionally sent into exile, prompting several appeals to the papacy and Byzantine authorities.

Second Iconoclasm

After a military coup in 813, Leo V assumed the throne as emperor and promptly set about reviving the iconoclastic policies of his predecessor Constantine V. As the most prominent opponent of iconoclasm, Theodore was once again banished in 815. Patriarch Nicephorus (758–828) was deposed, and many other monks

▲ Empress Theodora is credited with the restoration of icons within Orthodoxy. Mosaic from the Basilica San Vitale, Ravenna, Italy.   mountainpix/Shutterstock

📍 FEAST OF ORTHODOXY

The feast established to celebrate the defeat of iconoclasm is a major point in the Orthodox calendar. On the first Sunday of Lent, hymns composed by martyrs are chanted during the procession of icons, and a list of heretics, saints, and devout emperors (called the *Synodicon*) is read out in litany.

▲ A modern Feast of Orthodoxy in Russia
Fotosearch RM/age fotostock

▲ Late fourteenth- early fifteenth-century icon illustrating the "Triumph of Orthodoxy" under the Byzantine empress Theodora over iconoclasm   Wikimedia Commons

were imprisoned or killed when they opposed the removal of icons from their churches and buildings.

Leo was assassinated in 820. His successor, Michael II, continued a milder iconoclasm, prohibiting only the worship of images in the capital city. In 829 his son and successor, Theophilus, brought back violent opposition to icons—a persecution that only ended with Theophilus's death in 842.

Theophilus's widow Theodora (?–c. 867) announced an end to iconoclasm and ordered that the icons be restored. She supported the election of the pro-icon monk Methodius (?–847) to the office of patriarch in 843, and a great feast was celebrated in honour of the event.

Rejuvenation of Orthodoxy

The iconoclastic controversies laid the ground for the final schism between the Eastern and Western Churches. The theological implications of images aroused less interest in the West than did the worrying tendency for Eastern emperors to exert political control over the church, a trend that was largely welcomed and unopposed in principle by the Byzantine clergy. In addition, Roman and Byzantine Christianity inhabited very different contexts. The growing vitality of the Papal States in Rome and of the Christian culture of Frankish Europe in the West was matched by a confident Orthodox Church firmly entwined with the Eastern Empire and Greek culture.

Photius and Nicholas

Byzantine court intrigues in 858 resulted in Emperor Michael III deposing Ignatius as patriarch of Constantinople and installing the layman Photius (c. 820–c. 893) in his place.

▲ Photius   Historia/Shutterstock

📍 **MUSLIM, JEWISH, AND CHRISTIAN CONFLICT**

837   Christians and Jews revolt under Moorish rule in Toledo.

846   The Basilica of St. Peter's in Rome sacked by Muslim raiders.

847   Pope Leo IV erects walls around Rome in defence of further raids.

871–879   Continuing war with Muslim armies in the East. Eastern Empire also at war with the Christian Paulicians who aid the Saracens.

878   Periodic persecution of Christians and Jews under Egyptian Muslim rule of Jerusalem.

This Byzantine sect probably earned its name from the third-century heretical bishop Paul of Samosata. They rejected the Old Testament and professed dualistic belief in a Good, spiritual God and an Evil God who created material things. As a result of being persecuted between 842 and 857, many Paulicians assisted the Muslims against the Byzantine armies. Popular and widespread, Paulicianism developed into the Bogomil, Cathar, and Albigensian heresies of the medieval era.

📖 **ENCYCLICAL LETTER OF ST. PHOTIUS**

Photius's 867 encyclical opposing the *Filioque* clause and other aspects of Roman Catholic theology is the first of a series of major statements of Orthodox doctrine that would come to be known as the Symbolical Books. The last statement was written in 1952.

Constantinople appealed to Rome for confirmation of the installation, and under pressure from the emperor, the papal legates approved of Photius. Pope Nicholas I (?–867) rejected the decision that had been made in his name, and in 863 he affirmed Ignatius as patriarch and attempted to depose Photius and all his supporters.

The Western intervention caused great offence in the East. The rift was compounded by debates about whether the current mission to Bulgaria should be carried out under the auspices of Rome or Constantinople. In 867 Photius (who, supported by Emperor Michael, had remained patriarch despite Nicholas's objections) denounced the presence of Roman missionaries in Bulgaria and officially objected to Latin practices such as the *Filioque* clause in the Nicene Creed. Furthermore, Photius issued an excommunication against Pope Nicholas. Tentative peace between East and West would be established, broken, and established again, but the Photian controversy marks a major milestone in the road towards permanent schism.

Slavic Missions

In the ninth century, missions to the pagan Bulgarian, Croatian, Serbian, and Czech peoples were largely conducted by the Eastern churches. The Western influence was always present, however, and local kings often prevaricated between Constantinople and Rome.

CROATS

Prince Viseslav reigned in the Croatian port city of Nin c. 800. A Christian, Viseslav was in power when a Frankish bishopric was established c. 803 and the Croatians officially became a Christian people. Inspired by Pope John VIII (?–882), missions to establish Croatian clergy and the Croatian Church were organised between 879 and 892.

CZECHS AND MORAVIANS

Christianity was evident amongst the Czech peoples from early in the century. In 845, fourteen Czech princes presented themselves before the German prince Louis in Regensburg, demanding to be baptised. The move, although probably motivated by political and military reasons, nonetheless would have brought considerable changes to the fabric of Czech society, as the princes represented the majority of the Czech power base at the time.

However, it was the 863 mission of Cyril and Methodius to Greater Moravia that would fully entrench Christianity amongst the Slavic people.

"Apostles to the Slavs"

These Greek brothers from Thessalonica were the era's most celebrated missionaries. Before becoming a monk, Methodius (c. 815–885) was a governor of a Slavic province in the Byzantine Empire. A theologian, linguist, and minister, Cyril (826–869) was originally called "Constantine" but changed his name when he became a monk shortly before his death.

Their first mission was to the Khazars in 860. In 862 Emperor Michael III and Patriarch Photius recruited the brothers to lead the mission to the Slavs of Bohemia and Moravia. Cyril and Methodius enjoyed great success preaching in Slavic, translating the liturgy, and organising church services according to the local language. The Orthodox mission also gained the support of Rome and acted under full papal authority, although Germanic churchmen sometimes resented their influence.

After Cyril died in a Roman monastery in 868, Methodius was consecrated bishop to the Slavs by Pope Adrian II (792–872). On his return to Moravia, Methodius was opposed by the German bishops already there, and he was imprisoned by the local Slav prince Sviatopolk. Pope John VIII secured his release, and Methodius went on to work in Pannonia and Velehrad (modern-day Czech Republic), where he died in 885.

Serbs

Under the influence of Cyril and Methodius, the Serbian prince Mutimir (reigned c. 860–891) converted to Christianity and was baptised.

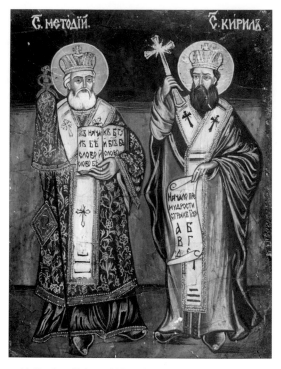

▲ Methodius, Bishop of Moravia and "Apostle to the Slavs." Fourteenth-century fresco from the Monastery of St. Mark, Skopje, Macedonia. Adam Jan Figel/Shutterstock

From this point the Serbs became an officially Christian people, but the transition was not always easy. In 866, under orders from Emperor Basil I, Serbs living in the Narenta Valley were forcibly baptised. Serbian Christianisation continued from 867 to 874, with the country wavering between allegiance to Constantinople and to Rome.

Bulgarians

Christian missionaries had seen some success in Bulgaria from as early as the seventh century. Later concerted missionary efforts led to Boris (?–907), the khan (or king) of Bulgaria, being baptised in 864. As Greek and German Christian missionaries were already an influence

▲ Tsarevets fortress, Veliko Tarnovo, Bulgaria

nstanev/iStock

THE CYRILLIC ALPHABET

Tradition ascribes the invention of the alphabet used by the Slavonic peoples to Cyril. The vernacular work of Cyril and Methodius opened the way for the rich tradition of Slavonic literature, liturgy, and scriptural translations.

▲ Cyrillic writing

in Bulgaria, Boris too prevaricated between Rome and Constantinople. Boris favoured an independent Bulgarian Church, and for this reason ran afoul of both the patriarch and the pope. Eventually Boris joined with Constantinople c. 870. In 885 the Bulgarian Church received a native liturgy under the auspices of Clement of Ochrid (?–916), a disciple of Cyril

and Methodius and founder of the first Slavic university teaching language and theology. Bulgarian pagan reaction against forced baptisms led to violent conflicts in 889–893. The rebellion was short-lived however, and under the rule of the Christian khan Simeon (893–927), Bulgaria enjoyed a golden age of literature and culture. It was also under Simeon's rule that the Bulgarian Church became autocephalous ("self-headed" or autonomous) early in the following century.

West

Persistent Scandinavian raiding undoubtedly unsettled much of society in the West; however, the English and Frankish Churches retained a strong influence on the religion, administration, education, and culture of the European peoples.

Louis the Pious

Charlemagne died in 814. Louis, his third and youngest son, assumed the empire in 814.

Louis (778–840) took a great interest in mission and monastic reform. In 815 he built a model abbey at Aachen and handed the rule of it over to Benedict of Aniane (c. 750–821). As the founder of a monastery at Languedoc that emphasised manual labour rather than study, Benedict had already earned a reputation as a strict enforcer of the Benedictine Rule. Through regular councils held at the Aachen community in 816, 817, and 818, Benedict enforced conformity of the surrounding monasteries. Benedict died before the reform scheme could fully take root, and Louis's attempt at monastic unity was further disrupted by constant Viking raids.

Scandinavian Missions

Louis did not allow the Scandinavian threat to thwart his attempts at Christian expansion. A royal visit to Denmark led to the conversion and baptism of the Danish chief Harald. Louis followed up this initial missionary endeavour by creating the archbishopric of Hamburg and Bremen and sending Anskar (801–865), a Frankish monk, to establish a church and school in Hedeby (modern-day Schleswig) in c. 826. Although he saw little success during his missionary career, Anskar would become known as the "Apostle to the North" and would be seen as the foundational influence for Scandinavian Christianity.

Heathen opposition forced Anskar to return to Louis's court in 829, only to be sent out again to Sweden at the request of Björn, a local chief. Anskar founded Sweden's first church at Birka in 830. In 854 Anskar returned to Denmark, providing a Christian influence on the Jutland king Erik (or Horik) and opposing the Viking slave trade. Anskar continually faced stiff challenge from the local people and warlords.

CONTINUED VIKING ATTACKS

800	In Britain, Vikings attack the shrine of the tomb of St. Andrew.
807	Iona monastery abandoned as a result of Viking raids.
840	Ireland becomes the centre for Norse trade with Europe. Settled Vikings begin to adopt Christianity.
866	Vikings destroy the Great Library of York.
870	Danish raiders destroy Ely Monastery.

PILGRIMAGE

The pilgrimage of Santiago de Compostela began in 899, following the purported discovery of the relics of James the Apostle in north-western Spain. The Shrine of St. James remains a major pilgrimage destination for travellers from all over the world.

▲ The scallop shell is the symbol of James the apostle. Here it is at the start of the Camino de Santiago or "The Way of Saint James" famous rout in Bilbao, Spain. Train_Arrival/iStock

After his death, Scandinavian Christianity collapsed back into paganism, not to resurge until a century later.

Alfred the Great

For Christianity, the last half of the ninth century in England was a time of culture and learning set against the backdrop of devastating Viking incursions. Alfred "the Great" (849–899) became King of Wessex in 871. His plans for the reform of the parish system and

the revival of monasticism were thwarted by the crippling cost of defence against the Danish. Instead, Alfred turned to literacy as a way of maintaining the links with wider Christendom and civilisation that the pagan raiders threatened to sever. A great work of dissemination and preservation of key Latin Christian texts was undertaken. Alfred himself did many of the translations, as did the team of international scholars he assembled for the purpose.

Alfred set the pattern for Christian kingship as well as instituted a high standard of education for clergymen and nobles. He also began the work of Christianising the Danish invaders. Despite the threat of dissolution at the hands of the barbarians, he helped Christianity in the Western Isles to thrive, leaving it in good health upon his death at the end of the century in 899.

▲ King Alfred ordered copies of the "Alfred Jewel" to accompany the texts that he sent out around the country. It was probably used as a pointer to aid in reading. Only one Jewel remains and is kept in the Ashmolean Museum, Oxford.

Universal History Archive/Universal Images Group/Shutterstock

 KING GUTHRUM (?–890)

In 878 the Danish warlord Guthrum overran Wessex in a surprise attack on Alfred's forces. Alfred's successful counterattack brought Guthrum to terms under a treaty known as the Peace of Wedmore. Guthrum accepted conversion and was baptised under the name "Aethelstan." In 880 he withdrew to East Anglia and ruled as a Christian king.

10 GREEN SHOOTS, DEAD BRANCHES: 900–1000

In the last century before the new millennium, the church in the West endures a string of bad popes. Yet even as the centre of Western Christendom suffers, the faith is kept alive at the fringes. Monks preserve the ideals and culture of Christianity, while the official hierarchy is largely concerned with its own temporal power. In the East, significant developments are also made due to a thriving monasticism, which exerts its influence on Orthodox rulers and leads the charge in the Christianisation of the Slavic peoples. Bulgaria especially benefits from its adoption of Orthodox Christianity. This is also the century of the Christianisation of Russia—an event that will come to be of great significance for the Eastern Church. Meanwhile, territorial wars between Christians and Muslims rage on, preparing the ground for the Crusades of the following century and beyond.

▶ Domes of St. Mark's Basilica in Piazza San Marco or St. Mark's Square, Venice, Italy
bpperry/iStock

West

Disastrous Popes

The year 900 saw yet another tenuous renewal of the relationship between Rome and Constantinople. However, reconciliation was hampered by the reputation of the hierarchy of the Western Church, which was suffering under a series of corrupt, worldly, or simply incompetent popes.

As the Papal States grew in temporal and economic influence, they became more entrenched in the political power plays of the day. The office of the papacy had become a desirable acquisition for rival aristocratic Italian families, who jockeyed to get their own family members in the position. The trend began in the previous century with publicly corrupt popes such as Sergius II (in office 844–847) and John VIII, who held office for ten years before becoming the first pope to be assassinated in 882. Other mad or bad popes followed, including Stephen VI (strangled in 897 after presiding over an infamous synod that condemned the exhumed corpse of his predecessor Pope Formosus), Leo V (pope for thirty days before being killed in 903), and his successor (and executioner) Sergius III (presided 904–911). Other ineffectual or political popes included John X (914–928), Stephen VII (c. 929–931), and Stephen VIII (939–942).

Pope John XII

The reputation of the papacy reached one of many low points with the career of Pope John XII. Octavian (?–964) was the aristocratic son of Alberic, the ruler of Rome. As part of his consolidation of power, Alberic arranged for his son to be made pope in 955. Octavian was eighteen years old when he took the name John XII.

John XII's pontificate was marked by the worldliness and political intrigues that began his reign. In 962 John enlisted the help of the Germanic prince Otto I against the rival king Berengar from northern Italy. John crowned Otto the Roman emperor and in return offered his fealty to the new emperor. The *Privilegium Ottonianum*, a legal document detailing the treaty,

▲ Octavian became Pope John XII when he was eighteen years old. His time in office marks a low point in the history of the papacy. Zvonimir Atletic/123RF.com

was based in part on the forged *Donation of Constantine*. It offered Otto effective control over the Papal States, putting the authority of the pope under the emperor. John reneged on his agreement and turned to Berengar and to the Byzantines for help against Otto's troops. The help was not forthcoming, and John was deposed for "immorality" in 963. He returned to Rome a year later but died suddenly under mysterious circumstances in 964.

Subordination of the Papacy

John's case is significant because he placed in power Otto and his successors. This dynasty installed a number of unsuitable popes, including Benedict VI (reigned 973–974), John XIV (983–984), John XV (985–996), and Gregory V (996–999), without consultation of the clergy or thought for the church.

This time of the general discrediting of the papacy is important to note, for it acted as a catalyst for renewal and reform in the West. These movements were often led by churchmen or secular rulers operating outside of Rome.

ANTIPHONARY OF ST. BENIGNE

Probably written c. 980, the manuscript records Gregorian plainsong and is one of our earliest surviving pieces of written music. Its obscure method of notation predates the invention of the musical stave in the eleventh century.

▲ An example of the obscure method of notation

Wikimedia Commons

▲ The Church of St. Peter and St. Paul forms part of Cluny Abbey in Burgundy, France. Other monasteries were quick to follow Cluny's moral and spiritual example.

Wikimedia Commons

Monastic Reform

Corrupt popes, constant invasions, and the complacency that often accompanies material success had contributed to the disarray of many monastic houses in Western Europe. It was against this backdrop that William, Duke of Aquitaine, founded the monastery of Cluny in Burgundy in 909–910.

Cluny Abbey

Cluny grew in importance largely due to its strict observance of the Benedictine rule. The Cluniac model valued education and learning, stressed the cultivation of a pure spiritual life in individuals, and emphasised good administration and organisation. Neighbouring monasteries quickly adopted the high standards set by the Cluniacs. Under its second abbot, Odo

(927–942), many of the houses of southern France allied themselves with Cluny, and its reforming influence also spread to the great Italian monasteries of Monte Cassino and Subiaco. Under the fifth abbot, Odilo (c. 961–1049), the number of monasteries doubled to sixty-five. Valued by churchmen, kings, and emperors, Odilo's influence was felt across Western Christendom.

Glastonbury Abbey

Celtic Christian communities of some description had been in existence in Glastonbury

"TRUCE OF GOD"

Abbot Odilo was instrumental in establishing the *pax, treuga Dei* between warring factions of southern France and Italy. The Truce of God was a formal suspension of fighting on holy days or seasons. In 1027 fighting between Saturday night and Monday morning was forbidden. The medieval church would eventually extend the truce to cover Advent and Lent.

AELFRIC (C. 955–C. 1020)

The Benedictine abbot Aelfric is chiefly known for his concern to educate English clergy in their own language and for the high quality of his writing, such as his *Lives of the Saints* (c. 998).

CHURCHMAN'S CIGARETTES

THE GLASTONBURY THORN

▲ Glastonbury thorn. The legendary Levantine hawthorne that flowers twice a year was cut down by Cromwell's soldiers but remained alive.

Historia Collection 56/Shutterstock

in England since the seventh century. By the early tenth century, attacks by Danish invaders had reduced the monastery considerably, and indeed monasticism was waning throughout the country. In 943 Dunstan (c. 909–988) was made abbot of Glastonbury. A strict ascetic, Dunstan brought the monastery back under the Benedictine rule. A revival of learning, piety, and organisational excellence ensued. Glastonbury became the main religious centre of the land, leading the restoration of regular monasticism in England. Later medieval legends would connect the abbey to Joseph of Arimathaea, St. Patrick, and King Arthur, instituting Glastonbury as a major site of pilgrimage.

Codes of Conduct

Dunstan was a royal counsellor to Prince Edgar (c. 943–975). When Edgar became king of all England in 959 he appointed Dunstan archbishop of Canterbury in the same year. Together the two undertook a programme of major reform of church and state. A key product

▲ Roussanou Monastery on a cliff, Mount Athos, Meteora, Greece
Artsy/iStock

of this reformation was the *Regularis Concordia* (c. 973). As well as regulating Benedictine observance across the country, the code also detailed the role of the sovereign as the patron of monastic life.

East

Mount Athos

A rocky peninsula jutting into the Aegean Sea off the coast of Macedonia, the "Holy Mountain" was already home to some monks before Athanasius (c. 920–1003) founded the Great Lavra community in 961. With the strong backing of Emperor Nicephorus Phocas, Athanasius instituted a monastic system following the ascetic, coenobitic rule of Basil the Great. Instead of living in isolation, the coenobite monks gathered in supportive communities, a system that led to the increase in power and influence of Mount Athos.

When the emperor died in 969, Athanasius was forced into exile on the grounds that his reform project was too closely aligned with imperial power. However, the new emperor John Tzimisces lent his support, and Athanasius returned to become abbot-general of the entire mountain. Under his influence, Athos would grow to eclipse Stoudios as the most important monastic centre of the Byzantine Church. The mountain, which admitted (and still admits) no women, was home to 58 (now 20) semi-independent Orthodox communities and 900 places of worship, serving, at the height of its popularity, up to 40,000 monks.

Bulgarians

Symeon I (c. 864–927) was the first Bulgarian ruler to adopt the title "Tsar" in 917.

WENCESLAS (C. 907–C. 935)

The Bohemian prince became king in 922 and was known for his Christian piety and learning. He favoured relationships with the West, and he forged ties with the German princes, a move that was not approved of by some of his pagan subjects. After Wenceslas was murdered by his brother Boleslav, he soon became revered as a martyr and Czech national hero. The English Christmas carol by J. M. Neale (1818–1866) celebrates "Good King Wenceslas," although the events of the song are imaginary.

▲ The mounted statue of Wenceslas, Duke of Bohemia, towers over Wenceslas Square in the Czech city of Prague.

Alex Cimbal/Shutterstock

Symeon's reign was marked by constant warring with the Byzantium Empire, the Serbs, and the Magyars. Under his rule Bulgaria grew to be a major power in the region. It was also during his time that Constantinople was compelled to recognise the Bulgarian Orthodox Church as an independent entity c. 924.

Instead of using Greek, the autocephalous Bulgarian Orthodox Church adopted Slavic as its official language. Christian books translated from Greek to Slavic soon spread from Bulgaria to neighbouring nations. In this way the Bulgarians played a key role in the spread of both Orthodoxy and the Cyrillic alphabet to the Serbs and other Eastern Slavic peoples.

Bogomils

The vigorous Orthodox Bulgarian Church also produced an equally vigorous heresy. The Manichaeistic movement seems to have taken root in the Balkans from the Paulicians who had settled in Thrace. The Bogomils, who

ROYAL CONVERSIONS

The tenth century saw the conversion of a number of rulers, leading to significant Christianisation of the cultures concerned. The Danish king Harold Bluetooth converted in c. 965, sparking a renewed interest in Christianity that had lain dormant for a century. In 966 Prince Mieszko of Poland adopted Christianity, probably under the influence of Catholic missionaries from Moravia. Stephen, the first king of Hungary, was baptised in 985 by the Czech missionary and Prussian martyr Adalbert.

demonised created matter and did not recognise the authority of church or state, earned a reputation for immorality and licentiousness.

Bogomilism spread quickly, prompting the Bulgarian tsar Peter to request help from

85

▲ Princess Olga was one of the first to sow the seeds of Christianity in her nation, although she saw little success in her lifetime. Wikimedia Commons

> ### 👤 ADALBERT OF PRAGUE (956–997)
>
> Adalbert became bishop of his native Prague in 982. His attempts at moral reform led to much opposition from local princes, and he was forced from the city in 996. Adalbert led missions to Hungary, Pomerania, and possibly Russia. He was martyred by pagan Prussians in 997, and his burial site became a major centre of pilgrimage.

Patriarch Theophylact of Constantinople (915–956) in 950. The efforts were ultimately unsuccessful and by 972 the Bogomils were condemned again by the Bulgarian priest Cosmos. Eventually the sect would grow to be the dominant religion in the Balkans and Asia Minor, extinguished only by Islam in the fifteenth century. Bogomil ideas in Italy and France also influenced the Cathars and Albigensians, heretical movements that would have a significant impact on church and state in medieval Europe.

Russians

Christianity had been introduced to the people of Russia before, but the impact had been negligible. In 955 Princess Olga of Kiev (890–969) was baptised after a visit to Constantinople. Neither her subjects nor her son Sviatoslav accepted the faith, and in fact the period following the end of Olga's reign in 964 was marked by a strong pagan revival. The Christianisation of the country would not begin in earnest until the conversion and regency of Sviatoslav's son Vladimir (956–1015).

Prince Vladimir

Prince Vladimir came to power in 980. According to tradition, the pagan Vladimir investigated various other faiths and Christian traditions before adopting Eastern Orthodoxy in 988. The following year he married Anna, the sister of the Byzantine emperor Basil II, and began his campaign promoting Christianity. The success of the religion in Russia can be attributed in part to Vladimir's extensive church-building projects; however, he also imposed forced baptisms. The upper classes and nobility accepted Christianity, but the countryside would remain largely pagan for another 500 years.

POPES, KINGS, AND PEASANTS: 1000–1100

The first century of the new millennium sees Christianity spread to more corners of the map thanks in part to a restored and rejuvenated Roman Church. The reformed papacy consolidates power in Rome, leading to conflicts with secular rulers and a final breach with the church in Constantinople. The advances in Christian architecture, philosophy, and music made in this era remain into the present age. Military conquests by the Normans in the north and the continuing Iberian Christian reconquest in the south will form the contours of European Christendom and prepare the ground for Christian expansion into the New World. Territorial and religious conflict with Muslims in the east also leads to the first of many Crusades in the Holy Land.

Iceland

Iceland had known sporadic Celtic, Viking, and Saxon Christian missionary activity since the early ninth century. The first concerted

KING OF TIDES

The Danish warlord Canute (c. 994–1035) conquered England in 1016. After his conversion to Christianity, Canute earned a reputation as a wise and humble ruler. Legend has it that some of his subjects once attempted to praise Canute by claiming that he could command even the sea and it would obey him. To quiet their flattery, Canute placed his throne in the water and ordered the tide to turn back. When it did not, he forced his followers to admit that there was a limit to his reign: "Let all men know how empty and worthless is the power of kings. For there is none worthy of the name but God, whom heaven, earth, and sea obey."

effort to institute Christianity as the official religion in Iceland came by way of the Norwegian king Olaf Tryggvason in 1000. Isleifur Gizurarson (1006–1080) became Iceland's first

▲ Psalms and hymns from a sixteenth century Icelandic manuscript

The British Library, The Catalogue of Illuminated Manuscripts, CCO 1.0

bishop in 1056, and his son and successor Gissur (1042–1118) presided as the second bishop from 1082 until his death. While the influence of Christianity on the culture and morals of the Icelandic people can be known from stories and sagas of the time, the official church was relatively weak, often subservient to the civil powers of the day. The country was also politically unstable and often under the sway of other Scandinavian powers. As a result, the monastic and intellectual pursuits that sustained much of Christianity in early medieval Europe were bypassed in Iceland. It would not be until the Reformation in the sixteenth century that a stronger Icelandic Church came into its own.

Hungary

Stephen (c. 975–1038) was made the first king of Hungary in 1001 with the blessing of Pope Sylvester II. Stephen's programme of Christianisation was opposed by pagan factions, and he quashed an anti-Christian revolt in Transylvania in 1002. Stephen laid down a constitution, creating ten new bishoprics and instituting Gran as the site of the archbishop's seat.

Restoration of Papacy

By 1046 the papacy had once again fallen into disrepute. Three men, backed by different factions and noble families, vied for the position of pope. Seeking a legitimate pope who could crown him Holy Roman emperor, the German king Henry III convened a council in the Italian town of Sutri to settle the dispute between Benedict IX (c. 1012–c. 1085), Sylvester III (?–1063), and Gregory VI (?–1048).

The claims of all three were quickly dismissed, and Suidger, a bishop from the German town of Bamberg, reluctantly accepted the position. Suidger (?–1047), who took the name Clement II, marks the first in a long line of subsequent German popes who brought a Cluniac reforming influence to the Roman Church.

Further Reforms

Clement II's first major council met in Rome in 1047. Strict measures were put into place, including strong decrees supporting clerical celibacy and condemning simony, a practice that was widespread in the West at the time.

Clement's successor Leo IX (1002–1054) is seen as the man who provided a new ideal for the office of pope. He travelled extensively, promoting the reform programme instituted by his predecessor and working closely with a host of rigorous-minded clergy. Two of these men (Stephen IX and Gregory VII) would go on to become reforming popes themselves in the pattern of Leo.

The College of Cardinals

Many of the problems plaguing the papacy arose from the way that new popes were appointed. In the face of growing popular and clerical demand, 113 bishops met at the Lateran Synod in 1059 to work out a new system for papal elections. The synod set out laws governing the election of a new pope by a congregation of bishops known as the College of Cardinals.

This important development saw the appointment of the pope arising primarily from inside the church. This went against the old system, which relied heavily on sponsorship from noble families or selection by the Holy Roman emperor.

One of the central architects of Lateran was the papal adviser Hildebrand (?–1085).

POPE SYLVESTER II (C. 945–1003)

Sylvester became pope in 999, the first Frenchman to hold that office. An avid reformer, Sylvester assumed responsibility for a papacy that had been plagued by years of corruption. Sylvester encouraged the spread of Christianity in Poland and Hungary, and he led the revival of philosophical, scientific, and mathematical studies in Europe. He is credited with the introduction of Arabic numerals to the West, and with the invention of the pendulum clock.

▲ The first French pope, Sylvester II, did much to restore the damaged reputation of the papacy and to aid learning throughout Europe.

Zvonimir Atletic/123RF.com

▲ Cardinals attend the Religious Mass 'Pro Eligendo Romano Pontifice' at Saint Peter's Basilica in the Vatican Vatican City, 2013   Michael Kappeler/Epa/Shutterstock

◀ A modern-day cardinal. Since the medieval era, cardinals meeting together in a process called the Conclave have been responsible for electing the new pope.

Paolo_Toffanin/iStock

The decisions made here laid the groundwork for Hildebrand's major push for reordering the church. He continued the policy of organisation and consolidation of power when he became pope in 1073.

Hildebrandian Discipline

Hildebrand became pope by popular consensus, taking the name Gregory VII. Hildebrand had earned his reputation as a bishop and chief administrator, working for Pope Leo IX from 1049. Even before assuming the role of pope himself, he exerted great influence over the papacy, and the programme of structural reform that followed in his wake is known as *Hildebrandian*.

Hildebrandian reforms were driven by the belief that the papacy functioned as a governmental institution, and thus legal and clerical structures were of utmost importance. To enforce discipline in the hierarchy, Gregory managed the higher clergy by strengthening decrees against simony and clerical marriage in 1074. Also central to the reforms was a ban on *lay investiture*—the appointment of bishops and clerics by authorities outside of the church. The reforms served to lessen the ties a bishop might have to his local ruler and thus increased his allegiance to Rome.

The measures were opposed, sometimes violently. King William I of England balked at the full extent of Gregory's attempts to focus power in Rome. Philip I of France and Henry IV of Germany also proved especially resistant to the Hildebrandian regime.

The Investiture Struggle

In 1075 Henry IV objected to Pope Gregory's ban on investiture, as it meant that Henry had no control over powerful official appointments in his empire. In 1076 Henry sponsored two synods at Worms and, later, Piacenza at which Gregory's papacy was declared invalid. However, Gregory enjoyed more support and his position remained secure. In the same year, he responded by excommunicating the king. Not only did this remove Henry from the church and deny him Christian communion, it also had the effect of releasing other German and Saxon nobles from their oaths of allegiance.

Henry the Penitent

The threat to Henry's claim to the throne was severe, and in the face of an imminent rebellion, Henry travelled to Italy to subject himself to a programme of public penance in 1077. The event was historically significant for it indicated to the other rulers of Western Europe the superior position of the church in matters of authority, as well as the political consequences of excommunication.

Gregory restored Henry into the church, but the reconciliation was short-lived. In 1080 Henry forced Gregory into exile (where he died in 1085) and set up Clement III

 NORMAN EXPANSION

The Normans were a people largely from Viking and Frankish stock. Their outward expansion from the regions of northern France to Italy (1054), England (1066), and Sicily (1091) would have a comprehensive effect on the culture and Christian traditions of Western Europe.

(1050–1100) as a rival pope. Henry's actions were disastrous for the stability of his reign. The resulting unrest in church and state led to constant revolts and a looming civil war averted only by Henry's death in 1106. The investiture struggle and its aftereffects contributed to the rise of feudalism and prince-fiefdoms in the medieval era.

Road to Schism

With the improved fortunes of Rome came an increase, once again, in tensions with Constantinople. The Western and Eastern traditions of the Christian church had long been at odds politically, linguistically, and theologically. Occasionally these differences had resulted in temporary schisms, but until now the conflicts had eventually been resolved.

The Power of Constantinople

The Eastern emperor Constantine IX Monomachos (c. 980–1055) was seeking allies to defend against Norman expansion in southern Italy. In negotiations with Pope Leo IX, Monomachos agreed to hand over jurisdiction of the Italian churches of the region to the pope.

Patriarch Michael Cerularius (?–c. 1059) objected to the agreement and feared the dominance of papal influence. In defiance of his emperor's perceived sympathy with Rome, Cerularius enacted strict anti-Western measures. He forced all churches in the East to use Greek and attacked Latin liturgical practices such as the use of the *Filioque* clause. The churches that refused to comply were shut down in 1052.

ANSELM

Anselm was archbishop of Canterbury in England from 1093. He was an influential church reformer and educator. As a philosopher, Anselm built on the Platonic tradition received through Augustine. He is a key figure in the school of "realism," and is also the source of the ontological argument for the existence of God.

The Primacy of Rome

The papacy responded by sending a legation led by Cardinal Humbert (?–1061). Humbert was a key Hildebrandian reformer and a champion of centralised Roman Church authority. He objected to Cerularius's use of the title "Ecumenical Patriarch," and he demanded that Constantinople recognise the primacy of Rome. Cerularius refused. The failure of Humbert's legation resulted in declarations of excommunication from both sides, thus establishing the permanent breach between East and West in 1054 and formalising the division of the church into the traditions now known as Orthodoxy and Roman Catholicism.

The Reconquest of Iberia

The Iberian Peninsula (modern-day Spain and Portugal) had been under Muslim control since the beginning of the eighth century. Known as Al-Andalus by the Moorish rulers, by the eleventh century the region was largely controlled by Caliphs from the Umayyad dynasty based in the southern city of Cordoba.

The *Reconquista* refers to the long period since the eighth century when Christians (mostly from small northern kingdoms) attempted to retake Al-Andalus. Due to constant pressure from these assaults, the Arab Caliphs recruited the Berbers—North African Muslim mercenaries—to aid in the defence of the realm. As the Berbers grew in numbers and strength, they too began to compete with their Arab rulers. Under these pressures the Umayyad Caliphate collapsed in 1031, and the disparate armies of the *Reconquista* (often fighting with each other as much as with the Moors) began their advance southwards.

Iberian Christian Advances

By 1034 the Christian Portuguese frontier was established at the river of Mondego. This in turn contributed to the creation of the Kingdom of Galicia and Portugal in 1065.

The year 1034 also marked the height of the power of the king of Navarre, Sancho "the Great" (c. 970–1035). Along with uniting various Iberian regions, Sancho also did much to revive the church in Spain, including re-establishing the See of Pamplona, which was governed along Cluniac principles.

By 1077 the Castilian king Alfonso VI (c. 1040–1109) proclaimed himself "Emperor of All Spain." In 1085 Alfonso took back the city of Toledo from the Moors. There he reinstated the influential diocese of Toledo under Archbishop Bernard de Sedirac (c. 1050–c. 1125). Bernard, a Frenchman, was a Cluniac monk who also supported the reforming programme of Pope Gregory VII and did much to draw the Spanish Church closer to Rome.

Iberian Muslim Challenge

Alfonso's success and the Christian advance southwards were halted by the reinvigorated Berber armies of the Almoravid dynasty, which had come to power after the collapse of the Umayyad Caliphate and which practiced a more vigorous form of Islam than their predecessors. Eventually, the combined armies of the Spanish kingdoms were soundly defeated by the Berbers under the command of Yusuf ibn Tashfin in 1086.

The Mercenary Chief

It would only be under the influence of the mercenary Rodrigo Díaz (c. 1040–1099) that Christian fortunes were revived. Díaz had earned his reputation as a soldier of fortune leading both Muslim and Christian armies, and he was popularly known as El Cid ("The Chief"). In 1094 a major victory was won for the Christians when El Cid conquered the Moorish city of Valencia after a two-year siege. El Cid ruled the city as his own principality, employing both Christians and Muslims in his army and city administration until his death in 1099.

Road to Crusade

In 1028 the Eastern emperor Romanus III (c. 968–1034) allowed for the persecution of Monophysite Christians living in Syria. The subsequent flood of Monophysite refugees relocating to the surrounding Muslim territories sparked unrest in the regions that aided the eventual rise of the Seljuk dynasty. The Seljuks grew powerful, battling other Muslims for control of Jerusalem in 1070 before going on to defeat the forces of Constantinople in the Battle of Manzikert in 1071.

▲ Statue of the Castillian military commander El Cid, Burgos, Spain
Carlos Soler Martinez/123RF.com

▲ The Byzantine emperor Alexius Commenus
Kayıhan Bölükbaşı/123RF.com

GREAT BUILDINGS

A number of significant religious buildings and sites were either founded or destroyed in the eleventh century.

1009 Systematic destruction of the Church of the Holy Sepulchre in Jerusalem by the Caliph Hakim. Rebuilding was completed in 1048.

1037 Building of the Cathedral of Holy Wisdom in Kiev.

c. 1050 Pecherska Lavra (Monastery of the Caves) founded in Kiev.

1065 King Edward the Confessor consecrates Westminster Abbey in England.

1070 The cathedral at the pilgrimage city Santiago de Compostela begins construction in Spain.

▲ Saint Sophia Cathedral, Kiev, Ukraine

vvoennyy/123RF.com

First Crusade

The significant victory paved the way for Seljuk forces to control Asia Minor and Syria, regions that had previously served as recruiting grounds for the Byzantium army. Starved of resources and facing the increasing threat of Muslim forces, Emperor Alexius Comnenus (1048–1118) requested help from the West. In spite of the breach that existed between Constantinople and Rome, Pope Urban II (c. 1042–1099) answered the appeal. His proclamation of the First Crusade in 1095 called for Christian soldiers to liberate Jerusalem and protect Christendom against the Muslim invaders.

CANUTE THE HOLY (C. 1043–1086)

Canute IV became king of Denmark in 1080. He was a fervent supporter of Christianity and passed laws for the care of the poor and sick. His aborted 1085 invasion of England marked one of the last times in history that a Viking army was assembled to invade another European country. Canute was killed by pagan rebels in 1086 and is considered a martyr and the patron saint of Denmark by the Roman Catholic Church.

▲ View of Jerusalem and the Mount of Olives
Renata Sedmakova/Shutterstock

People's Crusade

The Crusade was immediately popular and sparked a religious revival, especially amongst the poor. The promotion of war against non-Christians also led to violent outbreaks against European Jews, who were plundered to help pay for the armed pilgrimage to the Holy Land.

Many fighting groups were organised. One zealous preacher, Peter the Hermit (c. 1050–1115), gained a massive following and in 1096 headed up an excursion to the Middle East. Composed of over 20,000 untrained and ill-disciplined peasants, his "People's Crusade" proved to be a threat and a burden to the very regions it was supposed to protect. Despite the Turks' comprehensive defeat of the ragged army at Civetot in 1096, Peter escaped and was present at the crusaders' capture of Jerusalem.

Capturing the Holy Lands

The official fighting force that Pope Urban assembled was composed of several armies from France and southern Italy. They fared better than Peter's untrained mob, and the city of Antioch was recaptured in 1098 with Jerusalem taken a year later. Victory was accompanied by mass slaughter of the Jews and Muslims living in the city.

The First Crusade had achieved its main aims, but the European occupation of the Holy Land was not complete and the Muslim presence remained in force in the region. A number of Latin city-states were set up at Antioch, Tripoli, Edessa, and Jerusalem. Duke Godfrey of Bouillon (1058–1100) was made the first Latin ruler of the Holy City in 1099, although he declined to assume a royal title. When Godfrey died, his brother Baldwin was not so reluctant, and he was crowned king of Jerusalem on Christmas Day in the year 1100.

12 WAR AND PEACE: 1100–1200

An apparently ceaseless procession of war and struggle dominates Christian concerns in the twelfth century. Three Crusades mobilise Western forces in an attempt to reconquer the Holy Lands, exacerbating tensions with the East in the process. The Moors are fought in Spain, and Islam continues to threaten Constantinople. Slavic pagans and Christian heretics invite violent suppression in the East. The West resists repeated attempts made by European kings for the state to dominate the church. Yet the era is not totally characterised by violence. Monastic traditions embrace simplicity, learning, and radical service to the poor. Mystics advise princes and kings in the practice of Christian meditation. Hospitals and universities come to prominence. Literacy and art advance. Legal systems become more sophisticated. Indeed, alongside war, the twelfth century witnesses some of the greatest advances in peaceful pursuits yet seen in Christian civilisation.

The Latin States

The crusaders imposed a brutal rule over their newly captured city-states, with many Muslim and Jewish residents massacred. Control over the Latin states proved difficult to maintain, and

▲ The power and wealth of the Church was displayed through its art and architecture. Here, gold-leaf mosaics adorn the Byzantine Basilica of San Marco, Venice, Italy.

emicristea/123RF.com

TEMPLES AND HOSPITALS

The Knights Templar were a military religious order founded by Hughes de Payens (c. 1070–c. 1136) c. 1118 with the original purpose of protecting crusaders and pilgrims as they travelled to the Holy Lands. The Templars soon became powerful throughout the Holy Lands and Europe, contributing to political tensions and their eventual suppression in the fourteenth century.

◄ Nineteenth-century artist's representation of the Knights Templar, who are wearing their distinctive tabard with the cross of St. George.

Historia/Shutterstock

The Knights Hospitaller were founded no later than c. 1108 with the original intent of caring for sick, poor, and wounded pilgrims. Under the organisational leadership of Raymond du Puy (1083–1160), the influence of the order (made up of men and women) soon spread throughout the region and Western Europe. The Order of Knights of the Hospital of St. John continue today as the Knights of Malta. The order lies behind the foundation of many hospitals and the creation of the St. John Ambulance service of the modern era.

▲ The eight-pointed Maltese cross, symbol of the Knights Hospitaller of St. John
Jan Marijs/123RF.com

▶ The Grand Master's Palace for the Knights of Malta, in La Valletta, Malta. Built 1570–80 by Girolmu Cassar.

sergeyp/123RF.com

Muslim armies led by Sultan Zeuzhi captured Edessa in 1144. Fear that Jerusalem would also soon fall provoked Pope Eugenius III (?–1153) to proclaim a Second Crusade in 1147.

Second Crusade

The influential abbot Bernard of Clairvaux was commissioned to organise and preach the Second Crusade. The army—a joint venture of French and German troops led by the French king Louis VII and the German king Conrad III—ransacked Byzantine territory as it marched through on its way to Jerusalem, leading to deeper mistrust between East and West. Furthermore, when the crusaders reached their destination, they did not meet with success. Conrad was defeated in 1147 by Seljuk Turks, Louis was defeated the following year, and the crusaders were forced to withdraw

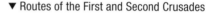

THE CRUSADES

The crusaders' ostensible aim had been to defend the Byzantine Empire against the Muslim threat, yet conflicts between Western and Eastern Christendom continued in the Middle East. After a successful crusading campaign, the Norman prince Bohemond (c. 1052–1111) took control of Antioch rather than returning it to the possession of Emperor Alexius I in Constantinople. Alexius and Bohemond warred over the territory between 1105 and 1107, with Bohemond even gaining papal blessing for his "Crusade" against the Christian emperor.

▼ Routes of the First and Second Crusades

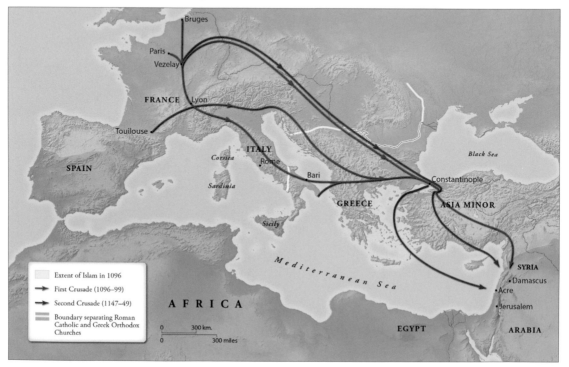

from Damascus. Edessa was totally lost in 1151. In October 1187 the celebrated Muslim leader Saladin captured Jerusalem and subsequently routed the crusaders from many of their fortified cities.

Third Crusade

The rise of Saladin led to panic in Christendom. Faced with the prospect of losing all Christian presence in the Holy Lands, Pope Gregory VIII (?–1187) strove to unite warring European kingdoms in a renewed effort to take Jerusalem. Gregory's efforts led to European truces and the organisation of the Third Crusade under his successor Pope Clement III (?–1191). Running between 1189 and 1192, this venture became known as the "Crusade of Kings" due to the involvement of Emperor Frederick I ("Barbarossa"), Philip II of France, and the "Lionhearted" Richard I of England.

Even though much lost territory was regained, the Third Crusade is not considered a success.

NORTHERN CRUSADES

The crusades against Islam were accompanied by military adventures against pagans of northern Europe and the Baltic states. The missionary Vicelin (c. 1090–1154) had already been preaching peacefully amongst the tribes of northern Germany, but his small successes were swept away by Saxon and Danish crusades against the Wends in 1147. Eric, the king of Sweden (?–1160), is reputed to have led a crusade against the Finns in the 1150s. King Canute VI of Denmark (c. 1163–1202), with the strong support of his archbishop Absalon, conquered the Pomeranian Slavs in 1184. The Baltic regions (present-day Latvia, Lithuania, and Estonia) were also subjected to forced conversions and military conquest following the crusade in 1193 sponsored by Pope Celestine III (1106–1198).

IBERIAN CRUSADE

The 1147 crusade was also waged against Moorish Spain and Portugal as part of the *Reconquista*. That year, English crusaders aided Afonso, first king of Portugal, in the siege and conquest of Lisbon. Some crusaders continued their travel to the Holy Lands, but most stayed and fought the Moors throughout the region. Also starting in 1147 as part of the crusade, the Count of Barcelona Ramón Bérenger IV invaded Moorish Valencia with the help of the French and reconquered Catalonia by 1148.

◀ The sultan Saladin. He led his armies against the Crusaders, taking many cities including Jerusalem.

Alfredo Dagli Orti/Shutterstock

When the German army collapsed after the drowning death of Barbarossa in 1190, the French and English quarrelled, leaving Richard in sole command. Acre was retaken after a long and costly siege, but Jerusalem remained under Muslim control, with Richard and Saladin coming to a three-year truce under which unarmed Christian pilgrims were allowed to enter the city. The failures and unrest following the Third Crusade would lead to the formation of the Fourth Crusade and the Western sack of Constantinople in 1204.

East

The effect of the Crusades on an already fractious Eastern Europe meant that both the Byzantine Empire and the Byzantine Church encountered considerable challenges in the twelfth century. Faced with wars of aggression from the Muslims in the south, as well as the ever-present threat of crusader invasion from the west, Constantinople looked to exert its dominance over its frontier territories.

Emperor Manuel Comnenus led successful campaigns against Serbia (1151–1153) and Hungary (1163–1168), doing much to revive the fortunes of Constantinople. However, his reign represents the last high point of the empire. After his death a succession of poor leaders would contribute to the permanent decline of Byzantium and the dissipation of all that had been gained.

Byzantine Rebellions

The heretical Bogomil movement had spread rapidly throughout the Balkans and Asia Minor. Amongst the Bulgarians, Bosnians, and Serbs, the Bogomil religion was closely connected to patriotic ideas of independence from Constantinople. The rebellious feelings were exacerbated with the imprisonment and execution of Bogomil leaders in Constantinople in 1110 and with violent repression in Serbia in 1180.

In that same year, unpopular and badly administered tax increases led to major revolts in Bulgaria and the loss of Byzantine control over the region. Years of campaigns of rebellion

BERNARD OF CLAIRVAUX (1090–1153)

The French Cistercian monk stands as a towering figure in the twelfth century, and he was involved in most of the significant disputes of the day. As a theologian, Bernard is known primarily for developing the concept of the church as the Bride of Christ and for being a forerunner to the movement of the Devotion to the Blessed Virgin Mary. Unlike most of his contemporaries, Bernard opposed the persecution of the Jews.

MARONITE CHURCH

This Syrian Christian church is predominately based in Lebanon (where they currently constitute the largest single religious group), with members found throughout the Middle East as well as in North and South America. The Maronites trace their foundations to the fifth-century teaching of Maro. In the seventh and eighth centuries, the Maronites rejected the Third Council of Constantinople and were estranged from the wider church. Following their assistance to the crusaders in Syria, the Maronites were brought back into communion with Rome in 1182.

followed, leading to the Byzantine Empire's recognition of the independence of Bulgaria and Serbia in 1186.

West

In the West as well, the historical relationship between church and state is one filled with examples of mutual dependence and antagonism.

LALIBELA

In 1189 the ruling member of the Ethiopian Zagwe dynasty, Emperor Gebre Mesqel Lalibela, ordered the construction of the stone monolithic churches at Roha (now known as Lalibela). The eleven churches were hewn from the rock, with their construction probably not completed for the next two centuries.

▲ The sunken, rock-hewn church of Bet Giyorgis (St. George), Lalibela, northern Ethiopia

Hakan Can Yalcin/123RF.com

Kings and emperors needed the church to legitimise their claims to rule and valued the vast material resources and moral authority that came with an alliance with the papacy. Yet at the same time, secular rulers often resented the power of the church, which claimed, in principle, to be serving a Master higher than any earthly ruler. Likewise, the church often appealed to the king's coffers when it needed money and to the emperor's troops when it needed protection, although popes and bishops were loath to give over all their authority to the state.

The investiture struggle of Henry IV did not end with his death in 1106. Various European kings found themselves embroiled in conflict with bishops who refused to pay homage to or accept priests who had been placed in their position by state rulers rather than the church.

Bishops against Kings

In England, Archbishop Anselm of Canterbury (c. 1033–1109) excommunicated any layperson who installed priests and any priest who accepted the commission. Going against the feudal system that demanded fealty in return for land, in 1100 Anselm refused to pay homage to the English king Henry I for his landholdings, an act that seriously undermined the king's rightful claim to rule. A compromise was reached with Henry in 1107 when the king agreed to give up his claim to lay investiture, and in return, priests would pay homage to him before being consecrated. Similar conflicts occurred between the pope and Philip in France and, most significantly, Emperor Henry V in Germany.

The Concordat of Worms

Pope Callistus II (?–1124) came to office in Cluny in 1119. That year he excommunicated

Henry V and opposed Gregory VIII (1106–1125), the "antipope" endorsed by the emperor. With the aid of German princes, Henry and Callistus eventually came to a peaceful agreement, and the investiture struggle was formally resolved at a meeting in the German city of Worms in 1122. As a result of the Concordat of Worms, the emperor renounced his right to investiture and granted free elections of bishops to the church. The pope agreed to allow the emperor's presence at consecrations and formalised the extent to which the emperor could adjudicate in the selection process of church officials.

The English Pope

Nicholas Breakspear (c. 1100–1159) became Pope Hadrian IV in 1154, the only Englishman ever to hold that office. Before becoming pope, Hadrian had spent time as a missionary in Scandinavia. There he organised and reformed the churches of Norway and Sweden. In 1155 Hadrian expelled, and then executed, the troublesome Arnold of Brescia. That same year Hadrian also exerted papal authority over Emperor Frederick I.

Emperor Barbarossa

As German king and emperor, Frederick Barbarossa reignited the state-church tensions that persisted after the Concordat of Worms. He was crowned emperor in 1155 by Hadrian, but soon came to resent the pope's assertion that the crown was a gift of the church. In 1157 Barbarossa distinguished between the *sacrum imperium* (Holy Empire) and the *sancta ecclesia*, the spiritual jurisdiction of the Holy Church. In 1160, after an internal church debate over who should become the next pope, Barbarossa supported Victor IV (?–1164) against the more popular

THE TROUBLESOME PRIEST

Archbishop of Canterbury from 1162, Thomas Becket (c. 1118–1170) opposed the attempts of King Henry II to exert authority over the English Church. In 1170 he was murdered in Canterbury Cathedral by four zealous knights, probably acting on an intemperate pronouncement from Henry. Thomas's martyrdom sparked outrage throughout Europe, and Henry was forced to do public penance in 1172. Becket's shrine remained a principal pilgrimage destination until dissolved by Henry VIII in 1538.

▲ Cantebury Cathedral. Archbishop Thomas Becket's martyrdom here in 1170 sent shockwaves throughout European Christendom.

Philip Bird/123RF.com

candidate Alexander III (c. 1104–1181). The resulting church schism lasted seventeen years and politically served to isolate Germany against the Lombards, French, and Anglo-Normans. Finally, Barbarossa was forced to submit to Pope Alexander with the Treaty of Venice in 1177.

The Simple Life

As the church grew richer and more powerful, so too did reform-minded movements led by churchmen attempting to restore the original purity and simplicity of Christianity. Some of these movements were sanctioned by the church, while others attracted opposition and sometimes violent persecution.

Cistercians

Known as the White Monks, the Cistercian Order was founded in 1098 and grew to prominence under the influence of the Cistercian monk Bernard of Clairvaux. By Bernard's death in 1153, 345 monasteries and nunneries had been established throughout Europe and the Eastern regions loyal to Rome. Cistercians promoted a strict rule and forbade ostentatious displays of wealth or power. They encouraged instead the practice of simplicity and manual labour, and Cistercians became known for their agricultural expertise. The Cistercian way of life and the organisation of its monasteries profoundly influenced other monastic movements in the Middle Ages.

Arnoldists

Arnold of Brescia (1100–1155) was a student of Peter Abelard (1079–1142) and a radical church reformer. He preached simplicity and poverty for the clergy and rejected any papal claims to authority over territory or government. Some of the more severe extremes of his preaching and his opposition to the church earned condemnation from Rome. In 1152 he was captured by Emperor Barbarossa and eventually sentenced to death by Pope Hadrian. His followers (who became known as "Arnoldists") exhibited Donatist tendencies, rejecting the legitimacy of any priest who did not live up to their strict ideals.

Waldenses

The exact origins of the Waldense (or Valdense) movement are uncertain, and the term describes a number of similar groups operating throughout Europe. The most prominent of these centred around Peter Waldo (or Valdes, ?–c. 1218), a rich merchant from Lyons who gave away all his money to the poor and taught a life of simplicity. In 1179 Pope Alexander III gave Waldo his approval, provided only that he preach with the permission of the clergy. When Waldo and his followers broke this ban on unofficial preaching, they were excommunicated and expelled in 1183. The Waldenses were considered to be schismatics and heretics, and they themselves soon splintered into different factions after the death of their leader. In later centuries, many of the groups connected to the Protestant Reformation would claim affinity with the Waldensian movement.

Rise of the University

Alongside Christian warfare and conflict in this era must be placed the flowering of Christian philosophy, debate, and reason. Great universities, such as those in Paris, Oxford, and Bologna, had their beginnings in the twelfth century. Originally founded as centres for theological study and the education of clergy, the universities soon became focal points for academic controversy, with some lecturers attaining fame or notoriety beyond the walls of the lecture hall.

Yes and No

Peter Abelard was lecturing in Paris c. 1115. He attracted large audiences for his dialectical style of teaching and the daring theological conclusions that he reached. In 1121 the Council of Soissons

SCHOLASTICISM

This method of enquiry was first developed in the schools of medieval learning established by Alcuin (c. 735–804) under Charlemagne (742–814). Scholastics approached theology and philosophy through dialectical reasoning, whereby opposite (or apparently opposite) positions are contrasted to come to the truth. The method drew largely from Aristotle and Plato, and the scholastic period saw the rediscovery of many Greek philosophical works that had been lost in the West. Early figures include Johannes Scotus Eriugena (815–877), Anselm of Canterbury (c. 1033–1109), and Peter Abelard (1079–1142). The later, or high, period of scholasticism led to the foundation of universities and the rise of thinkers such as Roger Bacon (1214–1292), Thomas Aquinas (1224–1274), and William of Ockham (c. 1280–1349). Opposition to scholasticism was a key part of much of the renewal, reformation, and renaissance movements in the Middle Ages.

HILDEGARD OF BINGEN (1098–1179)

A German Benedictine abbess, Hildegard was famous for her mystical theology, writing, and wide learning, which included natural history, musical compositions, and medicine. From 1141 Hildegard experienced a number of visions, or "showings," which she wrote down in her principal work *Scivias*. The mystical homilies were closely scrutinised (and approved) by Pope Eugenius III and Bernard of Clairvaux in 1147 and again by the archbishop of Mainz c. 1150.

▲ This medieval illustration depicts Hildegard of Bingen receiving and recording one of her visions of the Divine. Gianni Dagli Orti/Shutterstock

condemned his views on the Trinity without Abelard being present to defend himself, but he continued to work. His most influential theological training manual, the *Sic et Non* ("Yes and No"), was produced in 1122. The book collected apparently contradictory statements from the Bible and from early church fathers and required students to reconcile them while recognising different expressions of authority. Abelard was condemned again in 1140 by Bernard of Clairvaux, but after the intervention of some of his supporters, Abelard was reconciled to Bernard before his death at a Cluniac priory in 1142.

The Laws of the Church

The monk and papal adviser Gratian (?–c. 1160) is considered to be the "father of canon law." Like Abelard, Gratian collected together the occasionally contradictory thoughts of disparate authorities throughout the ages. However, where Abelard was interested in theological

HÉLOÏSE (1101–1164)

While teaching in Paris, Abelard met and secretly married Héloïse, the niece of Fulbert, Canon of Notre Dame. The affair sparked an outcry; Héloïse was sent off to a convent and, notoriously, Abelard was castrated by a gang of men hired by Fulbert. Abelard retreated to a monastery afterwards in 1117.

THE LATIN QUR'AN

The abbot of Cluny Peter the Venerable (c. 1092–1156) was a friend of Peter Abelard and Bernard of Clairvaux and celebrated as an educational reformer. Peter wrote theological arguments against Judaism and Islam and was responsible for the first translation of the Qur'an into Latin, a work completed in 1143.

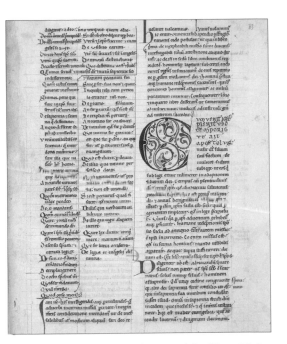

▲ Details from an illuminated manuscript edition of Peter Lombard's Sentences. The book remained a standard university text for 500 years.

The British Library, The Catalogue of Illuminated Manuscripts, CCO 1.0

Master of the Sentences

The "Master of the Sentences," Peter Lombard (c. 1095–1160) trained at Bologna before moving to Paris, where he was elected bishop in 1159. His *Book of Sentences* (completed c. 1158) compiled the thoughts of Christian writers from the church fathers all the way up to near contemporaries, including Abelard and Gratian. The *Sentences* also introduced to Western readers the thoughts of Greek fathers, such as John of Damascus. By applying objective organisational principles and avoiding extremes on either side, the *Sentences* provided a clear summary of Christian thought and doctrine that became the standard textbook for university education throughout Europe well into the seventeenth century.

debate, Gratian focused on issues of church discipline. His *Decreta* (written no earlier than 1139) is a collection of almost 4,000 texts and pronouncements from church fathers, popes, and councils, presented in a structured and harmonious form. Gratian's contribution was to make canon law (the regulations of the Christian church) a subject separate from theological doctrine and to provide a legal framework for the church's organisation. The *Decreta* was taught in Oxford and Paris and was a principal text for the University of Bologna in northern Italy, which became the centre for canon and civil law throughout Europe.

EMPIRE AND WILDERNESS: 1200–1300

The thirteenth century sees the reigns of the great medieval popes and the births of major religious orders. It brings the developments of technologies, philosophies, and theologies that continue to affect Christian thought and practice. Despite attempts at reconciliation, the gap between the cultures of Eastern and Western Christianity proves too great to close, especially following the disastrous events of the Fourth Crusade. Christians in large swathes of the east and south adapt to life outside of Christendom. Paradoxically, the Russian Orthodox Church enjoys resurgence under the rule of the pagan Mongolian Empire, while the Roman Church struggles at the hands of its Christian kings and rulers.

West

Vicar of Christ

Giovanni Lotario de' Conti (1160–1216) became Pope Innocent III in 1198. Historians consider his time in office a climax to the papacy

▲ Pope Innocent III with Dominic and another friar (possibly Francis) supporting the collapsing basilica of Saint John Lateran.

of the Middle Ages. As the head of Christendom, Innocent saw himself as occupying a space below God but above other men, and he was the first pope to make regular use of the title "Vicar of Christ." Innocent oversaw the reform and reorganisation of church hierarchy and administration. He supported Francis of Assisi, aided Dominic in establishing his new order, and convened the influential Fourth Lateran Council in 1215.

Lateran

The council that met at the Lateran Palace in Rome marks the pinnacle of much Christian thought and practice of the era. It established policies that would shape the church's agenda for centuries to come. Lateran confirmed the official doctrine of the Eucharist, using the term *transubstantiation* for the first time. Yearly confession and Communion were made mandatory. Orthodox rebuttals of the Albigensian, Cathari, and Waldensian heresies were formulated. Clerical abuse of indulgences was curbed, and the church's participation in trial by ordeal was forbidden. The new Franciscan order was confirmed, provision was made for the rule of the Dominicans, and the creation of future orders was curtailed in an effort to encourage church discipline and unity.

Political Intervention

Politically, Innocent asserted the right of the Roman Church to oversee the affairs of kings, princes, and governors. He intervened in the coronation of the Holy Roman emperor, supporting first Otto IV (c. 1182–1218) and then Frederick II (1194–1250) according to the strength of their fealty to the church. In English affairs, Innocent excommunicated King John (1167–1216) in 1209 when the king refused to

ELIZABETH OF HUNGARY (1207–1231)

The daughter of King Andrew of Hungary, Elizabeth gained a reputation from an early age as an extreme ascetic and holy woman. When her husband Louis IV of Thuringia died on crusade in 1227, Elizabeth became a Franciscan nun. She served the poor in Marburg, Germany, and was responsible for building one of Europe's first orphanages. The Gothic cathedral Elisabethkirche was built in her honour, and her remains were interned there in 1236.

▲ Elizabeth of Hungary   Wikimedia Commons

accept Stephen Langton (?–1228) as archbishop of Canterbury. John was forced to submit, and Langton was duly installed in 1213. Innocent's considerable influence was also known in France,

Denmark, Spain, Portugal, Italy, the Germanic and Baltic states, Cyprus, and Armenia. However, it was the unintended consequences of Innocent's earliest intervention that proved to have the greatest impact on Christendom.

Fourth Crusade

The previous crusades had failed to secure Jerusalem or halt the advancement of Islam. In 1202 Innocent launched the Fourth Crusade in yet another attempt to recover Egypt, North Africa, and the Holy Lands. Drained and weary from previous campaigns, Europe's nobility did not meet the call enthusiastically, and relatively few knights joined the crusade. In addition, a great burden was placed on the territories through which the crusaders had to march on their way to Jerusalem, leading once again to friction and instability within Christendom's borders. As a result, the army mustered by the pope was soon deflected from its original purpose.

▲ The expense of transporting large numbers of troops was one of the main reasons the Fourth Crusade failed. *Departure of a Boat for the Crusades*, detail from a Galacian vellum manuscript, mid-thirteenth century.

Fol.53r Departure of a Boat for the Crusades, written in Galacian for Alfonso X (1221–84), Spanish School/Biblioteca Monasterio del Escorial, Madrid, Spain/Bridgeman Images

📖 MAJOR ORDERS

The thirteenth century saw the creation of three major religious orders that remain active to this day.

Dominicans

Dominic (1170–1221) had been active in preaching against the Albigensians since 1203. In 1206, with the support of the bishop of Toulouse, he founded a teaching convent for women. In 1216 Dominic established the Order of Preachers (also known as Black Friars). Dominican men and women became known for their great learning, and many universities were founded under their auspices. Dominicans were at the forefront of missionary activities in the New World and the East.

Franciscans

Francis of Assisi (1182–1226) renounced worldly possessions after a pilgrimage to Rome in 1205, after which he founded a

▲ *Saint Francis and Saint Clare at Supper in the Convent of Saint Damian* Wikimedia Commons

society for preaching, poverty, and penance in 1209. From 1245 onwards, adherents to the original ideal of poverty clashed with moderates who allowed corporate ownership of property. Today the Franciscans are composed of three orders —the Conventuals, the Observants, and the Capuchins.

Poor Clares

Francis founded a second order in partnership with Clare of Assisi (c. 1193–1253). Established c. 1213, the Poor Clare communities spread rapidly through Italy, France, and Spain. The Poor Clares' strict rule included perpetual fasting, sleeping on boards, and complete silence. Adherents to a milder version of the rule instituted by Pope Urban IV (c. 1195–1264) in 1263 became known as Urbanists. A reform in the fifteenth century led by Abbess Collete led to the Colletines and another reform in the sixteenth century produced the Capuchinesses. The three branches are in effect today. Devoted to prayer, fasting, penance, and manual labour, together they constitute the most austere order for women in the Roman Catholic Church.

▲ Clare of Assisi with the order of Poor Clares

Historia/Shutterstock

▲ A Poor Clare nun in Japan

Wikimedia Commons

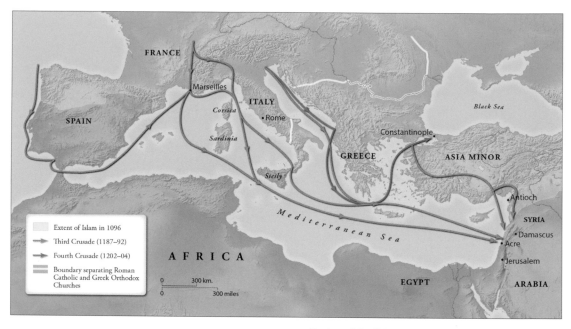

Extent of Islam in 1096

Third Crusade (1187–92)

Fourth Crusade (1202–04)

Boundary separating Roman
Catholic and Greek Orthodox
Churches

▲ Routes of the Third and Fourth Crusades

▼ *How Constantinople was Attacked and Taken* by Loyset Liefet (1420–79).
Kharbine-Tapabor/Shutterstock

Sack of Constantinople

The route to the Holy Land required the assistance of Venetian ships. When the crusaders could not afford to pay the charges demanded of them, their leader Boniface of Montferrat (c. 1150–1207), and the Venetian ruler Enrico Dandolo (c. 1107–1205) agreed instead to join forces and invade Constantinople. In 1204, against the express commands of the pope and of some of the commanders present, the armies of the Christian West sacked and conquered the principal city of the Christian East. The Greek patriarch was removed from power, and the Venetian Thomas Morosini (dates unknown) was installed in his place.

With the creation of the Latin Empire of Constantinople, the advance of the Fourth Crusade on the Holy Land was abandoned and a union of sorts between the Eastern and Western Churches was established under Innocent. However, the situation was unpopular, unstable, and temporary, with the Byzantines repeatedly attempting to regain control. The events of the Latin Empire cast a long shadow over the future development of church and state in the West and in the East, entrenching bitterness between the two cultures and undermining Byzantium's ability to defend against future threats to its territory.

CATHARS AND ALBIGENSIANS

Since the time of the early church fathers, several heretical sects have been known as *Cathari*, a term that derives from the Greek word for "pure." By the medieval era, the label was exclusively applied to those who followed a Manichaean dualistic religion that demonised the body and denied the incarnation of Christ. The Cathars of the twelfth century were heavily influenced by the Bogomils from the East, and they shared the politically subversive nature of that Bulgarian sect. The movement was widespread throughout Germany, Italy, and France, and the term *heretic* is synonymous with *Cathar* in medieval church documents. Many of the findings of the Fourth Lateran Council of 1215, the formation of the Dominican Preaching Order in 1216, and the institution of the Inquisition from 1233 came about in large part in opposition to the Cathar heresy.

In France the Cathars were known as Albigensians because they were based around the town of Albi in the Languedoc region. In 1208 Pope Innocent III sent Peter of Castelnau to Albi on a preaching mission. When Peter was murdered, a long and bloody war followed. By 1229 the Languedoc culture had been decimated and the region incorporated under the rule of northern France. Further action by way of the Inquisition ensured that the Albigensian religion all but disappeared by 1300.

East

Orthodoxy and Union

In 1261 Michael VIII Palaeologus (1223–1282) regained control of Constantinople, finally bringing an end to the Latin Empire of the East. To protect against further threat, especially from Charles of Anjou (king of Naples and Sicily), Emperor Michael sought an expedient alliance with Rome. In return for the allegiance of the Orthodox Church, Pope Gregory X (1210–1276) agreed to provide financial support and check the ambitions of Latin warlords with designs on Constantinople.

Official Union

In 1274 Pope Gregory convened the Second Council of Lyons, which some 1,600 churchmen attended, including 500 bishops. Legates from

THE FINAL CRUSADES

The abortive Fourth Crusade gave rise to further popular movements, not all of them welcomed or sanctioned by the church. The spontaneous Children's Crusade of 1212 involved thousands of poor children and peasants marching to Jerusalem. The ragged group dissolved at Genoa, with many participants returning home at the urging of the pope. From 1219 three more military crusades were raised in the attempt to win Egypt, retake Jerusalem, and defend Christian territories in Syria. The decisive loss of the last Christian stronghold in Acre in 1291 brought an end to the era of official crusades, though crusading ideals continued to influence Christian military and missionary endeavours well into the sixteenth century and beyond.

📖 INQUISITION

The growing threat of heretical groups gave rise to the formation of the dedicated tribunal known as the Inquisition, formalised by Pope Gregory IX (c. 1170–1241) between 1231 and 1235. Suspects were invited to voluntarily confess. Those who did not were subject to examination, with the testimony of two witnesses considered sufficient for conviction. The use of torture was permitted by Pope Innocent IV (?–1254) in 1252. The church oversaw mild penalties, but obstinate heretics were occasionally handed over to the state authorities for execution.

the emperor and representatives of the Orthodox Church were also present, providing assurances that they were ready to submit to the authority of the Roman Church. The Orthodox churchmen accepted the Roman doctrines of purgatory, the sacraments, and the primacy of the pope. At a special High Mass celebrated by Pope Gregory on June 29, the Greek clergy recited the Nicene Creed and sang the *Filioque* clause three times.

Popular Opposition

The Byzantine emperor and the Roman pope had achieved their aim of closing the schism between East and West. Yet the politically motivated union was not popular with wider Orthodoxy, and the submission to Rome was soon repudiated by Greek clergy in defiance of their emperor's wishes.

The patriarch of Constantinople Joseph I Galesiotes (?–1283) abdicated in 1275 and was replaced by John XI Bekkos (c. 1230–1297),

📍 CHRISTIANITY AND THE MONGOLIAN EMPIRE

Nestorian Christianity had been present in Mongolian culture since the seventh century, but it was the rapid expansion of the Mongolian Empire under Genghis Khan (c. 1165–1227) and his successors that brought the most significant opportunities for Christian contact.

▲ A Nestorian wall painting of Palm Sunday found in Chotscho, Chinese Turkestan.

China: Nestorian priests in a procession on Palm Sunday, in a 7th-or 8th-century wall painting from Gaochang (Khocho), Xinjiang/Pictures from History/Bridgeman Images

a patriarch loyal to the union. Bekkos defended the Council of Lyons on intellectual and theological grounds, while the emperor used military might to enforce his will. Ultimately this combination of argument and compulsion was unsuccessful in converting the majority of Orthodoxy to the cause. After Michael's death in 1282, Bekkos was considered by many to be a traitor to the Orthodox faith. He was forced into exile where he died in 1297.

1240 Pope Gregory IX (c. 1170–1241) sends a mission group of Dominicans to the Georgian city of Tiflis, where they encounter the Mongolian court.

1245 Pope Innocent IV (?–1254) sends four Franciscan missions, one of which is led by Giovanni da Plano Carpini (c. 1180–1252). He became an early and important Western chronicler of Central Asia, although the mission was not a success.

1240 Pope Gregory IX (c. 1170–1241) sends a mission group of Dominicans to the Georgian city of Tiflis, where they encounter the Mongolian court.

1245 Pope Innocent IV (?–1254) sends four Franciscan missions, one of which is led by Giovanni da Plano Carpini (c. 1180–1252). He became an early and important Western chronicler of Central Asia, although the mission was not a success.

1253 The Franciscan William of Rubruck (c. 1200–after 1256) travels to the Mongolian capital Karakorum, finding a religiously tolerant culture with evidence of Nestorian, Cathar, and Muslim religions.

1271 Kublai Khan (1215–1294) sends a letter to Pope Gregory X (1210–1276) requesting Christian teachers be sent to aid the Nestorian Church already present in the Chinese Mongolian Empire.

1275 Marco Polo (1245–1324) journeys to the home of Kublai Khan (near modern-day Beijing).

1289 Pope Nicholas IV (1227–1292) sends the Franciscan Giovanni of Monte Corvino (1246–1328) to China. En route, Giovanni sees some missionary success in India in 1291. Despite Nestorian resistance, he builds a Catholic church in Peking (Beijing) in 1299 and translates the Psalms and the New Testament into Mongolian. By the time of his death, Giovanni is reported to have overseen the conversion of 6,000 people. With the Chinese overthrow of the Mongolians and the establishment of the Ming dynasty in 1369, Christianity is once again driven underground.

1295 Ghazan Khan (1271–1303) declares Islam the official religion of the Middle Eastern (Ilkhanid) division of the Mongolian Empire.

▶ Genghis Khan
Universal History Archive/
UIG/Shutterstock

Serbia

The consequences of Latin influence in Constantinople were being felt elsewhere in the realms of Eastern Orthodoxy.

Sometime between 1206 and 1208 the monk Sava (c. 1175–1236) left his Mount Athos monastery to return to his native Serbia. The country was in disarray, due in part to power struggles prompted by the Western presence. As king of Serbia, Sava's brother Stefan enjoyed close ties with Rome (having been crowned by the pope in 1217), but the political situation proved unstable and the nation was on the verge of civil war. Sava countered the Latin influence by forging strong links with the patriarch of Nicaea and organising an independent Serbian church hierarchy loyal to Eastern Orthodoxy. The autocephalous Serbian Church was established in 1219, with the Orthodox Church in Bosnia and Herzegovina also tracing its roots back

TEUTONIC KNIGHTS

The German religious and military order was initially founded as a hospital order confirmed by Pope Clement III in 1199. The knights were active in Hungary (1211–1225) and Prussia (from 1231), becoming powerful rulers in their own right. The character and importance of the order were decisively altered by the Reformation in the sixteenth century and the French Napoleonic advance in the nineteenth century.

◀ A Teutonic Knight

INTERFOTO/Sammlung
Rauch/Mary Evans

EASTERN RITE CATHOLIC CHURCH

The division between Eastern and Western Christianity has not always been clear. Some churches retained Orthodox structures and liturgy while remaining under the authority of Rome. These groups are sometimes called Uniate churches. Early development of the Eastern Rite Catholic Church arose from the 1246 agreement reached between Pope Innocent III and Daniel Romanovich (1201–1264), ruler of the territory comprising much of modern-day Ukraine and Poland. Romanovich sought protection from the Mongolian invaders and accepted the sovereignty of the pope in return for assistance. These early Uniate steps would come to fruition in the Union of Brest-Litovsk in 1596.

to this event. Sava made a number of pilgrimages to Egypt, Palestine, and Constantinople. He died in Bulgaria while returning from a pilgrimage in 1236 and is considered the patron saint of Serbia.

Russia

In Russia, two main military-political factors shaped the development of the Orthodox Church. One was Mongolian advance and rule under Batu Khan (c. 1205–1255); the other was the actions of Prince Alexander Nevsky (c. 1220–1263) against the Latin armies of the West.

THE GOLDEN HORDE

By 1223 Mongol invaders had begun raids on Russian territory. By 1237 the invasion was

fully underway. In 1238 the invaders sacked and burnt Moscow. In 1240 the principal city of Kiev was conquered, and Russia came under the rule of the Mongolian "Golden Horde" led by Batu, grandson of Genghis Khan.

Initially, the sweep of the Mongolian army across Russia wreaked havoc on the church. Monasteries and church buildings were burnt and looted while monks and priests were killed or captured. Yet the social instability brought by the raiders eventually led to the rise of the church as the sole remaining national, cultural, and political centre of Russian life. This was recognised by the new Mongolian rulers, who granted the church special privileges. A charter of immunity (*iarlyk*) was granted to the church in 1267. The decree meant that the clergy were free from being pressed into labour or military service, and it exempted the church from taxation by Mongol or Russian authorities.

Mongolian Alliance

While the Mongols were consolidating their rule over Russian territories, Prince Alexander Nevsky governed the principalities of Novgorod (1236–1252), Kiev (1246–1252), and Vladimir (1252–1263). He allied himself with Batu Khan, suppressing rebellions and collecting taxes for the new rulers of Russia. Through his alliance with the Mongolians, Nevsky is credited with preserving and uniting much of Russian culture that otherwise would have been decimated. He was especially supported by the Russian Orthodox Church, which considers him a national saint.

The Battle on the Ice

Nevsky's contribution to Orthodoxy arises primarily from his defeat of Western invaders, which prevented Rome from dominating the Russian Church. In 1240 Nevsky's army prevented Swedish forces from crossing the River Neva. At the same time, Pope Gregory IX (c. 1170–1241) sent German soldiers on a crusade to the Baltic, with the intent of Christianising the pagans and exerting Roman control over the region. The Teutonic Knights continued their campaign into Russia. In 1242 Nevsky decisively defeated the mounted soldiers as they struggled on frozen ground near Lake Peipus in a fight known as the "Battle on the Ice." As a result, Orthodoxy affirmed its position as the predominate church tradition in Russia.

From Kiev to Vladimir

The greatest churchman from this era, Kirill III (or Cyril, ?–c. 1282), was consecrated

▲ Alexander Nevsky is celebrated for stopping the Teutonic Knights from invading Russia. Fresco from the Archangel Cathedral, Moscow, Russia.   SPUTNIK/Alamy Stock Photo

metropolitan c. 1245. Under Kirill, the centre of the Orthodox Church migrated from the devastated city of Kiev to the city of Vladimir, setting in motion a series of relocations that would end only when Moscow became the home of the Russian Church in the 1320s.

Kirill was convinced that the Mongolian occupation was a punishment from God on the Russian Church, which had grown lax and immoral. During his long service, Kirill worked to reorganise the church, taking advantage of its favoured status and forging close relationships with the khan in order to bring about restoration.

Council of Vladimir

Sometime around 1270 Kirill obtained a copy of the *Nomocanon* from the Bulgarian Church. This valuable Greek document collected Orthodox doctrines, decrees, and interpretations dating from the twelfth century. With the *Nomocanon* as the template, in 1274 the Council of Vladimir issued a strict code rectifying errors in the liturgy and practice of the church in Russia. In addition, immoral practices such as simony, slave ownership, and alcoholism were addressed. Under Kirill, Orthodox Christianity enjoyed a time of resurgence, and the institution of the church grew in wealth and power.

West

At the same time, the fortunes of the Roman Church in the West were not faring so well. In 1277 Giovanni Gaetani Orsini (c. 1216–1280) became Pope Nicholas III. As pope, Nicholas fought to protect Rome's independence from ambitious rulers such as Charles of Anjou and King Rudolph I of Germany. He was the first pope to make the Vatican his central residence, and he expanded the papacy's territories, granting governorship to members of the Orsini family. Nicholas earned a reputation for nepotism and was portrayed in Dante's *Inferno* as the chief example of simony.

Boniface Supreme

The ongoing power struggle between the church and various European kingdoms came to a crisis point during the papacy of Boniface VIII (c. 1234–1303). When he became pope in 1294, Boniface inherited a situation already unstable due to internal and external conflicts.

THOMAS AQUINAS (1224–1274)

The influence of this doctor of the church on Western philosophy, theology, and ethics continues to be felt. Born in Italy, Thomas Aquinas spent most of his working life teaching in Paris. His *Summa contra Gentiles* (1261–1264) is a compendium of Christian apologetics, and his *Summa Theologiae* (1265–1273) systematises Christian thought following the philosophy of Aristotle.

Boniface sought to uphold the tradition of supreme papal power practiced by predecessors such as Gregory VII and Innocent III, but the political mood towards the church had shifted, and he was unable to continue in the same vein.

Boniface Humiliated

In 1296 Boniface issued the bull *Clericis laicos*. The document was directed primarily against the kingdoms of England and France. It forbade any secular power from exacting taxes of revenue from the clergy without prior papal consent. Furthermore, any layman who accepted this money was threatened with excommunication.

Edward I "Longshanks" (1239–1307) and Philip IV "the Fair" (1268–1314) refused to comply. Edward effectively outlawed all clergy by withdrawing royal protection from the church in England. Philip halted the export of gold and valuables from France, thus depriving the church of its revenues from the realm. In the face of these challenges, Boniface was forced to concede in a humiliating, and public, climb-down.

▲ The medieval Sainte Marie-Madeleine basilica in Vezelay, France. The Church in France struggled bitterly against King Philip IV.　　TokioMarineLife/iStock

Waning of the Papacy

Boniface persisted in making claims for the papacy that were resisted by secular rulers. The struggle with Philip of France continued when Boniface issued the bull *Unam Sanctam* in 1302, proclaiming: "It is altogether necessary to salvation for every human creature to be subject to the Roman pontiff." Philip responded by sending a force to arrest the pope. Boniface was briefly taken prisoner in 1303 and died a few weeks later. His passing marks the last in the line of medieval popes who could expect to enjoy absolute authority, and his failure is seen as a turning point in the history of Christianity in the West, leading to new ways that Christians would think about their relation to the world.

HUMILITY AND POWER: 1300–1400

Christians in the fourteenth century continue to wrestle with the tensions and contradictions that arise when a religion of humility, peace, and powerlessness assumes responsibility for the accumulation of wealth, the enforcement of law, and the exercise of power. As the Western Church grows closer to

Cupola of the Church of San Lorenzo, Florence, Italy
isogood/123RF.com

rulers and kings, Europe sees an advance in cultural and political pursuits. Yet at the same time, Christian groups emphasising reform, poverty, and study flourish. Nationalistic forces as much as theological debate fuel the Great Catholic Schism. In the East, the last of the pagan Slavic people convert to Christianity, Constantinople faces the real prospect of life under Muslim rule, and the Russian Orthodox Church enjoys a mystical revival as it prepares to throw off the Mongol yoke.

West

Philip and Boniface

The events of the new century were not auspicious for the Roman Church. Under the leadership of Pope Boniface VIII, the 1302 papal bull *Unam Sanctam* failed to exert power over the secular states of Europe, instead resulting in a humiliating climb-down for the papacy. In 1303 further conflicts with Philip IV of France led to Boniface's capture at the hands of the

▲ Pope Boniface VIII died after being held in captivity by men acting for Philip IV of France.

Alfredo Dagli Orti/Shutterstock

BABYLONIAN CAPTIVITY

The phrase alludes to the capture and deportation of the Hebrew people under the ruler Nebuchadnezzar as told in 2 Kings 24–25. It was first coined by the poet Francesco Petrarch with reference to the situation of the church in Avignon. During the Protestant Reformation in 1520, Martin Luther would use the phrase to denounce various doctrines that he thought held the church in bondage. The life of the Orthodox Church under Ottoman rule in the sixteenth century is sometimes referred to along similar lines.

mercenary agents William de Nogaret and Sciarra Colonna. Boniface died shortly thereafter and his successor, Benedict XI (1240–1304), held the office for only a year until 1304. Following Benedict, the cardinals of the church were divided, and the position of the papacy was left in a precarious position. Further challenges to the integrity of the church came with the 1305 election of Pope Clement V (1264–1314).

Captivity of the Church

Clement founded the universities at Orléans (1306) and Perugia (1308) in support of the study of medicine and oriental languages. Furthermore, his Council of Vienne (1312) provided for the study of Arabic, Chaldee, Hebrew, and Greek in the universities of Paris, Oxford, Salamanca, Bologna, and Rome. However, Clement is best known not as a scholar but as the pope who was responsible for bringing the church under the sphere of French and other Western European interests. In 1309 the centre of the church was moved from Rome to Avignon—a French region that had only relatively recently been cleared of Albigensians. Avignon would become the home for the papacy until 1377, inaugurating a seventy-year period that is often referred to as the "Babylonian Captivity of the Church."

Templars Suppressed

The riches amassed by the Knights Templar proved too much of a temptation for Philip IV. In 1311 Pope Clement inaugurated the Council of Vienne, which, besides furthering the work of universities, met primarily to settle the future of the military and religious order. At first, the council held that the charges of immorality and heresy levelled against the Templars were baseless. Yet when Philip and his army arrived at Vienne in 1312, Pope Clement issued a decree suppressing the order and allowing Philip to appropriate much of their property.

Poverty or Wealth?

Struggle over property would also become the flashpoint for Clement's successor, except in the case of Pope John XXII (1249–1334), the owner in question was not a warlord or a king, but Jesus Christ.

When Jacques Duèse became Pope John in 1316 he continued to bind the church closer to the kingdom of France. He strengthened the papal presence in Avignon, following the policy that when it came to the heart of the church, "Rome" was where the pope lived. Under John, Avignon became a centre for wealth, learning, and culture. It was here that many of the artists and scholars resided who would later be considered the founders of the humanist movement known as the Renaissance. Yet this celebration of the wealth and culture of Christian civilisation led once again to a clash with those who sought to maintain the original Christian ideal of poverty and humility.

Spiritual Franciscans

Debates between Franciscans over the exact rule and purpose of the order had been

---

📍 RENAISSANCE AND HUMANISM

The European Renaissance began in the fourteenth century. The culture experienced a rebirth of interest in the classical world of Greek history, poetry, and philosophy. This emphasis on the classical "humanities" is also known as humanism. Humanist writers of this period were not necessarily setting themselves against religion. Indeed, the leading lights of Renaissance humanism were often clergy or those closely allied with Christian movements and ideas. Nevertheless, humanists tended to treat the church as a secular institution, and their interest in pagan culture led them into tension with other Christian schools of thought.

Francesco Petrarch (1304–1374) is considered the "father of humanism." In addition to describing the "Babylonian Captivity" of the church, he is credited with being the first to label the early medieval period as the "Dark Ages" due to its lack of classical culture. Petrarch's *Secretum* (1352) described an imaginary conversation with Augustine in which the poet attempts to reconcile his love of worldly things with Christian piety.

Dante Alighieri (1265–1321) was an Italian poet, exiled from Florence when he opposed the political ambitions of Pope Boniface VIII. His *La Divina Commedia* (*The Divine Comedy*, written between c. 1308 and 1320) is a magisterial work imaginatively describing the circles of hell, purgatory, and heaven in three volumes, *The Inferno*, *The Purgatory*, and *The Paradise*.

▶ Francesco Petrarch, Italian poet, was the first to describe the early medieval era as "the Dark Ages."

Wikimedia Commons

in existence since the middle of the previous century. The main split was between the *Conventuals*, who supported a moderate rule, and the *Spirituals*, who wanted to retain Francis's original ideas of simplicity and complete poverty. In 1317 Pope John dissolved the Spiritual party and denounced their teaching. Closely related to their ideals was the question of whether Christ and his apostles owned property, and whether the complete renunciation of possessions was required to live a life in imitation of Christ. In 1322 and 1323 Pope John issued further decrees, allowing for the ownership of property and declaring it heretical to claim that Christ lived in absolute poverty.

Bavarian Challenge

The decision did not quell the debate. A group of Spiritual Franciscans fled to Bavaria, accepting the protection of King Louis IV (c. 1283–1347). In response, Pope John excommunicated Louis in 1324. In 1328 Louis invaded Rome and had himself crowned Holy Roman emperor.

▼ The Palais des Papes and Pont Saint Benezet, Avignon
alxpin/iStock

Louis set up a Spiritual Franciscan named Nicholas V (?–1333) as pope, claiming that as John resided in Avignon, he had abandoned any claim to head the Roman Church. Louis eventually returned to Bavaria after he was unable to gain the support of the city's population, and Nicholas submitted to the authority of Pope John in 1330.

Supremacy of the State

In addition to the action of soldiers, a fierce literary debate arose over the issue of the state's supremacy, with major theologians including John of Jandun (c. 1286–1328) and William of Ockham (c. 1280–1349) taking sides. The war of ideas culminated in the publication of Marsiglio of Padua's *Defensor pacis* ("Defender of the Peace") in 1324. The influential book took a strongly anti-papal line, maintaining that it was the state, and not the church, that formed the unifying element of any society. Marsiglio argued theologically that the pope only had spiritual power—any earthly power he enjoyed was a gift from kings, princes, and emperors. The book was condemned by the pope in 1327 but won the favour of King Louis, who made Marsiglio his chief vicar when he seized control of Rome. When Louis's attempt to re-create the Holy Roman Empire failed, Marsiglio returned to Bavaria and relative obscurity. However, his *Defensor* was carefully studied by later reformers in the sixteenth century.

Brethren of the Common Life

Elsewhere in Europe, dissatisfaction with the opulence and power of the church led to the growth of movements emphasising the Christian values of simplicity, charity, and learning. In 1374 the Dutch theologian Geert

BLACK DEATH

This name was given to the bubonic plague that swept through China, India, and Europe between 1347 and 1351. The plague may have originated amongst the Kirgiz in central Asia (modern-day Kirgizstan), where Nestorian tombstones dating from 1338 provide the earliest evidence of plague fatalities. The Black Death gave rise to some extreme religious responses, including the practice of *flagellation*, whereby groups of men publicly scourged themselves in penance for the sins of the population. In 1349 Pope Clement VI called on church and state authorities to suppress the movement. The Black Death had a cataclysmic effect on the populations it touched, with some urban centres in Europe losing up to 40 percent of their population. The church was directly involved in care for the sick and dying, and a large number of educated priests and scholars were lost to the plague. As a result, the quality of Christian teaching and practice for the following generations was affected as the church was forced to take on many incompetent or illiterate clergy to fill the ranks.

▲ The massive scale of the Black Death affected every facet of European life for generations to come. Here, Death is depicted reaping his victims in an illuminated manuscript from the early sixteenth century.

Wikimedia Commons

Groote (1340–1384) was converted under the influence of a Carthusian monk who preached strict contemplation. Although Groote never became a priest, he began to call for repentance, speaking against corruption and clerical self-indulgence. Hostile factions of the church managed to have him banned from preaching in 1383, and he died from the plague the following year before he could appeal. People drawn to Groote's message later became known as the Brethren of the Common Life. The Brethren demanded no vows, and the clerical and lay members remained in their original vocations. Nevertheless, they became an influential presence, paying for their acts of charity by copying manuscripts and founding schools. Later Brethren would count amongst their numbers Thomas à Kempis (c. 1380–1471), Nicholas of Cusa (1401–1464), and Erasmus (c. 1466–1536).

John Wycliffe

Marsiglio, based in Bavaria, had challenged the authority of the church by appealing to the state. Fifty years later in England, similar ideas

JULIAN OF NORWICH (C. 1342–AFTER 1413)

A mystic and anchoress, Julian lived in a cell built into the wall of her church. In 1373 she experienced a series of "showings," or mystical visions, which were then written up as *Revelations of Divine Love*. In 1393 Julian produced a major theological reflection on her experiences, drawing parallels between divine action in the world and human motherhood.

were promoted by the Christian priest and theologian John Wycliffe (c. 1329–1384).

In 1375 Wycliffe published *De civili dominio* ("On Civil Dominion"), which distinguished between the "invisible," eternal, and true aspects of the church and the "material" reality of the daily life of its members. When the material church went wrong, Wycliffe argued, it was the duty of the civil government to put it right by punishing immoral clerics. Wycliffe's ideas were condemned in 1377 by Pope Gregory XI (1329–1378). Wycliffe carried his attack further, arguing in 1378 that the Bible, not the pope, was the sole authority of Christian doctrine and calling again in 1382 for the king to disband religious institutions and reform the church in England. Wycliffe and his followers also translated the Bible from Latin into English and attacked the doctrine of transubstantiation. His influence was felt in later English reforming movements in the sixteenth century, but his writings had the most effect on the Czech theologian and national hero Jan Hus (c. 1372–1415) in the first years of the following century.

The Great Western Schism

In an effort to restore order amongst the populace in Italy, Pope Gregory returned the papacy to Rome in 1377. His death a year later and the events surrounding the appointment of his successor led to considerable division within the Western Church: a time known as the *Great* (or *Western*) *Schism*.

Urban VI

Under popular pressure from the people of Rome, the Italian Bartolomeo Prignano (c. 1318–1389) was appointed Pope Urban VI in 1378. Yet four months into his time in office it began to be suspected that Urban was not mentally stable, as he displayed frequent outbursts and extravagant rages as he attempted to carry out his desired church reforms. The French members of the Sacred College of Cardinals questioned the validity of Urban's papacy and claimed that they had been forced to vote for an Italian.

Clement VII

The cardinals returned to France, where they installed Robert of Geneva (c. 1342–1394) as Pope Clement VII in 1378. The University of Paris recognised his election as legitimate, the king of France welcomed the decision, and Clement established Avignon once again as the centre for the church. Clement is now considered an anti-pope by the Roman Catholic Church, but at the time he divided the loyalties of Western Christendom, commanding the support of France, Naples, Scotland, Spain, and Sicily. For his part, Pope Urban in Rome was recognised by the Germans, English, Hungarians, Scandinavians, and Italians.

THREE POPES

The Great Schism lasted for decades, with successions of popes and anti-popes along both lines claiming their legitimacy over the other. In 1409 attempts to resolve the conflict led to the creation of a third line of popes based in the city of Pisa, beginning with Alexander V (c. 1339–1410). The schism would not be healed until the Council of Constance in 1417 and the unanimous election of Pope Martin V (1368–1431). By this time a generation or more of European laity, clergy, and theologians had known only a divided Christendom of competing claims undergirded by nationalistic allegiances, thus preparing the political, spiritual, and intellectual ground for the events of the Reformation.

OTTOMAN ADVANCE ON CONSTANTINOPLE

1321   Ottoman Turk armies reach the Sea of Marmara, threatening Byzantium.

1329   Ottomans control Nicaea.

1352   Serb army defeated by Ottomans at Maritza River.

1363   The Byzantine emperor John V Palaeologus formally recognises Ottoman rule of its conquered European territories.

1389   Overthrow of Serbian Empire. Prince Lazar defeated at Kosovo by Turkish forces led by Murad I.

1396   First Ottoman siege of Constantinople is called off when Ottoman army is diverted to fight Battle of Nicopolis instead.

East

The Crusades and the Latin rule of Constantinople of the previous centuries had taken their toll on the resources and confidence of the Byzantine Empire and its Orthodox Church. The relationship with Western Christendom was marked by continued mistrust and hostility. In the north, Constantinople struggled with the growing power of the Slavic kingdoms and their drive for political and religious autonomy. In the south, pressure from the armies of Islam was ever present, with the advance of Ottoman Turks threatening the very existence of Eastern Christendom.

Outer Turmoil, Inner Peace

In the face of this outward military, ecclesial, and political instability, Orthodoxy began to focus on the inward, mystical aspects of Christianity more than ever before. The tradition of inner meditation and mystical experience had always been present in the East, especially in the prayer practices of the monks of Mount

THE JESUS PRAYER

"Lord Jesus Christ, Son of the Living God, have mercy upon me, a sinner." The prayer has its roots in Greek mystical writers of the sixth and seventh centuries, but saw full flowering in the fourteenth century where it was recited repetitively and accompanied by a "physical method" of controlled breathing and the bowing of the head towards the heart. The prayer continues to be important within Orthodoxy and is also widely practiced in the West.

Athos. The monks drew from the writings of Gregory of Nyssa (?–c. 394), John Climacus (c. 579–649), and Maximus the Confessor (c. 580–662), amongst others.

Hesychasm

The practice known as Hesychasm (from the Greek for "quietness") primarily involved the constant repetition of the Jesus Prayer and strict discipline of body posture and breathing. The aim was to align the thoughts of the head with the movements of the heart in order to attain a material vision of the Divine Light—that is, the mystics believed that they were witnesses to the light of the transfiguration of Christ as described in Matthew 17. In the fourteenth century the development of this mystical tradition reached its height under the influence of Gregory of Sinai (c. 1265–c. 1346), Nicephorus of Mount Athos (dates unknown), and especially Gregory Palamas (c. 1296–1359).

Criticism of Superstition

The Hesychasts came under intense criticism in 1337, led by a prominent monk in Constantinople. Barlaam (c. 1290–1348) was born into an Orthodox family from Calavria in southern Italy. He had earlier been involved in the movement to reunite the Orthodox and Catholic churches. Upon his return to Constantinople, Barlaam accused the Mount Athos monks of encouraging superstition. He and his followers were particularly dismissive of the Hesychasts' physical practices and their claims to directly experience the Divine through their meditations. When the Council of Constantinople sided with the Hesychasts in 1341, Barlaam returned to the West, where he served as a Catholic bishop until his death.

The Energies of God

Barlaam's main opponent in this debate was the monk and archbishop of Thessalonica Gregory Palamas. In response to Barlaam's claim that God was completely unknowable, Gregory wrote the *Triads in Defence of the Holy Hesychasts* (1338). Here he differentiated between the *energies* of God, which could be experienced, and the *essence* of God, which could not. Gregory also defended the disciplines and physical practices of prayer on the grounds that as humans are bodily creatures, they must use their whole bodies to be in communion with God. The monks of Mount Athos accepted the teaching in 1340. Constantinople followed in 1341. Further councils in 1347 and 1351 served to confirm the Hesychast practice as an essential part of Orthodox Christianity.

Pagan Lithuania

The last officially pagan nation in Europe at this time was Lithuania. Christianity had been present amongst the people for a number of generations but had not made significant inroads. King Mindaugas (?–1263), an uncertain Catholic convert himself, had attempted to Christianise his people, but the exercise was short-lived. Even before his assassination, paganism had quickly reasserted itself. In addition, various Slavic aristocratic families had close ties with the Orthodox Church. Through them Byzantium exercised some influence over the Russian territories of Lithuania, leading to a period of vacillation between East and West. The prevarications came to a climax with the crusade of the Teutonic Knights in 1336. A succession of pagan Lithuanian kings resisted the Christian invaders, but the pressure was too great. In 1384 Grand Duke Jogaila (Jagiełło in

▲ The domes of St. Basil's Cathedral, Moscow

PhotoDisc

Polish, c. 1351–1434) sought an alliance with Polish nobility who, although Catholic, were also hostile to the German Knights. Jogaila was baptised into the Catholic Church in 1386 and, in return for ceding Lithuanian lands to the Polish Empire, was made temporary protector of Poland. Although the conversion was instigated for political reasons, Lithuanian Christian culture flourished under Polish Franciscan influence, leading to the foundation of schools and hospitals as well as closer integration with Western Europe. However, tensions with the East—especially Russia—remained.

Mother Moscow

Although Russia was under Mongol rule, the Orthodox Church enjoyed a favoured position and was allowed to operate relatively freely. In 1325 the Metropolitan Bishop Peter (1308–1326) moved his see from Kiev to Moscow. In 1326 construction began on the Cathedral of the Assumption (or Dormition Cathedral) in Moscow, and by 1328 the transfer of power was complete. Moscow became the official seat of Russian Orthodoxy, and the Cathedral became known as its "mother church."

Sergius

Born in Rostov, Bartholomew (c. 1314–1392) adopted the name Sergius when he became a monk in 1336. In the 1350s he founded a community in the forest of Radonezh that would later become the great Monastery of the Holy Trinity. The community reintroduced the practice of monastic life that had been disrupted by Tartar rule, and it established Sergius as leading church authority and reformer. Sergius intervened in Russian politics and averted four civil wars through his relationship with Muscovite princes. As a result, Russia was more able to resist the Tartar invaders.

Battle of Kulikovo

In 1380 Sergius gave aid to Prince Dmitri (c. 1350–1389) in fending off the Mongol army amassing at Kulikovo, south of Moscow. Following Sergius's encouragement and counsel, Dmitri was victorious over the Golden Horde and its Lithuanian allies. The battle led to the liberation of the Russian people and church from Mongolian rule, an event that would have lasting significance for Europe and for the future of the Orthodox Church. For this reason, after his death in 1392, Sergius came to be considered one of the greatest patron saints of Russia.

CHURCH AND STATE: 1400–1500

In the fifteenth century in the West, the idea that the pope represents a universal authority that transcends national boundaries is increasingly challenged by the rise of nation-states and independent Christian groups. The various reformations that would arise in the following century have their roots in these developments. Rapid exploration too will give rise to new expressions of Christianity as Christendom spreads to the New World at the end of the century. In the East, with the victory of the Ottoman Empire, Byzantine Orthodoxy enters a time of "Great Captivity." As Constantinople loses influence under Muslim conquest, Moscow comes into its own as Russia emerges from Mongolian rule.

East

Second Siege of Constantinople

In 1422 Turks led by Sultan Murad II resumed their siege of the city of Constantinople. The siege was unsuccessful, but it served to entrench the Ottoman invaders even further into the Byzantine territories.

Temporary Unity

In the face of the Ottoman threat, unity within Christendom was the best policy for halting further expansion. The Council of Florence met between 1438 and 1445 with the primary

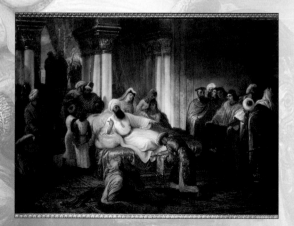

▲ Murad II, Sultan of Turkey. His rule over Constantinople marked the end of the Eastern Roman Empire.

Alfredo Dagli Orti/Shutterstock

aim of once again seeking rapprochement between the Western and Eastern Churches. The East was represented by the likes of Emperor John VIII Palaeologus (1392–1448) and Patriarch Joseph II of Constantinople (1360–1439), and the West by Pope Eugenius IV (1383–1447) and Cardinal Julian Cesarini (1398–1444). After long discussions and disagreements, a union of sorts was established in 1439, although it never enjoyed popular approval in Constantinople and many Orthodox bishops refused their support.

Collapse of Eastern Christendom

As part of his project of unification, in 1442 Cardinal Cesarini travelled to Hungary to preach a crusade against the Ottomans. In 1444 he convinced the king of Hungary and Poland, Władysław III (or Vladislaus, 1424–1444), to break the Peace of Szeged, the uneasy truce that existed between the Christians and the Turks.

Instead of the intended aim of reinvigorating Eastern and Western Christian opposition to the invaders, the renewed war led to a rout of the would-be crusaders. The Christian army was defeated and Cesarini and Władysław were killed at the battle of Varna in Bulgaria in 1444. The collapse of this force paved the way for a string of Ottoman victories, including success in Kosovo in 1448, which ensured Turkish rule over the Balkans. In 1453 Ottoman soldiers led by Sultan Mehmed II conquered Constantinople. Turkish rule went on to be consolidated farther into the Balkans, including Moldavia (1455), southern Greece (1456–1460), southern Serbia (1459), and Wallachia (1474). Successful wars with the Polish (1497–1499) and the Venetians (1499–1503) threatened Western Christendom while decisively demonstrating the collapse of Byzantium and the end of the Eastern Roman Empire.

FALL OF CONSTANTINOPLE

The Turks invaded the city of Constantinople by land and sea in 1453. Although significantly outnumbered, the Byzantine forces held off the invaders for seven weeks before the city was captured. Even though the Church of the Holy Wisdom was turned into a mosque, the Ottomans treated the Christians with a fair degree of tolerance. Agreements between the patriarch and the sultan allowed the Orthodox Church to continue, although Christians were heavily taxed, forbidden to serve in the army, and banned from missionary work or proselytising.

▲ After a siege lasting for seven weeks, the city of Constantinople fell to Ottoman turks in 1453.

Alfredo Dagli Orti/Shutterstock

The Great Captivity

For the Eastern Church, the period under Muslim rule is sometimes known as the Great Captivity. In return for political obedience, the church was allowed to continue exercising its spiritual and civil authority. This concordat reached between the Ottoman rulers and the Orthodox Church would govern relations until 1923.

Patriarchy under Islam

The first patriarch of Constantinople under this new arrangement was George Scholarius (c. 1405–c. 1472). Sultan Mehmed II himself invested Scholarius as Patriarch Gennadius II in 1454. Gennadius had supported Cesarini's scheme for church union at the Council of Florence (1439), but by this stage he was a bitter opponent of Rome—a position attractive to Constantinople's new Ottoman ruler. Gennadius resigned, or attempted to resign, the patriarchy a number of times but was ordered by the sultan to occupy the office. Gennadius wrote a number of theological and philosophical works, including a translation of Thomas Aquinas from Latin into Greek. His *Confessions* comprise an apologetic dialogue with Mehmed II.

The Rise of Russia

As the Byzantine Greeks adapted to their new life under non-Christian rule, the Russians—already used to living with Mongolian rulers—assumed greater prominence within Orthodox Christianity. The Russians had wholly refused the 1439 union compromises of the Council of Florence. As a result, they considered themselves to be more authentic preservers of the Orthodox faith than the Greeks. In 1448 Russian bishops elected Jonas (?–c. 1461) as metropolitan of Moscow without making any reference to the hierarchy in Constantinople. The action effectively created an autocephalous Russian Church, although this was not formally recognised by Constantinople until 1589.

Ivan the Great

Ivan III "the Great" (1440–1505) ruled in Russia between 1462 and 1505. The 1472 marriage between Ivan and Sophia (1455–1503), niece

▲ Ivan III, Grand Duke of Russia, did much to make the Russian Church assume the mantle of Byzantine Orthodoxy.

Universal History Archive/Universal Images Group/Shutterstock

of the last Byzantine emperor, helped strengthen Russia's claim to be the natural successor to Byzantine Orthodoxy. When the Russians under the leadership of Ivan defeated their Mongolian rulers in 1480, these claims were further enhanced. This laid the foundation for the idea of Moscow as "third Rome," which would rise to prominence in the following century.

West

Closing of the Schism

The Great Schism had divided Europe since 1378, with allegiance to the different popes falling along nationalist and political lines. The situation was untenable for the church, and in 1409 the

ETHIOPIAN CHURCH

Although the Abyssinian Church operated largely independently of the main Catholic and Orthodox traditions, a small group of Ethiopian monks are recorded as attending the Council of Florence in 1441. The Ethiopian Church at this time was experiencing cultural revival and reform, especially under the influence of the Christian emperor Zar'a Ya'qob (Zara Jacob, c. 1399–1468). The emperor wrote hymns and theological reflections on the creed of the Ethiopian Church. In addition, many Arabic and Western European texts were translated into Ge'ez (Ethiopic) in this era, and most of the copies of the ancient Ethiopic Bible date from the fourteenth and fifteenth centuries.

CONCILIAR MOVEMENT

By creating three papal lines, Pisa had made the schism worse. Yet the attempts to heal the breach led to the foundation of the 1414–1418 Council of Constance and the end of the Great Schism. Two French theologians figured prominently at Constance. Pierre d'Ailly (1350–1420) and Jean Gerson (1363–1429) helped to formulate a radical cure for the problems by arguing that the office of pope only existed as the "head" of the "body" of the church. If the head was failing the body, the faithful church had the right to call it to account. The family of doctrines maintaining that the supreme authority of the church lies with the General Council of Bishops, rather than the one pope, is known as *Conciliar Theory*. The failure of the movement to flourish much past the fifteenth century was a contributing factor to the Protestant reformations of the following century.

cardinals convened the Council of Pisa to resolve the matter. The council declared the papacy of both Gregory XII (c. 1327–1417) and Benedict XIII (1328–1423) invalid and unanimously elected a third pope, Alexander V (c. 1339–1410), who died before he could fulfil his promises to unite the Catholic Church. He was succeeded by John XXIII (1370–1419). Despite the validity of his election being contested, John commanded more support than the other popes. The Roman Catholic Church now considers John, Benedict, and Alexander to be anti-pope and reused the name John XXIII in the twentieth century.

Council of Constance

At the instigation of the Holy Roman emperor Sigismund (1368–1437), John XXIII agreed to call the Council of Constance in 1414. The council, which was well attended, fully

embraced Conciliarism by decreeing, "This Council holds its power direct from Christ; everyone, no matter his rank or office, even if it be Papal, is bound to obey it in whatever pertains to faith."

John was the first pope to be persuaded to abdicate in 1415. Gregory XII followed three months later, and Benedict XIII was deposed in 1417. Finally, Oddo Colonna (1368–1431) was elected Pope Martin V in 1417, bringing an end to the Great Schism. Martin returned the seat of the papacy to Rome, re-established control over the Italian Papal States, and resumed authority over the Western Church.

Jan Hus

In addition to uniting a schismatic church, the Council of Constance also met to deal with an antipapal Christian movement that had taken root amongst the Czechs of Bohemia.

Jan Hus (1373–1415) had been teaching at the University of Prague for five years before he encountered the radical theology of the English Reformer John Wycliffe in 1401. Wycliffe's ideas inspired a Czech reforming party, encouraging a more rigorous obedience to Scripture and opposing German political and religious dominance in their country. In 1409 the Czechs sided with the election of Pope Alexander V against the German favourite Pope Gregory XII. Further conflict arose when Hus opposed the indulgence policies of Pope John XXIII, resulting in his exile from Prague in 1412. The conflict reached its climax when Hus was called to attend the Council of Constance in 1414.

Betrayal

Jan Hus travelled under assurances of safe conduct from Emperor Sigismund, with the belief that he would be given an opportunity to defend his views. Despite the emperor's efforts, shortly after his arrival at Constance, Hus was imprisoned and charged with heresy. After a public hearing in which Hus was not permitted to present or defend his own views, he was denounced as a heretic, charged with being a "Wycliffite," and handed over to the secular government for execution in 1415.

The Hussites

Following these events, Hus became a national hero, with the University of Prague declaring him a martyr. Hus became a focal point for Czech grievances against the dominating

▲ Ponte St. Angelo and St. Peter's Basilica in Rome at night
Songquan Deng/123RF.com

◄ Christian reformer and national hero Jan Hus was betrayed and executed in 1415.
Public Doman; Krl, Josef Ji, b. 1870

▼ The radical English theologian John Wycliffe insisted that the Bible should be translated into local languages. He influenced later generations of Reformers across Europe.
Public Domain

JOHN WICLIF.

THOMAS À KEMPIS (C. 1380–1471)

A German priest and mystic, Thomas spent his life in the Augustinian monastery at Zwolle where he was a celebrated author and spiritual adviser. Thomas is most known for *The Imitation of Christ* (although a minority of scholars question his authorship). *The Imitation* is a manual of spiritual devotion. It is popular with many different Christian traditions and has never gone out of print since it first began to be circulated in 1418.

NICHOLAS OF CUSA (1401–1464)

The German priest and theologian was also a celebrated humanist and philosopher. His *De concordantia catholica* (1433) argued for the superiority of the General Council over the pope. Nicholas worked for reconciliation with the Hussites, and he supported union between East and West, travelling to Constantinople in 1437–1438. A scholar of mathematics, astronomy, and history, Nicholas is also responsible for creating the first geographical map of central Europe. In 1459, together with his father and sister, he founded a hospital in his native town of Cusa.

Catholic Church and the German influence in Bohemia. Part of the Hussite programme was laid out in the *Four Articles of Prague* (1420), which anticipated later Protestant Reformation developments in some key ways. The Hussites argued for a more disciplined clergy, the allowance of Communion of both kinds (that is, bread and wine) for all people, the liturgy in the local language, and a mutual independence of church and state. Their religious concerns thus had a political dimension. With the Hussites reacting violently against Catholic Europe, Holy Roman Emperor Sigismund launched a number of "crusades" against the Czechs from 1420 to 1434.

The Anti-Papal Council of Basel

The agitation of the Hussite Wars coincided with the growing Conciliar movements within the church. The controversial Council of Basel was convened in 1431 and was presided over by Cardinal Cesarini. When the newly elected Pope Eugenius IV tried to dissolve the meeting, Cesarini and the other bishops disregarded the order, reaffirming the idea that the General Council was superior to the pope. In this action, the cardinals were widely supported by the European princes, the great universities, and humanist thinkers such as Nicholas of Cusa.

Basel enforced a number of anti-papal decrees and placed strict limitations on the office of the pope while enhancing the authority of bishops and lower orders of clergy. In 1437 the council found in favour of some Hussite demands, allowing a degree of independence to the Bohemian Church that the papal party tried to oppose. In the face of these tensions, in 1438 Eugenius transferred the council from Basel first to Ferrara and then to Florence, where a short-lived union between the Eastern and Western Churches was achieved.

France

The papacy's relations with France were especially estranged, due to the French Church's

JOAN OF ARC (1412–1431)

This peasant "Maid of Orléans" was born into the context of the Hundred Years' War with England and the ongoing civil strife between the great houses of France. In 1425 she had the first of many visions, claiming from these experiences a supernatural mission to fight for France. In 1429 she convinced King Charles VII and his court theologians and was allowed to lead a successful military campaign to liberate the city of Orléans. Captured in 1430 by her enemies, Joan was eventually executed for witchcraft in 1431. Pope Callixtus III reviewed her case in 1456 and declared her to have been wrongly condemned. She is considered a national hero and is a secondary patron saint of France.

WITCHCRAFT

Classical, early medieval, and Orthodox Christianity was generally cautious about encouraging belief in the power of witches. However, Western European interest in witchcraft steadily increased in the fifteenth century, largely as a result of the 1486 publication of *Malleus Maleficarum* ("Hammer of Witches"). Written by German Dominicans, the book singled out women as the main culprits and would go on to have popular influence in later years. Its content and style were controversial even in its own time, and it was never fully accepted by the church.

increasing assertions of autonomy from Rome, a tendency known as Gallicanism. In 1438, while Eugenius was preparing to relocate the council from Basel, the French clergy issued the *Pragmatic Sanction of Bourges*. The declaration upheld the right of the French Church to administer its own affairs, avoided taxation, and denied the pope a say in the appointment of French bishops. The French king Charles VII (1403–1461) endorsed the anti-papal decrees of Basel and supported the *Sanctions*, which halted the flow of money from France to Rome.

England

The victory over the French at Agincourt in 1415 contributed significantly to the growing national self-consciousness of the English. The protracted Hundred Years' War with papacy-controlled France, the physical distance from Rome, and the controversies of the Babylonian Captivity and the Great Schism all meant that the English Church in the fifteenth century operated largely independently of the mainland Catholic hierarchy. The result was a stronger relation between the English monarchy and the English Church, at the expense of allegiance to the papacy.

The Lollards

The English Church faced opposition of its own in the guise of the Lollards, the followers of John Wycliffe. (The name "Lollard" is probably a derogative term meaning "mumbler.") The Lollards supported the translation of the Bible into the local vernacular rather than Latin and believed that church practices should be drawn only from Scripture. For this reason they disapproved of church hierarchical systems, clerical celibacy, transubstantiation,

READING AND LEARNING

Books and their study flourished in Western Christendom.

c. 1448 Johannes Gutenberg (c. 1398–1468) develops his printing press invention using moveable type.

1456 Appearance of the "Gutenberg Bible," the first printed book in Europe.

1448 Pope Nicholas V establishes the Vatican Library. A census in 1481 establishes it as the largest collection of manuscripts in the West.

c. 1475 Foundation of Copenhagen University.

1494 Bishop Elphinstone (1431–1514) founds King's College, Aberdeen.

▶ The Gutenberg Bible

Universal History Archive/Universal Images Group/Shutterstock

praying for the dead, and Christian participation in war. In 1401 William Sawtrey became the first Lollard martyr when he was burned at the stake. Lollardy increased and became associated with disaffection with the English government, culminating in a march on London that was dispersed by the soldiers of King Henry V in 1414. There is evidence of Lollard activity in 1431, 1455, and beyond, with some historians linking the movement with the regions where the sixteenth-century Anglican Reformation was most enthusiastically received.

Portugal

Under the influence of leaders such as King Henry "the Navigator" (1394–1460), the Portuguese undertook many voyages of discovery during the fifteenth century, establishing their empire's reach in India, Africa, and East Asia, with the Americas soon to follow. In 1452 Pope Nicholas V issued the papal bull *Dum Diversas*, which granted the Portuguese crown rights over all the persons and property they discovered on their overseas explorations.

The Spanish Inquisition

An inquisition in Spain was instituted through papal bulls issued by Pope Sixtus IV in 1478 and 1483. Its inception was due largely to the encouragement of Ferdinand II (1452–1516) and Isabella I (1451–1504), dubbed the "Catholic King and Queen" for their enthusiastic political

SIXTUS IV (1414–1484)

The Franciscan Francesco della Rovere became Pope Sixtus IV in 1471. He soon earned a reputation for nepotism and corruption, including dealings with his nephew, the future "Warrior Pope" Julius II (1443–1513). Sixtus was a great Renaissance patron of art, and he built the Sistine Chapel (1471–1484), which bears his name.

▶ Assembly of the clergy with Pope Sixtus IV

Gianni Dagli Orti/Shutterstock

▲ The Spanish Inquisition reached all corners of Spain's empire, including Mexico as depicted here.

Gianni Dagli Orti/Shutterstock

protection of the church. In contrast to previous inquisitions, the Spanish Inquisition was characterised by its subservience to the secular authorities, who appointed the examiners and conducted trials.

Inquisitor Torquemada

The Inquisitor General was nominally under the authority of the pope, although in reality he served the policy of the Spanish crown. Tomás de Torquemada (1420–1498) took charge of the Inquisition in 1483, establishing by his *Ordinances* (1484) an organisational system that would remain in place for the best part of three centuries. The earliest phase of the Spanish Inquisition was the bloodiest, with the principal targets being Catholic heretics (deemed enemies of the state), Moors, Moriscos (converts from Islam whose Christianity was suspect), and Marranos (converts from Judaism). Under his reign, some thousands were interrogated and some 2,000 executed, earning Torquemada a reputation for cruelty throughout the wider church. Successive appeals to the pope to curb Torquemada's excesses were often unfruitful, as the papacy had limited influence over the Inquisition.

The New Spanish Empire

In 1492 the absorption of Granada was complete, leading to the union of the Spanish kingdoms of Aragon and Castile and the final defeat of the Moors by the Catholic monarchs.

That year, as part of the reconquest, the Inquisition also oversaw the expulsion of all unconverted Jews from Spain. Also in 1492, explorer Christopher Columbus claimed the newly discovered Americas in the name of Ferdinand, Isabella, and Catholic Spain. The explosion of Spanish exploration prompted Pope Alexander VI (1431–1503) to issue *Inter Caetera Eximiae Devotionis* in 1493, the papal bulls granting the Spanish crown the responsibility for spreading Christianity in all its territories. The 1494 Treaty of Tordesillas divided the newly discovered territories in South America between Spain and Portugal, giving the conquistadores free rein over their expansion. That same year a service was held at the settlement of La Isabela on the island of the Dominican Republic—the first Mass to be celebrated in the New World.

▲ Florence's skyline in the fifteenth century was dominated by the newly erected cathedral dome. Designed by Brunelleschi, "The Duomo" remains one of the largest in the world. Construction of the cathedral was not completed until the nineteenth century.

Evgeniy Zakharov/123RF.com

GIROLAMO SAVONAROLA (1452–1498)

An Italian apocalyptic preacher and reformer, in 1490 Savonarola called for the repentance of city and church officials in Florence and spoke up for the poor and oppressed. His influence was so great that he helped establish Florence as an independent republic. When he denounced Pope Alexander VI and the entire papal court as servants of Satan, Savonarola was excommunicated in 1497. He was executed for schism and heresy a year later.

EXPANSION AND CONSOLIDATION: 1500-1600

The sixteenth century is, for Christianity, a time of revival and expansion in the New World, a time of massive reform in Europe, and a time of consolidation in Russia as power shifts from Constantinople to Moscow.

▲ Annunciation Cathedral of Kazan Kremlin is the first Orthodox church of the Kazan Kremlin. The Kazan Kremlin is the chief historic citadel of Tatarstan, Russia. In the sixteenth century Russia became a powerful Christian centre rivaling Rome and Constantinople.

saiko3p/123RF.com

East

Third Rome

Following the Turkish captivity of Constantinople in 1453, the Russian Church had become the largest and most influential church of the Orthodox communion.

In 1503 the Orthodox Church held a council to settle the dispute between the schools of Joseph of Volokolamsk (1440–1515) and Nil Sorsky (1433–1508). The council sided with Volokolamsk's advocacy of a strong national church, and Sorsky's suggestions that the church should avoid political engagement and ownership of property were condemned in 1504. The result was a stronger relationship than ever before between the church and the Russian state. By 1510 the monk Philotheus could write of Basil (Vasili) III, Grand Prince of Moscow, "[You are] on earth the sole emperor of the Christians, the leader of the Apostolic Church which no longer stands in Rome or in Constantinople, but in the blessed city of Moscow. . . .

JOHN OF IOANNINA (1522–1546)

Also known as John the Tailor, John was a craftsman living in Constantinople under Ottoman rule. Captured by angry apostates because he himself would not recant, he was burnt and beheaded in 1546. John is considered by the Orthodox Church to be a "New Martyr of the Great Captivity."

PHILOTHEI OF ATHENS (1522–1589)

During the Ottoman period in Greece, many women were forced into Turkish harems. The nun Philothei offered sanctuary to these women and was killed as a result. A "New Martyr," Philothei is considered a patron saint of Athens.

OTTOMAN EMPIRE

1517 Ottomans control Mecca and Jerusalem. (Ottoman rule in Jerusalem will last until defeated by the British in 1917.)

1529 Vienna successfully repels the first Ottoman siege.

1541 Suleiman "the Magnificent" conquers most of Hungary.

1551 Ottomans victorious in Tripoli against the Knights of Malta.

1571 Major Christian victory against the Ottoman navy at Lepanto.

Two Romes have fallen, but the third stands and a fourth there will not be."

Tsar of All Russia

With the new settlement, the state began to exert more influence over the church. In 1521 Basil deposed Metropolitan Varlaam from office when the churchman refused to allow Basil a divorce. Varlaam's successor Daniel proved more pliant, and Basil remarried in 1525. This new union produced the desired heir, Ivan IV, who would later be known as Ivan "the Terrible." He would be the first ruler to adopt the title "Tsar of All Russia" in 1547.

Seeing himself as "God's appointed" ruler, Ivan cultivated a close relationship with the Orthodox Church. In 1551 Ivan convened the Council of Moscow (also known as the Council of the Hundred Chapters) alongside Metropolitan Macarius. The council gave jurisdiction to church courts and strengthened church discipline. It also affirmed the tsar as the champion of the true faith and in turn gave the church a role in conducting domestic and foreign policy.

Constantinople

Although under foreign rule, Constantinople traditionally retained its primacy in Orthodox Christianity. The most significant figure at this time was Patriarch Jeremias II (c. 1530–1595). Between 1573 and 1581 Jeremias entered into serious correspondence with German Reformers from Tübingen when he was sent a copy of the *Augsburg Confession* (compiled by Martin Luther and Philipp Melanchthon). His reply, known as *The Three Answers*, made clear the points of agreement and difference between the two traditions, and the work remains influential in the Orthodox Church.

CALENDARS

The original calendar was mandated by Julius Caesar c. 45 BC. The Julian calendar introduced an error of one day every 128 years. Due to various innovations and additions, it had grown unwieldy and proved difficult to calculate accurate dates for Easter. Pope Gregory XIII decreed a reformed calendar in 1582. The Gregorian calendar shifts approximately one day every 3,300 years. It simplified the leap year process and attempted to provide uniformity for the calculation of Easter. Many Protestant and Orthodox countries resisted the new calendar as a Catholic imposition, but it has since been adopted as the civil calendar in most parts of the world. The national Orthodox churches continue to use a revised form of the Julian calendar for religious purposes.

▲ The highly decorated walls and ceiling of the Sistine Chapel
© 2015 by Zondervan

In 1582 Jeremias condemned the new papal calendar decreed by Pope Gregory XIII. It was also under Jeremias's rule that the growing autonomy of the Russian Church was formally recognised and the autocephalous patriarchate of Moscow was created in 1589. The death of Jeremias in 1595 led to a time of more chaos in the church during its time of Ottoman captivity. Until 1695 there would be sixty-one changes to the patriarchal throne, with many men being deposed and reinstated multiple times.

West

Protestant Reform

At the same time that Christianity was consolidating in Russia, the mood in Europe was for reform.

The authority of the papacy and the standing of the church in Rome had been weakened by the Great Schism and the Conciliar movements of the last century. Inside and outside Rome there was popular feeling that the Western Church was financially, secularly, and politically corrupt. Monastic communities were banding together, instituting rules for holy living. Throughout Europe, movements for clerical reform and a return to early Christian standards were coming to the fore.

Pre-Reformation

In 1508 Michelangelo was contributing to the church's earthly standing with his painting on the Sistine Chapel ceiling.

In the same year, the celebrated author Erasmus was attacking the church for losing its spiritual way in his *In Praise of Folly*. By 1511 the Congregation of Windesheim, a group of Dutch monasteries and convents dedicated to

DESIDERIUS ERASMUS (C. 1466–1536)

Europe's bestselling author, Erasmus held teaching posts in Oxford, Cambridge, and Basel. His satires, biblical translations, philosophical works, and theological writings were enormously influential. Although highly critical of the clergy and Roman Church of his day, Erasmus also distanced himself from the Protestants, and he wrote books critical of Martin Luther.

▲ Portrait of Erasmus by Hans Holbein the Younger
Public Domain

JOHANNES TRITHEMIUS (1462–1516)

Abbot of Sponheim in west Germany until 1506, Trithemius was a major figure for monastic reform and a precursor to the movements that would explode in the sixteenth century. His collection of manuscripts was one of the most famous libraries in the known world.

THE FIRST POLYGLOT BIBLE

In Alcalá in 1522 a team of compilers published the first full Bible to have parallel texts in Hebrew, Greek, and Latin. The work paved the way for serious textual study of the Old and New Testament Scriptures.

Indulgences

Lateran's calls for reform were ineffective. By its end in 1517 the situation of the church seemed hardly to have changed.

Years earlier, in conjunction with Albert, archbishop of Mainz, Pope Julius II had instituted a special indulgence in order to pay for the building of St. Peter's Church in Rome. After Julius died in 1513, his successor Leo X continued with the plan. Half the money was to pay off Albert's debts; the other half went to the lavish building project.

The German friar Johann Tetzel was employed to preach the indulgence. Tetzel promised that the indulgence would provide absolution for any crime and that anyone who bought an indulgence would instantly free their

reforming principles, had grown to ninety-seven member houses. Acknowledging the need for reform, the Fifth Lateran Council met in 1512. It called for improved clerical training and discipline and criticised the papacy for its over-involvement in temporal matters.

MARTIN LUTHER (1483–1546)

Luther was a German priest and theologian. Sometime between 1512 and 1515 Luther's reading of Augustine and the apostle Paul led to his conviction that "faith alone justifies without works." The idea that God's salvation could be received independently of obedience to religious demands and church hierarchy would become central to the political and spiritual aspects of the Protestant Reformation.

▲ Martin Luther nailed his Ninety-Five Theses on the door of Wittenberg Church. His action became symbolic for the new movement of "Protestants" opposed to the pope and some Roman Catholic practices.   Wikimedia Commons

loved ones from pain in the afterlife: "As soon as the coin in the coffer rings / The soul from Purgatory springs."

Wittenberg

Tetzel's success with the German peasants worried many reform-minded theologians. One of these was Martin Luther, a lecturer at the University of Wittenberg. Luther wrote up his concerns in 1517 and posted them in the usual way—by nailing them to the door of the main city church. Luther's *Ninety-Five Theses against Indulgences* caused an outcry. Rome's efforts at discipline failed, and in a public debate with the theologian Johann Eck in 1519, Luther formally denied the primacy of the pope. At the Diet of Worms in 1521, Luther was excommunicated by the church and outlawed by the emperor. All who followed his ideas were declared heretics.

Protest in Europe

Luther supported the close coalition of church and state, and he wrote to the German princes encouraging them to take reforms into their own hands. By the 1530s the rulers of Saxony, Hesse, Brandenburg, and Brunswick, along with a number of German "free cities," had adopted Lutheran principles. The movement also found European supporters keen on religious reform or political emancipation from Rome. By 1526 Sweden was seeing disputes between Catholics and the new reform-minded "evangelical" party, and Olaus Petri (1493–1552) had translated the New Testament into Swedish. In 1527 the Swedish crown assumed control of Catholic property. In 1534 Christian III (1503–1559) became the first Protestant king of Denmark, and shortly after, the Lutheran Church was established as the national church.

A NEW NAME

The First Diet of Speyer in 1526 had determined that each prince should be allowed to order church affairs within his sphere of influence, thus sanctioning the spread of Lutheranism. The toleration of religious innovation was reversed by the Second Diet of Speyer (1529), which was controlled by a council majority of Catholic leaders. Six Lutheran princes and representatives from fourteen German cities issued a formal letter of protest against the ruling, giving the new movement the name "Protestant."

ANABAPTISTS

"Anabaptist" was the general designation for those reform movements that refused to allow infant baptism and insisted on the rebaptism of adult believers. The main groups included the followers of Thomas Müntzer (active 1521), the Swiss Brethren of Zurich (active 1525), the Moravian communities founded by Jacob Hutter (?–1536), and the followers of the Dutch priest Menno Simons (1496–1561). Anabaptists tended towards pacifism. They practiced the communal sharing of property, and they encouraged non-participation in civic life, including the withholding of taxes. Both Roman Catholics and Protestants routinely persecuted Anabaptists, but their ideas continue in the Mennonite Church and in the exclusive Hutterite and Amish communities of North America.

Swiss Reformation

In 1520, writing under the influence of Erasmus (and probably also Luther), Huldrych Zwingli (1484–1531) developed his own evangelical teaching. After a series of public disputations in Zurich in 1523 and 1524, the civic authorities adopted his reforms for their city. The movement quickly spread to other Swiss cantons. In 1527 divisions between the Reformers were revealed when Zwingli and Luther clashed over the doctrine of the Eucharist.

In 1536 the leadership of the Swiss Reformation passed to John Calvin (1509–1564), a former priest fleeing persecution in his native France. By 1541 Calvin's *Ecclesiastical Ordinances* had established a highly organised theocracy in Geneva whereby the town council assumed the

▲ Huldrych Zwingli, theologian and leader of the Reformation in Switzerland
Public Domain

BARTHOLOMEW'S DAY MASSACRE

The events of August 23–26, 1572, represent the height of antagonism between Huguenots and Catholics in France. In order to quell unrest following an assassination attempt on the Protestant leader Gaspard de Coligny (1519–1572), Queen Catherine de' Medici allowed Catholic troops to attack the Huguenots. This in turn spurred further mob riots and led to the death of over 5,000 Parisian Protestants. The violence shocked all of Europe—Protestants and Catholics alike.

▲ *St. Bartholomew's Day* by François Dubois (1529–1584).

St. Bartholomew's Day Massacre, c.1572–84, Dubois, Francois (1529–1584)/Musee Cantonal des Beaux-Arts de Lausanne, Switzerland/De Agostini Picture Library/G. Dagli Orti/Bridgeman Images

 HUGUENOTS

The French Calvinist Huguenot Church was formalised at the Synod of Paris in 1559. The support of some Protestant territories against the Catholic majority resulted in a protracted civil war in France between 1562 and 1594.

UNITARIANISM

Some movements that emerged from the fervour of the radical reformation rejected the doctrine of the Trinity and the deity of Christ. Early Unitarians include Martin Cellarius (1499–1564) and Michael Servetus (1511–1553), who was executed for heresy in Calvin's Geneva. The decision was controversial, raising the issue of religious toleration amongst Protestants. Unitarianism persisted throughout Europe and thrived especially in nineteenth-century America.

authority for religious and moral discipline in the population. Calvinist reforms soon became the model for church and civic governance throughout Europe, especially in western Germany, Scotland, Holland, and France.

Catholic Revival

It was not only the Protestants who wished to reform the church. The revival of European Catholicism during this era is often referred to as the "Counter-Reformation"; however, many of the movements occurred independently of reaction to the Protestant schism.

New monastic orders such as the Theatines (1524) and the Capuchins (1529) were keen to restore original Christian practice. These orders

▶ Capuchin distinctive pointed cowl (*capuche*)

H.-D. Falkenstein/image BROKER/Shutterstock

WITCH TRIALS

Fear of sorcery was a constant feature of both Catholicism and Protestantism during this era. Prosecutions often involved multiple accusations and indictments. The vast majority of those tried and executed were women.

1532 Holy Roman Empire requires death for practitioners of black magic (*maleficia*).

1541 Luther approves of the burning of four witches in Wittenberg.

1550–c. 1560 Courts in Geneva try ninety witches.

1563 Johann Weyer's *De praestigiis daemonum* argues that witches are not demonic but merely deluded and of unsound mind and should not be prosecuted.

1580s England, France, Germany, and Sweden experience a surge in witch trials.

1588 Michel de Montaigne's essay "On Lameness" is critical of those who believe in witchcraft and diabolic forces.

1590–91 North Berwick witch trial. King James VI of Scotland (later James I of England) prosecutes women he thinks were using witchcraft to try to kill him.

THE ANGLICAN REFORMATION

The influence of the Reformation and national separation from Rome followed a different course in England than in the rest of Europe and led to the foundation of the Anglican Church.

1521 Pope Leo X awards King Henry VIII the title *Fidei Defensor* for Henry's published theological refutation of Luther.

1525 William Tyndale publishes his English translation of the New Testament.

1533 Against Rome's permission, Archbishop of Canterbury Thomas Cranmer annuls Henry VIII's marriage to Catherine of Aragon.

1534 *Act of Supremacy* establishes Henry VIII as supreme head of the Church of England.

1535 Execution of Thomas More and John Fisher for refusing to swear loyalty to the crown.

1539 Dissolution of the monasteries in England.

1547 Death of Henry VIII. German Reformers arrive in London.

1552 The revised *Book of Common Prayer* abolishes the Mass, prayers for the dead, and Latin liturgy.

1553 The Catholic Mary I assumes the English throne. English Reformers are deported or imprisoned.

1555 Execution of Hooper, Ridley, and Latimer amongst 300 other English Protestants. Cranmer burnt a year later.

1558 Death of Mary I and accession of Queen Elizabeth I. Restoration of English Protestant reforms and persecution of English Catholics.

were soon eclipsed by the "Society of Jesus" formally endorsed by Pope Paul III in 1540. The Jesuits had two aims: to reform the church while guarding against Protestant innovations and to engage in missionary activity. Governed by the *Constitutionales* of Ignatius Loyola, the Jesuits flourished, especially seeing success in Poland, southern Germany, East Asia, and the New World.

IGNATIUS LOYOLA (C. 1491–1556)

A nobleman, Ignatius, along with six companions, made a vow of poverty, chastity, and mission in 1534. He became the first Jesuit general in 1540. Loyola's *Spiritual Exercises* include rules for Christian meditation designed to aid prayer and self-discipline. Still influential, the *Exercises* have been in constant circulation since they were written c. 1522–1523.

◄ Ignatius of Loyola helped found the Jesuits. His main writings remain influential and have never been out of print.

Georgios Kollidas/Shutterstock

TERESA OF ÁVILA (1515–1582)

A Spanish Carmelite nun, Teresa was the author of *The Way of Perfection* (c. 1562) and *The Interior Castle* (1577) amongst other works. Her accounts of ecstatic "spiritual marriage" combined with practical discipline ushered in a new era of Christian mysticism.

JOHN OF THE CROSS (1542–1591)

A Spanish mystic and doctor of the church, John worked closely with Teresa of Ávila in reforming the Carmelite order. He wrote on the self's transformation in the presence of the Divine. John's idea of the "dark night of the soul" has subsequently influenced much Christian life and thought.

Tridentine Reforms

Jesuit influence was strong during the Councils of Trent of 1545–1563. Summoned by Pope Paul III, these councils marked the high point of the Counter-Reformation and ensured the impossibility of reconciliation with the Protestants. Trent renewed Catholic spiritual life by affirming that the church had the sole authority to interpret the Bible. It opposed Reformed doctrines of the Eucharist by upholding transubstantiation and affirming the Mass.

Trent also revised the Latin Vulgate Bible and paved the way for reform and simplification of the Breviary, the liturgical book of prayers, lessons, and psalms to be used in Catholic worship. In 1568 the Hail Mary was introduced to the Breviary. In 1577 the publication of Peter Canisius's *Incomparable Virgin Mary* (*De Maria Virgine Incomparabili*) further emphasised the difference between Catholic spirituality and Protestantism's increasing scepticism of devotion to the Virgin Mary.

New World Expansion

The revival of Catholic Christianity was not confined to the Old World. The century saw great mission projects to the New World, as well as to India, Japan, and China.

By 1500 Franciscan missions had been established in the Caribbean. The first bishoprics appeared in Hispaniola (modern-day Haiti and Dominican Republic) shortly thereafter. In 1508 the papal bull *Universalis Ecclesiae* granted the Spanish the right to appoint bishops and collect tithes across the New World.

Imperial expansion in the name of God brought much enslavement and abuse of the native populations. At the same time, many missionaries intervened on behalf of native peoples during the 1520s and 1530s, including the priests of newly created bishoprics in Mexico, Lima, Colombia, and Cuba. These bishops now some small success and sowed the seeds of restraint, but there was little immediate change to Spanish and Portuguese colonial excesses.

The Americas

In 1531, ten years after Hernán Cortés conquered Emperor Moctezuma II, recent Aztec Christian converts reported seeing visions of the Virgin Mary. The shrine of Our Lady of Guadalupe became a focal point for Mexican national identity as well as the emerging Devotion to Mary movement. An early supporter of Guadalupe, Mexico's first bishop Juan de Zumárraga (1468–1548), led campaigns to destroy pagan sites of worship, and in 1539 set up the Americas' first printing press.

Cuba had its first bishop in 1518, Nicaragua in 1531, and Bolivia in 1552. In Brazil, the 1549 Jesuit mission of Manuel de Nobréga led to the installation of a bishop also in 1552. Bogotá became Colombia's first diocese in 1564. Most mission work with the native inhabitants of the Americas was now undertaken by Jesuits, and they established the first parish in Florida in 1566, although the mission did not flourish.

India

In 1510 Afonso de Albuquerque began the Portuguese invasion of the Goa region of western India. Expansion continued through

ANTONIO DE MONTESINOS (C. 1486–C. 1540)

The Dominican priest was the first to preach against the abuse of indigenous peoples in Santo Domingo in 1511. He refused to offer the Eucharist to any slave owner, including Admiral Diego Columbus, son of Christopher Columbus. De Montesinos's protest led to the passing of the Laws of Burgos in 1512, guaranteeing certain basic rights to New World native peoples.

BARTOLOMÉ DE LAS CASAS (1474–1566)

"Protector of the Indians," Las Casas devoted himself to opposing the cruelty and exploitation of native peoples living under Spanish imperial rule. From 1543 to 1551 he was the Dominican bishop of Chiapa in Mexico. His *Destrucción de las Indias* (1552) detailed accounts of settler abuses.

FIRST AMERICAN MARTYR

A Spanish military chaplain, Juan de Padilla (c. 1500–1544) travelled with colonial explorers into what is modern-day Kansas. The explorers turned back in 1542, but Father Padilla elected to remain amongst the Tíguez people. Slain by a neighbouring tribe in 1544, he is considered to be the first Catholic martyr of the incipient United States.

▲ Palm trees sway over Palolem Beach in Goa, India. Goa was the main staging ground for missions to India, China, and Japan.

domin_domin/iStock

▼ Ruins of Sao Paulo Church, Macau, China. The church was built by the Jesuits between 1582 and 1602.

Leung Cho Pan/123RF.com

ŌMURA SUMITADA (1533–1587)

Sumitada was the first Japanese warlord to convert to Christianity in 1563. Taking the Christian name Bartholomew, he forged close links with the Jesuits, opened the port of Nagasaki to foreign trade, and waged an unpopular campaign against Buddhism and the Shinto religion.

Muslim and Hindu territories for the next two decades, establishing Goa as the trading and religious centre of the Portuguese Empire. In 1542 Francis Xavier (1506–1552) made Goa the headquarters for his Jesuit mission.

Xavier saw much success gaining Roman Catholic converts in southern India. Christianity had existed in India since at least the fourth century. However, until imperial influence began to make itself felt, the native Syrian and Thomas churches had been left alone. A Catholic bishopric was established at Cohin in 1577, and at the Synod of Diamper in 1599, the Portuguese archbishop of Goa, Alexis Menezes (1559–1617), ordered the Indian churches to swear an oath of loyalty to the pope. He faced stiff resistance from the patriarchs, and thus under Portuguese patronage, Christianity in India was divided into three groups: the Latin Catholics, the Syrians (who kept Syrian liturgy but obeyed Rome), and the Independent Thomas Christians.

Japan and Southeast Asia

In 1545 Xavier travelled to Malaysia, the Spice Islands, and Sri Lanka. In 1549 Xavier arrived in Japan and enjoyed early success. The Jesuits were followed by Franciscans, Dominicans, and Augustinians, and Christianity became accepted in the islands of Kyūshū and Honshū. By 1580 the Japanese Christian population was estimated to be around 150,000, and in 1587 Emperor Hideyoshi attempted to expel all Christian missionaries with their foreign ideas. He was not successful, and the next year a bishopric was created at Funai. Official hostility towards Christianity persisted. Six missionaries and twenty-six converts were crucified at Nagasaki in 1597, the persecution driving Christianity largely underground.

China

Francis Xavier died in Goa in 1552 while awaiting permission to enter China. A parish had been created in Macau in 1576, but it was not until the missionary journey of the Jesuits Michele Ruggieri and Matteo Ricci in 1582 that Christianity made an impact. Ricci (1552–1610) gained the esteem of his hosts through his method of adapting Christian concepts to Chinese systems and beliefs. He allowed the use of *tian* (an ancient Chinese term for "heaven") for God, and found a way to incorporate traditional Chinese ancestor worship into Christian forms. A Christian community flourished; however, the Jesuit method of accommodation would eventually draw censure from Rome, contributing to the overall suppression of the Jesuits and the collapse of Christianity in China until the Protestant missions of the nineteenth century.

17 REFORM AND REVIVAL: 1600–1700

The story of Christianity in this era can be told in three main strands. The revival and expansion of Catholicism continues, leading to a church stronger and more united in some key ways than before the Reformation. Protestantism too continues its trajectory set in the previous century by creating multiple, vibrant reforming groups in Europe and beyond. As Orthodoxy confirms its central statements of faith, the Russian Church grows from strength to strength, dealing with schismatic movements of its own in the process.

Wars of Religion?

In the seventeenth century, the emergence of nationalism and the sectarian strife of autonomous states would have profound (and bloody) consequences. The wars that wracked Europe during this time are sometimes referred to as the "Wars of Religion." Conflicting religious feelings were obviously exploited during these wars; however, the rifts tended to follow national allegiances rather than simply religious differences.

▲ Holy Tinity Church in Bavaria, Germany. It is a small pilgrimage church, built in 1689 by Georg Dietzenhofer.

wolfgang hertel/123RF.com

Thirty Years' War

The Thirty Years' War (1618–1648) was a protracted series of conflicts largely between the two great Catholic houses of Europe. The war began in Prague in 1618 when Protestant Bohemians rebelled against attempts by Emperor Ferdinand

II's (1578–1637) attempt to enforce uniformity on his territories. Fighting soon spread to include England, Holland, Denmark, and Sweden, with Ferdinand's actions alienating both Protestants and Catholics. In 1630 the conflict incorporated the ongoing struggle between Bourbon France and the Habsburg houses of Spain and Germany. The Bourbons and their Protestant allies represented the interests of the emerging independent nation-states; the Habsburgs and the Catholic League defended the old order of the imperialist Holy Roman Empire. Pope Urban VIII (1568–1644) did not interfere when French Cardinal Richelieu provided material support to the Protestant Swedish king Gustavus Adolphus (1594–1632), who invaded Habsburg Vienna in 1630. In 1635 Catholic France directly entered the war on the side of the Protestant groups opposed to imperial power.

The Peace of Westphalia

The two treaties of Westphalia brought a decisive end to the Thirty Years' War in 1648. Westphalia ushered in a new age of ideological nationalism by recognising the sovereignty of individual countries and by superseding the medieval notion that Christendom was united under the highest authority of the church. Westphalia endorsed the formula *cuius region eius religio* ("whose realm, his religion"): the subjects of each nation should follow the religion of their ruler. Protection was given to religious minorities, and the political legitimacy of the Calvinists was recognised along with the Lutherans and Catholics. Church land too was "secularised" (a term first used at Westphalia) and distributed among the several nations who participated in the war, to the chagrin of Pope Innocent X (1574–1655), whose protest was ignored.

ARMAND JEAN DU PLESSIS, DUKE OF RICHELIEU (1585–1642)

A trusted adviser to the Medici family, Richelieu exerted great power as the virtual ruler of France after he became a cardinal in 1622. A major patron of the arts, he built the Palais Royal and Sorbonne Chapel and founded the French Academy in 1635.

▶ Cardinal Richelieu (1585–1642) effectively ruled France and exerted enormous influence throughout Europe.

Wikimedia Commons

Catholicism

Catholic Christianity did not lose out entirely after the Thirty Years' War. Despite ceding some ground to the Reformers, the Hussites and other Protestants were outlawed in Bohemia, and the region was declared Catholic. The opening of the century also saw gains for Catholicism in Poland, which as of 1569 also included Ukraine.

Ruthenian Catholics

Since the 1596 Union of Brest-Litovsk, many significant Ukrainian Orthodox churches had placed themselves under the authority of Rome, with more bishoprics following in 1694 (Przemyśl) and 1700 (Lvov). Thus the majority of Ukrainian (also called Ruthenian) and Polish nobility in this era were Uniates, practicing Latin Christianity and suppressing Orthodoxy.

SACRED HEART

The practice of "Devotion to the Heart of Jesus" has its roots in the mystical and meditative tradition of the Middle Ages. John Eudes (1601–1680) and Margaret Mary Alacoque (1647–1690) provided theological shape to the practice, linking it closely with Devotion to the Sacred Heart of Mary. It would become one of the most popular Catholic devotional practices.

▲ An image of the Sacred Heart of Jesus

sedmak/iStock

Transylvanian Catholics

The Romanian principality of Transylvania had long been the target of Hungarian Catholic, then German Lutheran, missionary efforts. Though the majority of the population adhered to Orthodoxy, by the opening of the century

CATHOLIC MISSIONS

Catholicism rapidly expanded around the world, usually by way of Spanish and Portuguese Jesuit missionaries and often on the back of colonial expansion, leading to occasional tensions between native peoples, churchmen, and profiteering explorers.

Japan

c. 1600   Japanese Christian population estimated to be around 210,000.

1613   The Tokugawa Shogunate banishes all Europeans and issues decrees against Christianity.

1640   An estimated 150,000 secret Christians remain in the country.

China

1601   Matteo Ricci (1552–1610) arrives in Beijing.

1615   The Chinese Christian population estimated to be around 5,000.

a minority of nobility were Calvinists. When Romania was unified in 1600–1601 under the Greek Orthodox hierarchy, these Transylvanian Protestants forced the church to accept many points of Reformed doctrine. When the region came under Habsburg control in 1691, Catholicism was added to Calvinism, Lutheranism, and Unitarianism as a "received religion." Under Metropolitan Atanasie Anghel Popa (?–1713), the Transylvanian Greek Catholic Church was born in 1698. In return for accepting the *Filioque* clause and the authority of the pope, the new church was able to keep its liturgy intact and its clergy were also considered to be "received."

India

1600   First Portuguese bishopric established at Angamaly.

1606   Diocese of Mylapore established.

1623   Pope Gregory XV (1554–1623) intervenes in the controversy over Indian Christians who return Hindu social customs and cultural practices.

1637   Matheus de Castro of Divar (dates unknown), a native of Goa and member of the Brahmin caste, is appointed bishop over the regions not covered by the Portuguese mandate.

Southern Americas

c. 1600   Jesuits active in Paraguay.

1610   Establishment of the Inquisition in Colombia, Venezuela, and the Spanish Caribbean.

1617   Creation of the Diocese of Buenos Aires. Pedro Carranza (dates unknown) appointed first bishop in 1620.

c. 1638   Jesuits active in the Amazon region.

Northern Americas

1603   First activity of French Catholicism in Nova Scotia and Quebec.

1609   Missions established in Santa Fé (modern-day New Mexico).

1680   Indigenous Pueblo people's rebellion against colonial rule results in the destruction of the Santa Fé missions. They are restored in 1692.

1687   Eusebio Francisco Kino (1645–1711) establishes early missions in Arizona.

1697   Permanent mission outpost founded at Baja California.

▲ *The Black Madonna of Czestochowa.* The painting, housed in the Jasna Góra monastery, has long been a focus for Catholic pilgrimage and is a symbol of Polish national pride. Its ancient origins are obscure.   3LH/Superstock

The Uniate Transylvanian Church was not initially accepted by the majority of the population, but it would go on to become the centre of Romanian national identity in the eighteenth and nineteenth centuries.

The Jansenist Movement

France remained a bastion for Catholic Counter-Reformation ideas and movements, some of which went further than even Rome was willing to follow. One enthusiastic theologian was the bishop of Ypres, Cornelius Otto Jansen (1585–1638). Jansen's vision was to attack Protestantism with its own weapons and reshape

Catholic Christianity through a radical appeal to the writings of Augustine. In 1627 Jansen's project brought him into conflict with the Jesuits. Although Jansen's ideas were declared heretical by the University of Sorbonne in 1649 and by Pope Innocent X in 1653, the Jansenist movement retained its popularity and included amongst its numbers the scientist and philosopher Blaise Pascal (1623–1662).

Protestantism

Since the previous century, Protestantism had been embraced across Europe both as a vehicle for political freedom and as a vibrant expression of Christianity. Yet the hallmarks of Reformation theology (including the belief in the priesthood of all believers, the high value placed on individual interpretation of Scripture, and the rejection of many hierarchical systems) opened the way to a myriad of different expressions.

Calvinism

John Calvin died in 1564, leaving behind a sophisticated theological system and a wealth of literature, including the *Institutes of the Christian Religion* (1536–1559). In the seventeenth century, the majority of European Protestants who were not Lutherans were Calvinists of some description, and the movement thrived in France, parts of Germany, Romania, Hungary, Scotland, and the North American colonies. The English Puritans were greatly influenced by Calvinist thought. The Netherlands adopted Calvinism as the state religion in 1622.

📖 SLAVERY

A small band of churchmen stood against the exploitation and slavery that came with European colonial expansion. The Portuguese Jesuit missionary António Vieira (1608–1697) attracted controversy for his apocalyptic sermons and for his persistent defence of the native peoples of Brazil against colonial exploits. In 1622 the Caribbean Catholic Synod produced elaborate regulations for the right treatment of the native populations in the West Indies. From 1616 Pedro Claver (1580–1654), a Spanish missionary in Colombia, did much to alleviate the suffering of African slaves brought to the region. The success of his mission amongst the slave ships led to the condemnation of slavery in a bull issued by Pope Urban VIII in 1639.

👤 FRANCISCO SUÁREZ (1548–1617)

The Spanish Jesuit pioneered new methods of philosophy suited for the contemporary Christian mind. His 1613 *Defensio fidei* was directed against the church in England. As it undermined theories of absolute state power, the work was also banned by the *Parlement of Paris*.

▶ The Protestant Reformer John Calvin died in 1564. It was not long before Calvinist Christianity prevailed in continental Europe, the British Isles and North America

Georgios Kollidas/Shutterstock

Predestination

The doctrine that God's eternal plan requires that only the "elect" will be saved while others are predestined to damnation was not originally a central feature of Calvin's thought. It was under the influence of the theologian Theodore Beza (1519–1605) that "predestination" assumed greater importance. This picture of the Divine nature prompted opposition from some of Beza's former students. Jacobus Arminius (1560–1609) sparked controversy in his native Holland when he argued against Calvinist determinism in the university and before the legal courts.

FRANCIS DE SALES (1567–1622)

A Counter-Reformation missionary to the Swiss Calvinists in 1599, Francis is reported as saying, "Love alone will shake the walls of Geneva." In 1610, along with the nun Jane Frances de Chantal (1572–1641), he founded the charitable Order of the Visitation. He was declared a doctor of the church in 1877.

ROBERT DE NOBILI (1577–1656)

A Jesuit missionary, Robert arrived in India in 1605. He adopted local customs and became one of the first Europeans to have knowledge of Sanskrit and the primary sacred documents of the Hindu religion. Robert faced opposition, but by the time he retired in 1654, his unorthodox methods had resulted in several thousand converts from all social castes.

Arminianism

Shortly after Arminius's death his followers published the Remonstrance of 1610, which detailed their major divergence with Calvinism, namely, that Christ died for all people and thus it is possible for all men to be saved if they freely choose to believe. Theologically, the debate struck at the heart of doctrines of God and salvation. Politically, the situation threatened the stability of the Netherlands, which was engaged in ongoing hostilities with Spain.

Synod of Dort

Prince Maurice of Orange (1567–1625) convened the Synod of Dort in 1618–1619, welcoming delegates from England, Scotland, Switzerland, and Germany. Originally intended to settle the Arminian problem, Dort had the effect of crystallising the key doctrines of Calvinism and the theology of the Dutch Reformed Church. By finding the Remonstrance to be unorthodox, the synod ousted over 200 Arminian leaders from the country. However, Arminianism would go onto to exert considerable influence on Christian thought, including that of John Wesley and the Methodists of the following century.

Lutheranism

Martin Luther died in 1546. By the seventeenth century, the confessional movement that bore his name was flourishing in most of Germany, Scandinavia, Hungary, and Poland. The Lutheran churches and groups produced a variety of expressions, but they all took as their doctrinal guide the 1580 *Book of Concord*, a collection of Luther's Small and Large Catechisms, the Augsburg Confession, the Smalcald Articles, and other key texts of the German Reformation.

▲ Cathedral of St. Mary, a Lutheran church in Freiberg, Germany

Boris Breytman/123RF.com

Lutheranism at this time had a strong focus on intellectual argument, reason, and organisation. It was also closely allied with many of the newly emerged nation-states invigorated by the Peace of Westphalia.

Pious Longings

In reaction to the confessional strife of the Thirty Years' War, and the potentially stifling effect of Lutheran dogmatism on church and state, the German Lutheran pastor Philipp Jakob Spener (1635–1705) wrote *Pia desideria* ("Pious Longings") in 1675. The tract expressed a Reformed Christianity emphasising personal Bible study, the avoidance of religious arguments, fervent devotion, and faith expressed as love for neighbour rather than knowledge. It also counselled against engaging in political power struggles.

Pietism

The movement that arose from Spener's community and writings became known as Pietism.

Spener had not invented Pietism but was drawing from previous theologians such as Johann Arndt (1555–1621). Nevertheless, Spener became seen as the leader of the new subversive movement and was expelled from Leipzig by his mainstream Lutheran opponents in 1690. Pietism would reach its height under the leadership of Count Zinzendorf (1700–1760), and the Pietist influence would be felt in the Protestant revivals of the nineteenth and twentieth centuries.

Anglicanism

Anglicanism, while not generally so abrupt a change as the Protestant movements of the European continent, nevertheless existed as a distinct alternative to Roman Catholicism. The English Church experienced some of its most formative events in the seventeenth century.

King James

King James I of England and VI of Scotland (1566–1625) assumed the throne after the

▲ James I of England. His Authorized Version of the Bible is one of the most widely read books in the world.

Wikimedia Commons

The English Civil War

Charles I (1600 -1649) became king in 1625. He was pressured to adopt policies favourable to Catholicism and to move the church away from the Calvinist influence of his predecessors. A series of disastrous military expeditions abroad coupled with an authoritarian rule at home led to Charles's extreme unpopularity. In 1640 his powers were severely curtailed by Parliament. The ensuing English Civil War (1642–1651) saw the execution of the Anglican monarch and the imposition of a Puritan, Presbyterian republic under the rule of Oliver Cromwell (1599–1658).

Republic and Restoration

Cromwell's dissolution of the old Church of England and his attempt to impose a new, Puritan style of church and government ultimately proved unpopular with the people. In 1660 the exiled (and Catholic sympathiser) Charles II (1630–1685) was welcomed back as king, with the country and church forging a new settlement known as the Restoration.

death of Elizabeth I in 1603. During his reign, James opposed the Presbyterian movement in Scotland and sought compromise with the Puritans of England. In 1605 the discovery of the "Gunpowder Plot" to destroy the Houses of Parliament led to stricter laws against English Roman Catholics and exacerbated continuing tensions with other Catholic nations, especially Spain. James was keenly interested in church affairs, and his endorsement of a new English translation of the Bible led to the King James Authorised Version in 1611.

JOHN BUNYAN (1628–1688)

As a young Puritan, Bunyan fought in the Civil War. Following the Restoration, Bunyan was imprisoned between 1660 and 1672 for his dissenting preaching. While incarcerated he wrote *The Pilgrim's Progress* (published in 1678 and 1684), an allegory of the Christian life that would go on to become one of the most widely read books in the history of Christianity.

◀ *John Bunyan* by Thomas Sadler

Wikimedia Commons

QUAKERS

Also known as the Society of Friends, the Quakers were originally a Puritan sect from 1650 who earned their name for the way in which they trembled before the Word of God. Their founder, George Fox (1624–1691), preached that Christians should seek the Holy Spirit rather than the words of humans as the guide to Christian worship. As a result, Quakers became known for their silent meetings and for women sharing equal responsibility with men in leadership. They refused to participate in violence and were instrumental in the abolition of slavery in the eighteenth century.

Uniformity and Non-Conformity

The 1662 Act of Uniformity restored the establishment by commanding universal adoption of the Book of Common Prayer and Anglican ordination. The result for those churchmen who refused to comply was the creation of the Non-Conformists, a category including the English Presbyterians, Quakers, Congregationalists, Baptists, and, later, Methodists. It was largely Non-Conformism that provided the energising influence of Protestant Christianity in the New World.

CONGREGATIONALISTS

These Puritans contended that the church should consist only of those who have made the conscious decision to follow Christ, opposing on principle the idea of a national church and emphasising the independence of local congregations. The pilgrim fathers set off from a Congregationalist church in 1620, and since then the movement has been integral to the organisation of Christianity in America.

BAPTISTS

In 1609 the separatist Puritan John Smyth (c. 1565–1612) led his congregation in the practice of believer's baptism, establishing a church around freely converted adults rather than the practice of infant baptism. By 1660 there were around 300 Baptist churches in England and Wales. With their strong missionary focus, Baptist denominations have been hugely influential in the spread of Christianity throughout the world.

Orthodoxy

The influence of the Protestantism of Western Europe was also felt in the East, which was still living largely under Ottoman Muslim rule.

The Calvinist Patriarch

Cyril Lucar (1572–1638) became ecumenical patriarch of Constantinople in 1620. Lucar was familiar with the controversies of the Reformation, having used some Protestant writings during his conflict with Rome at the 1596 Synod of Brest-Litovsk. He forged close ties with European Protestants, especially in England, in 1628 presenting to the English court the *Codex Alexandrinus*—a fifth-century copy of the Bible and the earliest surviving example of Byzantine text. As a result of Ottoman opposition, Lucar was deposed numerous times during the course of his patriarchy but was restored to the position partly with the aid of Dutch and English ambassadors to Constantinople.

In 1629 Lucar published the thoroughly Calvinist *Confession of Faith*, which laid out his vision for an Orthodox Church following Reformed doctrine. In 1638 he sponsored a translation of the Bible into contemporary vernacular, the same year that he was put to death by Sultan Murad IV for treason against the Ottoman Turks.

DEMETRIOS OF PHILADELPHIA (?–1657)

A young Christian man living in Asia Minor, Demetrios was granted considerable favour by the ruling Ottomans upon his conversion to Islam. When he returned to Christianity in 1657, he was executed for his newfound faith. Demetrios is celebrated as a "New Martyr" by the Orthodox Church.

PROTESTANT AMERICANS

1607 Anglican church established at first permanent American settlement in Jamestown, Virginia.

1620 Puritan pilgrims sail from England and Holland to America on the *Mayflower*.

1630 John Winthrop (1587–1649) founds Congregationalist settlement in Massachusetts.

1639 Roger Williams (c. 1603–1683) founds first Baptist church in Providence, Rhode Island.

1643 Catholicism outlawed in Virginia.

1663 John Eliot (1604–1690) publishes first Bible in North America. It is written in the dialect of the Algonquin native people.

1664 The Dutch colony New Amsterdam is taken over and renamed New York by the English. The Dutch Reformed Presbyterian Church (present since 1628) continues to flourish under English rule.

1682 William Penn (1644–1718) leads emigration of over 200 Welsh Quakers to the newly created state of Pennsylvania.

1692 Witch trials in Salem, Massachusetts.

1690s English Protestants are joined by French Huguenots, German Mennonites, and Dutch Calvinists in the American colonies.

Orthodox Reaction

Lucar's Calvinist leanings were more positively received in Western Europe than they were at home. Shortly after his death, a series of councils repudiated his attempted reforms. As a result, these councils helped to clarify Orthodox theology, leading to the establishment of key statements of Orthodox faith.

◀ Russian Orthodox church, Copenhagen, Denmark

Taras Verkhovynets/123RF.com

 DOSITHEUS II (1641–1707)

Patriarch since 1669, Dositheus used his considerable influence in Orthodoxy to combat Protestant innovations and continue to resist Roman Catholic inroads. He instituted printing presses to encourage Orthodox literature, limited Franciscan access to the Holy Places in Jerusalem, opposed the development of the Uniat churches, and sought to extend Greek influence over the Russian Church.

▲ A view of the Western Wall and the Dome of the Rock, Jerusalem   Karina Lopatina/Shutterstock

Synod of Jassy

Lesser Synods at Constantinople in 1638 and 1642 began the process, but it was the Synod of Jassy (also in 1642, in what is modern-day Romania) that did much to consolidate Orthodox tradition. The synod drew representatives from the Greek, Russian, and Slavic Orthodox churches. Jassy condemned the Calvinist teaching of Lucar while at the same time positively endorsing the *Orthodox Confession* of Peter Mogila (1596–1646).

Peter Mogila

The metropolitan of Kiev from 1633, Mogila is credited with doing much to educate the clergy and laity of the Orthodox Church. His *Confession* was first composed in 1638 and is regarded as a primary document of Orthodoxy, providing a comprehensive survey of the faith. Originally Mogila's text was criticised for its debt to Roman Catholic Thomist theology, but after revision it was accepted by Jassy and published in 1645. Mogila was able to further outline the Orthodox objections to both Catholic and Protestant claims, with the *Confession* eventually earning the endorsement of the great Synod of Jerusalem in 1672.

Synod of Jerusalem

Along with Jassy, the Synod of Jerusalem is the most important council in the history of the Orthodox Church. Seven metropolitans and sixty-eight Orthodox bishops convened at the Church of the Nativity in Bethlehem, near Jerusalem. The main acts of the synod fell into two categories. The "Six Chapters" put a conclusive end to the Protestant influence of Lucar's *Confessions* while the "Eighteen Articles" provided a detailed catechism of Orthodox faith. This included the single procession of the Spirit, the infallibility of the church along with Scripture, justification by faith working through love, an endorsement of the seven sacraments, and the inclusion (with care) of the Apocrypha into the biblical canon.

Russian Troubles

In Russia, the period between 1598 and 1613 is sometimes known as the "Time of Troubles" on account of the chaos following the death of Feodor I (1557–1598) and the institution of the new Romanov dynasty. The patriarchs of the Russian Church played an important part in leading the people through this time, including especially Germogen (c. 1530–1612) and Filaret (c. 1150–1633). Filaret was the father of the Romanov tsar Michael, and he dominated in national politics. Under Filaret and his successors, state and church became indistinguishable, leading to much material corruption and abuse of power.

Zealous Reform

The situation in the Russian Church produced a groundswell of clergy keen to return the faithful to a life of sincere devotion. One such zealous monk was Nikon (1605–1681), who in 1652 was appointed patriarch of Moscow by the new, reform-minded tsar Alexis (1629–1676). Alexis and Nikon revised Russian liturgy and corrected various corruptions that they felt had crept into the service. The detailed revisions extended even to an insistence that the sign of the cross be made with three fingers rather than two.

Old Believers

The deep reforms were enforced throughout the land, prompting much resentment. At times, Alexis and Nikon were even described as the antichrist and accused of bringing the church into further error. When the new liturgical practice was finally endorsed in 1666, a section of the church under the leadership of Archpriest Avvakum (1620–1682) refused to comply. Avvakum (whose *Autobiography* is considered a landmark in Russian literature) was imprisoned and martyred in 1682. His movement, dubbed the "Old Believers," or *Raskolniki* ("Schismatics"), included thousands of peasants, townsfolk, and priests, and they experienced fierce persecution. Old Believers fled to Serbia and Karelia, and many committed mass suicide rather than face execution at the hands of the tsar's soldiers. Despite sporadic persecution, especially under Peter the Great (1672–1725), the Old Believers persisted in various factions and remain a feature of the Russian religious landscape.

▲ Nikon (1605–1681)　　　Wikimedia Commons

18 REASON AND REVOLUTION: 1700–1800

Eighteenth-century Orthodoxy sees the Greeks continue to live under Muslim rule while developing some of the church's key features. As Russia becomes a world power under a series of visionary leaders, the church is drawn closer and closer to the governing authorities. For Protestantism, the philosophical Enlightenment will have a lasting effect on European Christian thought and practice. At the same time, evangelical revivals sweep England and America, prompting a new form of heartfelt, individualistic religion with radical consequences for society. Meanwhile, Roman Catholicism is thriving in India, China, and Korea, while the long-standing success of the worldwide Jesuit network leads to concerted efforts to dismantle their power. Related to this is the bloody French Revolution, an explosive rebellion against the old monarchical order that will have a lasting impact on modern relations between church and state throughout the world.

Orthodoxy

Russia

Nikon, the patriarch of Moscow between 1652 and 1658, had brought in controversial reforms striking at the heart of the old Russian way of religious life. In the process, Nikon had also claimed that the patriarch, not the tsar, should be the *Veliki Gosudar* ("Great Sovereign")

▲ The Preobrazhenskaya Church of Transfiguration on Kizhi Island, Russia, was built in 1714 and features twenty-two shingled domes.   jejim/iStock

of the state. Unsurprisingly, this claim to superiority was not welcomed by the imperial power, and Nikon was exiled and imprisoned for fourteen years. He was succeeded by a number of ineffectual patriarchs. The assertion of the power of the tsar over the church reached its height in the reign of Peter "the Great" (1672–1725).

Peter the Great

A secularist and admirer of Western innovations, Peter saw the church as an obstacle to his plans. But at the same time, he used the church to extend the ideology of complete obedience to the ruler and strengthened the practice of serfdom. When Patriarch Adrian died in 1700, Peter let the post remain vacant

for twenty-one years. As a way of enforcing the cultural influence of Orthodoxy, compulsory confession was introduced in 1716, and church attendance on Sundays and holidays was made a legal requirement throughout the land in 1718. In 1721, the same year that Peter proclaimed himself Emperor of All the Russias, he also concentrated all the power of the church under the tsar.

College of Spiritual Affairs

In 1721, along with Bishop Prokopovich (1681–1736), Peter abolished the Russian patriarchy, instituting the College of Spiritual Affairs in its place with himself at its head. The college was soon renamed the Holy Synod to make it more palatable to reluctant bishops; nevertheless, the church effectively became a wing of the Russian government. In 1722 Peter nullified the traditional practice of confidential confessions, ordering instead that priests report any insults or conspiracies against the tsar, handing over their parishioners to the state police. This system, by which the Holy Synod was closely bound to the interests of the state, would remain in

 TIKHON OF ZADONSK (1724–1783)

Tikhon was a writer and bishop who retired to the Zadonsk monastery in 1769. His humility and care for the poor inspired later Russian writers, including Tolstoy and Dostoevsky, and the latter used Tikhon as the model for the character of Father Zosima in *The Brothers Karamazov* (1880).

◀ Portrait of Russian Tsar Peter I the Great by Godfrey Kneller   Wikimedia Commons

Russia for the next two centuries, leading to divisions between the ruling elite of the church and the common clergy serving the majority population.

Catherine the Great

One beneficiary of the Holy Synod settlement was Catherine "the Great" (1729–1796), who reigned from 1762 until her death. Catherine, a German princess, continued to exert a Western, Enlightenment influence on the Russian Church. In 1764 Catherine confiscated much church and monastic land, thus depriving Russian Orthodoxy of more than three quarters of its annual income. In 1767 she issued an *Instruction* that called for the "prudent toleration of other Religions," and in 1771 Old Believers were allowed to set up limited communities in Moscow. Keen to maintain educational standards, Catherine also briefly welcomed back the Jesuits, allowing for the creation of a Catholic bishopric in Mogilëv in 1773.

◀ Empress Catherine II. Catherine "the Great" brought a measure of religious toleration to Russia.

Wikimedia Commons

Moscow's Reach Extends

The Russo-Turkish war of 1768–1774 ended with the Treaty of Kuchuk Kainarji (in Bulgaria), granting the victorious Catherine political and economic rights over vast swathes of the Ottoman Empire. Wider reaching was the right that was granted to the Russian tsar to intervene in the internal affairs of Christians living under Ottoman rule. Thus, in the 1780s Catherine assumed control over the kingdom of Georgia, bringing its church under the influence of the Russian Holy Synod. Furthermore, Greek Orthodox citizens in Moldavia, Walachia, the Aegean Islands, and elsewhere in the Ottoman Empire began to look forward to the prospect of protection under the Third Rome of Moscow.

The New Martyrs

Although the Ottoman sultan's power was waning, the majority of Orthodox Christians in the eighteenth century still lived under Muslim rule. The era witnessed a number of martyrs, who in subsequent Orthodox tradition would be celebrated as "New Martyrs." In 1716 Anthimos (?–1716), a Georgian monk, printer, and metropolitan of Wallachia, was executed by Turkish soldiers. Kosmas Aitolos (?–1779), a Greek monk and educator, was caught up in the 1770 Peloponnesian revolt against the Turks before he was captured and executed as a Russian sympathiser in Albania in 1779. The following year monks

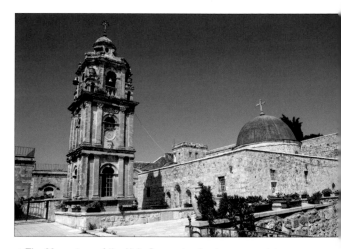

▲ The Monastery of the Holy Cross stands alone on a plot of land outside the Old City of Jerusalem.

Yevgenia Gorbulsky/123RF.com

at the Monastery of the Cross in Jerusalem were massacred. In 1788 the Bosnian Theodore Sladich (?–1788) and 150 of his followers were burnt at Moshtanica, a Serbian monastery. Sladich had agitated against Uniat movements towards Catholicism, Serbian secularisation, and Ottoman rule and was thus considered a disturber of the peace by the Turkish authorities.

Greek Decline

Despite sporadic persecution of Christians in the Ottoman Empire, the ecumenical patriarch of Constantinople worked under Ottoman permission and remained the nominal head of the Orthodox Church. For this reason, the 1774 Russian victory that weakened Ottoman power also led to a decline in Greek leadership of the church. Although in the new reality of the Eastern Church the Russians were becoming dominant, nevertheless the Greeks continued to assert their traditional authority within Orthodoxy.

Useless Waters

Opposition to the Latin influence was a continual theme in Orthodox life. Beginning in 1749 Ecumenical Patriarch Cyril V (?–1775) sought to counteract Protestant and French Catholic presence in Constantinople and in the Holy Lands. In 1755 he published the *Anathema of Those Who Accept Papal Sacraments*, a tract that was popularly received in the churches of the city. That same year, together with the patriarchs of Jerusalem and Alexandria, Cyril released the *Oros of the Holy Great Church of Christ*. The *Oros* ("Decree") was primarily concerned with the legitimacy of Catholic and Protestant baptism declaring: "We reject and abhor baptisms belonging to heretics. . . . They are useless waters."

Love of the Beautiful

Cyril died in retirement on Mount Athos in 1775, the same year that the Greek monk Nicodemus (c. 1749–1809) took up residence there. Nicodemus of the Holy Mountain produced a number of spiritual writings. He translated a Greek version of Ignatius of Loyola's *Spiritual Exercises*, keen to allow Western thought to illuminate the Eastern tradition where it could. In 1782, together with Macarius of Corinth (1731–1805), Nicodemus produced the *Philocalia* ("Love of the Beautiful"), a collection of spiritual writings from the fourth to the fifteenth centuries that dealt primarily with the Jesus Prayer and the Hesychast tradition. Through widespread distribution, with translations in Slavonic (1793) and later Russian (1876), the *Philocalia* became one of the most important texts for modern Orthodoxy, acting as a force for unification for a tradition that had seen much division.

Protestantism

Two, often opposing, intellectual and cultural forces affected the development of Protestant Christianity in the eighteenth century: Enlightenment and evangelicalism.

Enlightenment

The intellectual developments and ideals known as "the Enlightenment" built on the mechanistic and rationalist philosophies of René Descartes (1596–1650), John Locke (1632–1704), and other seventeenth-century thinkers. The German philosopher Immanuel Kant (1724–1804) defined the movement in the famous essay "What Is Enlightenment?" (1784): "Enlightenment is man's emergence from his self-imposed immaturity. . . . *Sapere Aude* ["dare to know"]! 'Have courage to use your own understanding!'—that is the motto of enlightenment."

Enlightenment thinkers were often opposed to orthodox Catholic and Protestant Christianity, and some philosophers supported deistic or atheistic worldviews. Leading figures include David Hume (1711–1776), Adam Smith (1723–1790), and Jean-Jacques Rousseau (1712–1778). Enlightenment thinkers were not uniformly anti-Christian, however, and many proponents (such as Kant) saw themselves as reforming traditional faith. The German theologian Friedrich Schleiermacher (1768–1834) appealed to Enlightenment principles while at the same time critiquing the excesses of intellectual rationalism. His 1799 *On Religion: Speeches to Its Cultured Despisers* has been enormously influential in the development of Protestant theology.

IMMANUEL KANT.

▲ Immanuel Kant, "Father of the Englightenment" and Professor of Logic and Metaphysics of Konigsberg University, Germany

📖 JOSEPHINISM

Josephinism was the programme of religious reform and Enlightenment principles in Austria initiated by the Holy Roman emperor Joseph II (1741–1790). The Toleration Edict (1781) restricted papal jurisdiction, dissolved over 700 monasteries, and extended toleration to Protestant groups and Greek Orthodox believers. In 1783 Joseph allowed divorce and made marriage a matter of civil contract.

📖 MORAVIANS

In 1722 the Moravian count Zinzendorf (1700–1760) established the Moravian Brotherhood when he welcomed a group of Czech pietists (known as "Bohemian Brethren") onto his estate at Herrnhut. Emphasising a "religion of the heart" rather than strict doctrine, Moravian missions were founded in the West Indies (1732), Greenland (1733), and South Africa (1736) and amongst the Inuit people of Labrador in 1752. The Moravian Church remains in existence, with a large proportion of members residing in Tanzania where a mission was established in the nineteenth century.

▶ Nikolaus Ludwig Graf von Zinzendorf, Moravian Count and pietist pastor

Evangelicals

The term *evangelical* (derived from the Greek *euaggelion* meaning "gospel" or "good news") had long been associated with the established Reformation churches of Germany and Switzerland. In the English-speaking world of the eighteenth century, the term began to refer not to a denomination but to those Christians who emphasised personal conversion and faith in the atoning death of Jesus Christ. Evangelical convictions were accompanied by a culture of mission and social activism, leading amongst other things to the institution of Sunday schools to promote literacy in England, social reform in India, and abolition of slavery in the British Empire in the nineteenth century. Formative evangelical influences included John Newton (1725–1807), the former slave trader who wrote the hymn "Amazing Grace," and Charles Simeon (1759–1836), the Cambridge Anglican clergyman who led the evangelical revival in the universities of Oxford and Cambridge. However, it was with the brothers John (1703–1791) and Charles Wesley (1707–1788) and their friend George Whitefield (1714–1770) that evangelical sentiments became closely identified with a new movement known as Methodism.

A Strange Warming

Methodism had its roots in a group of seriously minded Oxford theology students who gathered together to methodically pray and study the Bible. The group disappeared when John and Charles Wesley left Oxford for London in 1735, but was revived after John's contact with a Moravian group led by Peter Boehler (1712–1775). It was after one such meeting in 1738 that John described in his *Journal* how his heart was "strangely warmed."

SELINA, COUNTESS OF HUNTINGDON (1707–1791)

Lady Huntingdon did much to introduce Methodism to the upper classes, using her influence to employ many Methodist chaplains as priests in the Anglican Church. When barred from making more appointments, she registered her chapels as dissenting places of worship, thus founding the Countess of Huntingdon's Connexion in 1779.

Methodists

Finding the traditional churches closed to their style of worship, Whitefield and the Wesleys took their message of "vital practical religion" to the masses, preaching to great effect in the open air from 1739. The successful movement soon brought a separate sense of identity to the adherents, formed in large part by Charles Wesley, who penned over 9,000 Methodist hymns in his lifetime. John Wesley—theologically an Arminian—broke with the Calvinist George Whitefield in 1741. By 1751 Wesley's organisation of lay preachers spanned England, and the movement took root in America. In 1784 Wesley appointed Thomas Coke (1747–1814) as superintendent, or bishop, of the American Methodist Church. After Wesley's death a number of successions would lead to the formal separation between various Methodist groups and the Church of England in the first decades of the nineteenth century.

Protestant India

The first Protestant missionaries to India were sponsored by the Danish king Frederick IV.

▲ Luz Church at Mylapore in Chennai, Tamil Nadu, India

The India Today Group/Getty Images

Bartholomaeus Ziegenbalg (1682–1719) and Heinrich Plütschau (1677–1747) arrived at the Danish Indian settlement of Tranquebar in 1706. Despite facing severe opposition from Roman Catholics and Hindus, the Pietist missionaries managed to attract a Tamil congregation. Churches, schools, orphanages, and printing presses followed, with Ziegenbalg producing the first Tamil translation of the New Testament in 1714. Ziegenbalg and Plütschau's accounts of their exploits became popular in Britain, helping to stir up English enthusiasm for mission.

"English" Missions

Concurrent with the evangelical revival at home, the English sponsored many missions abroad, often employing non-British missionaries with a focus on South India. One of the most celebrated of these was Christian Friedrich Schwartz (1726–1798), a Prussian Pietist who arrived in India in 1750 having already learned Tamil. Schwartz was active in Ceylon (1760), Trichinopoly (1767), and the Kingdom of Tanjore (1772), where he was highly honoured by the rajah and given positions of political responsibility.

Mission and Social Reform

Schwartz was a great influence on Charles Grant (1746–1823), then superintendent of the British East India Trading Company. Grant was a driving force behind the British and Foreign Bible Society, the Church Missionary Society, and the Society for the Propagation of the Gospel. A member of the influential Clapham Sect, Grant opposed the British government's war policy against native Indians. He was an active proponent of evangelical social reform, calling for increased missionary and educational activity in India. His arguments brought him into opposition with the long-standing position of his own East India Trading Company, which opposed any Christian activity that would undermine their market dominance.

The Father of Modern Mission

The cobbler William Carey (1761–1834) became a Baptist in 1783; taught himself Latin, Greek, Hebrew, Dutch, and French; and founded the Baptist Missionary Society in 1792. As the East India Trading Company had banned missionaries travelling in British ships, in 1793 he journeyed to Bengal in a Danish vessel.

Carey was a prodigious translator, translating the entire Bible into Bengali and many other books into other Indian languages. In addition, Carey established a number of Christian communities, schools, and hospitals. His influence on the burgeoning missionary movement was immense.

📖 HALLELUJAH

The Lutheran composer George Frideric Handel (1685–1759) moved to England from Germany in 1712. His choral masterpiece *Messiah* was first performed in Dublin in 1742.

📖 *SUTTEE*

Carey waged a long campaign against infanticide and the traditional custom of *suttee*. This practice, whereby widows were expected to die on their husband's funeral pyres, was eventually abolished, the order being translated into Bengali by Carey's own hand in 1829.

American Colonies

Under the influence of theologians and pastors like Cotton Mather (1663–1728), whose *Magnalia Christi Americana* was published in 1702, America began to develop a Christian identity distinct from that of Europe. Catholicism retained a hold in the French and Spanish regions of North America; however, it was often suppressed or outlawed in the English colonies in favour of a growing Protestant, Puritan, and evangelical expression.

Great Awakenings

Between 1725 and 1760 a series of "stirrings" amongst Dutch Reformed and Presbyterian congregations followed the fervent preaching of pastors such as Theodore Frelinghuysen (1691–1747) and Gilbert Tennent

📍 AFRICAN AMERICAN CHURCHES

The Great Awakenings inspired white Christian missions and attracted increasing numbers of black slaves and freedmen to Christianity in the 1740s. Black-led churches were suppressed in the South, but after the Revolution a handful of black Methodist, Baptist, and other congregations grew up in the North. A coalition of Quakers and freed slaves founded the Free African Society in 1787, eventually leading to the opening of the "Mother Bethel" African Methodist Episcopal (AME) Church in 1794. The driving force for the project was Richard Allen (1760–1831), who would go on to become the first Methodist bishop of a fully independent African American denomination in 1816. The first American foreign missions were undertaken by black preachers such as George Liele (c. 1750–1820), a Baptist working in Jamaica, and David George (c. 1742–1810) in Sierra Leone.

▲ Richard Allen
Wikimedia Commons

(1703–1764) who emphasised personal conviction of sin and the need to be "born again." These evangelical movements became known as the "Great Awakening." Together the disparate spiritual revivals would have deep social implications for the 1776 Revolutionary War and the Declaration of Independence in 1783, and would influence the Civil War and abolitionist movements of the following century.

Edwards and Whitefield

The foremost Puritan theologian of this time was Jonathan Edwards (1703–1758). From 1735 the Great Awakening movement became closely identified with Edwards and his friend the English Methodist George Whitefield, who was seeing enthusiastic response during his preaching tour of the colonies. Both Edwards and Whitefield were conservative Calvinists opposed to Arminianism and cautious about excessive emotionalism. In 1746 Edwards published the *Treatise concerning Religious Affections*, an answer to criticisms that the revivals were merely products of emotional manipulation. While defending the movement as a work of the Holy Spirit, the study also took seriously the negative effects of the Awakening on Christian thought and practice, recognising the marked tendency for division amongst congregations affected by the revivals.

American Revolution

The feelings of individualism, voluntary religion, and moral seriousness sweeping the nation contributed to growing colonial political and economic disaffection with England. In turn, the American Revolution of 1776–1783 had a number of effects on Christianity in the United States. Congregationalists, Baptists, and

CANADA

Canadian Christianity had originally been established under the aegis of French Jesuits in the seventeenth century. The first German Lutherans arrived in 1750. Baptists, Quakers, and Moravians followed in the 1760s. British control over all Canadian territories in 1763 brought an influx of English-speaking Irish and Scottish Catholics as well as Presbyterians and other Protestants, making French Roman Catholics a significant minority. Methodist churches followed in 1775, and Loyalists swelled Anglican ranks after the American Revolution. The spread of the Anglican Church of Canada was further aided by the Constitutional Act of 1791, which divided Quebec into Upper and Lower Canada and reserved land, rent, and income for Anglicans. The Act contributed greatly to feelings of resentment amongst Roman Catholic French nationalists.

▲ Image of illuminated Mount Royal Cross, Montreal, Quebec. Quebec was founded as a Catholic colony in 1642.   Denis Roger/123RF.com

LAST OF THE WITCH HUNTS

In 1697 Judge Samuel Sewall publicly repented of his involvement in the Salem, Massachusetts, witch trials. Prussia (1714), England (1736), Germany (1755), and Poland (1776) all repealed capital laws against suspected witches during this time.

Presbyterians were largely behind the revolution and thus enjoyed cultural prominence, while the pacifist Quakers and Mennonites suffered persecution for refusing to fight for either side. With their clear connections to England, Anglicanism and Methodism were forced to adapt. Many Anglican Loyalists fled to Canada, while the American Methodist Church was "set apart" from the Wesley connection under the new superintendent Thomas Coke in 1784. However, the most significant and enduring legacy for the liberty and diversity of American Christianity came in 1791 with the adoption of Article I of the Bill of Rights: "Congress shall make no law respecting an establishment of religion."

Catholicism

Catholic India

At the opening of the century, Catholic Christianity was thriving in the South Indian regions of Madura and Mysore under Portuguese colonial rule. Christian practice followed the pattern set by the Jesuit Robert de Nobili and was overseen by popular priests like the Frenchman John Venantius Bouchet (1655–1732) and the Italian Constantine Joseph Beschi (1680–1742), who wrote and taught in Tamil.

Malabar Rites

The Capuchins (also active in India) questioned the "accommodation" methods of the Jesuits who adopted Hindu customs and allowed their converts to retain many of their cultural and religious practices. In 1703 Pope Clement XI (1649–1721) sent Cardinal de Tournon (1668–1710) to investigate. In sixteen articles, Tournon condemned the so-called Malabar Rites as mixing idolatry with Christianity and commanded the missionaries to serve all Indians regardless of caste distinctions. The Jesuits felt they had been misrepresented and challenged the practical worth of Tournon's recommendations. As a result the decree was revised in 1734 and in 1744 Pope Benedict XIV (1675–1758) issued *Omnium sollicitudinum*, a scheme creating missionaries specifically to work amongst the pariah or untouchable castes so as to not to offend Brahmin sensibilities.

Catholic China

Jesuit fortunes in China followed a path similar to those in India. Following the success of Matteo Ricci, Chinese Christianity flourished while retaining honour for Confucius and some forms of ancestor reverence. The Dominican missionaries present in China alleged that the Jesuit "Chinese Rites" constituted idolatry and superstition. In 1704 and again in 1715 Pope Clement XI issued bulls commanding the Jesuits to suppress all pagan practices. (Benedict XIV would confirm the ruling against the Jesuits in 1742.) The imposition of foreigners pronouncing on Chinese affairs drew the ire of Emperor Kanh Hsi, who banished all missionaries in 1717. This began a campaign against Christianity that would culminate in the Great Persecution in Shandong in 1784–1785.

Catholic Korea

Unlike neighbouring countries for which Christianity was a foreign import, Korea saw Christianity take root primarily through the initiative of Koreans. In 1783 Lee Sung-hun (1756–1801) was sent to China to learn more about Catholicism. He was baptised and upon his return in 1784 set about founding a new Korean church. The congregation had no formal priests, although in 1794 the Chinese Catholic priest Chu Munmo (1752–1801) began work baptising and ordaining. By 1801 there were an estimated 10,000 Korean Catholics. Christianity's opposition to ancestor worship was considered subversive, resulting in state opposition. The 1801 Shinyu persecutions claimed the lives of over 300 people, including Chu Munmo and Lee Sung-hun.

The Old Order

The opposition to Jesuit missionary tactics in India and China reflected a wider move against the Society of Jesus. Across Europe, all medieval institutions with their traditional economic, political, and religious ties were being replaced by new settlements. Symbolically, in some ways the Jesuits represented the height of this old older. With their international networks, educational establishments, and pledge of ultimate allegiance to the pope, the Jesuits also posed a material obstacle to the emerging nation-states and their corresponding empires.

Jesuit Suppression

In the eighteenth century, a number of local suppressions occurred. Russia expelled the Jesuits in 1719 (although Catherine the Great permitted them to return fifty years later; see

> ### NANO NAGLE (1718–1784)
>
> Ireland in the eighteenth century was largely under English Protestant rule, and Catholic schools were prohibited by law. Nano, the daughter of an Irish Catholic noble family, became concerned for the schooling of the poor, and established the first Presentation Convent in 1775. The teaching order is currently active in Ireland, England, Asia, Australia, and America.

above). In 1759 the Catholic king José I banished the society from Portugal and all Portuguese territories. In 1762 the French king Louis XV confiscated Jesuit property and forbade them to teach or recruit. Two years later the Jesuits were totally expelled from the country. In 1767 Charles III ordered the deportation of 5,000 Jesuits from the Spanish Empire. Finally, combined pressure from the great imperial and lesser state powers led Pope Clement XIV (1705–1774) to issue the bull *Dominus ac Redemptor*, dissolving the society in 1773.

Anti-Catholic Enlightenment

In Protestant Europe the Enlightenment was largely directed by Christians keen to reformulate religion along rationalist lines. Despite the cultural, scientific, and philosophical contributions arising from the Jesuit educational system, the Enlightenment of Catholic Europe tended to take a more explicitly anti-Christian turn. The appropriation of Enlightenment values as a way to attack the church was most evident in France. The French Church of the eighteenth century had been racked by disputes

▲ *The Taking of the Louvre, Paris* by Jean Louis Bezard (1799–1860) commemorates a scene from the French Revolution. Alfredo Dagli Orti/Shutterstock

over Protestantism, Gallicanism, the Counter-Reformation, and the rigor of Jansenism. The conflict between Jesuits and Jansenists soon became a focal point for many of the bitter divisions present in French society.

The Jansenist Revival

In 1713 Pope Clement XI, upon the instigation of King Louis XIV, vigorously condemned the Jansenists with the papal bull *Ungenitus*. However, the repression was unpopular and unsuccessful, and from 1727 a Jansenist revival swept through Paris. In 1729 the Parlement supported the Jansenists against the king and the church, declaring liberty of conscience for all France.

The Philosophes

These popular anti-papal sentiments soon morphed into a more explicitly anti-Christian movement, led by intellectuals and political theorists known collectively as the *philosophes*. The philosophes held a variety of opinions, but all agreed that Christianity was an obstacle to the rational reorganisation of society that they wished for. Some prominent figures such as the satirist Voltaire (the pen name of Francois-Marie Arouet, 1694–1778) were deist, while others like Denis Diderot (1713–1784), editor of the controversial *Encyclopédie*, were militant atheists. In an effort to counter the immoral and nihilistic implications of a godless society, Jean-Jacques Rousseau (1712–1778) devised a "civic religion." His *Du contrat social* (*The Social Contract*, 1762) set out a vision for society based on the general will of the people, making the state, and not the church, the ultimate object of a person's allegiance. Rousseau's ideas have had an enormous influence on the modern relationship between Christianity and government, and he helped define the new politics of revolutionary America and Europe.

French Revolution

France in the late eighteenth century faced financial ruin, in part following that country's support of the American War of Independence in 1776. With the aim of creating a national body capable of raising funds, King Louis XVI revived the institution of the States-General in 1789, incorporating the aristocracy, the clergy, and a third group of wealthy commoners. Louis's plan did not work. In rebellion against the king, this "Third Estate" created a separate National Assembly and that year passed the *Declaration of the Rights of Man*.

Oath of Obedience

The *Declaration* announced a break from the old order of the *ancien regime*, effectively creating a national church answerable to the (male, land-owning) electorate. In 1791 all the clergy were required to swear an Oath of Obedience to the Civil Constitution. Pope Pius VI (1717–1799) issued a formal condemnation of the Oath and half of the clergy refused to comply, bringing their parishioners with them and splitting the country between revolution and church.

The Terror

From 1792 the state enacted mass executions and violence against the aristocracy and clergy within France, as well as declaring war on the Holy Roman Empire and the Catholic Church. In 1793 the king and queen of France were executed. A bloody de-Christianising campaign was fully under way, including the drowning of priests, nuns, and monks; the destruction of churches; and the dismantling of all Christian institutions.

REVOLUTIONARY RELIGION

In the place of Christianity, the French revolutionaries instituted secular pageantry and ceremonies. In Paris, the Church of Ste Geneviève was rebuilt as the Parthenon in honour of humanistic heroes, an opera singer representing the Goddess of Reason was installed in the Notre-Dame Cathedral, and rationalist liturgy was produced to praise the Revolution.

▲ View of the facade of the Pantheon, Paris, France, built 1757–90.   Wanida Matmool/123RF.com

The Revolution Spreads

Instability within France affected the wider church. In retaliation against Pius VI's condemnation of the Oath of Obedience, the revolutionaries annexed the papal territories of Avignon and Venaissin in 1791. French troops, led by Napoleon Bonaparte (1769–1821), occupied the Papal States until 1797. That same year a French-sponsored revolution in Rome led to the capture of Pope Pius VI, marking the lowest point of prestige for the papacy.

Napoleonic Restoration

Pius died in exile in 1799, the same year that Napoleon staged a coup. He recognised that the dismantling of Christianity had alienated France from much of Europe and had led to disillusion amongst the people, especially the poor and weak who benefited most from church institutions. Accordingly, in 1801 Napoleon sought peace by reaching an agreement with the new pope Pius VII (1742–1823). The Concordat of 1801 restored the Catholic Church in France and reinstated the public standing of the papal office, signalling a new direction for Western Christendom in the nineteenth century.

PROGRESS AND PRESERVATION: 1800-1900

The nineteenth century is a time of radical upheaval, stemming largely from the unrest of Napoleon's march across Europe and culminating in a rash of political revolutions in 1848. During this time the Catholic Church tends towards conservatism and away from modernism. It is now that some of the most distinctive articles of Catholic faith are established as dogma. The Protestant world faces liberalism in different ways. Some mainstream branches embrace critical scepticism, while other groups bypass the debates in favour of practical, active religion. Mission and social reform thrive in the nineteenth century, often coalescing around the vexatious issue of slavery. Slavery also features in Orthodox debates over the treatment of serfs and the merits of peasant, national religion. Indeed, the entire Orthodox world is taken up with the issue of national autonomous churches emerging from under Ottoman rule and the domination of the Constantinople patriarchate.

Catholicism

Napoleon

The 1801 Concordat between Napoleon Bonaparte and Pope Pius VII (1742–1823) had the immediate effect of restoring the Catholic Church as the religion of France. However, with the *Organic Articles* of 1802, the terms were soon altered to the extent that the government retained firm control over public worship and religious education. Napoleon had Pius crown him emperor of the French in 1804. By 1808 Napoleon's troops occupied Rome and the Papal States, and he had abolished the Inquisition after assuming control over Spain and Italy. In 1813 he engaged Pius in intense negotiations, eventually forcing the pope to sign another concordat granting the emperor control over the bishops of France and Italy. The church resisted the clergy placed there by Napoleon, with the Belgians especially proving intransigent. In 1814, weakened by defeat in Russia and challenged on many military fronts throughout Europe, the emperor

▲ Napoleon Bonaparte, emperor of the French. His military advance across Europe unsettled church and state and set the stage for future revolution. Wikimedia Commons

KULTURKAMPF

Under Otto von Bismarck (1815–1898) Germany in the 1870s underwent an anti-Catholic movement known as *Kulturkampf*, or the "culture-struggle." Bismarck suppressed many areas of public Catholic life and imprisoned leading bishops. A peace agreement was eventually reached with Pope Leo XIII (1810–1903) and finalised in 1887.

▲ Prince Otto von Bismarck presided over a unified Germany as the "Iron Chancellor."

Wikimedia Commons

was forced to release the pope, restore the papal territories, and repudiate the concordat. A coalition of British, French, Prussian, Russian, and other forces defeated Napoleon at the Battle of Waterloo and forced him to abdicate in 1815. Napoleon left behind a shell-shocked, fragmented Europe, a fresh legacy of unstable church-state relations, and a culture of revolutionary idealism.

Revolutionary Spain

The 1808 French occupation of Spain had brought revolutionary ideas of anti-clericalism and political liberalism to the country, sowing the seeds for the socialist, anarchist, republican, and regional nationalist movements that would define the cultural landscape for the following century and beyond. In these ideological and military conflicts, the Catholic Church in Spain was firmly associated with conservatism and support for royalty.

Anti-Clericalism and Its Discontents

As a result, the church often suffered under revolutionary liberal governments, such as that of Prime Minister Juan Álvarez Mendizábal (1790–1853), who confiscated church lands in

1835 and 1836. This programme of confiscations was accompanied by fierce sentiments of anti-clericalism in which monks and priests were murdered, convents dissolved, and churches destroyed. In reaction to these populist negative views of the church, a wave of "neo-Catholic" thinkers thrived at this time, with political writers such as Juan Donoso Cortés (1809–1853) and the philosopher Jaime Luciano Balmes (1810–1848) writing spirited defences of conservative Catholicism in the face of liberal, secular and Protestant challenges. With the restoration of the monarchy in 1874 and the Spanish Constitution of 1876, Catholicism was once again recognised as the religion of Spain.

Revolutionary Italy

Social instability also continued in Italy, and a revolution broke out in the Italian Papal States shortly after the election of Pope Gregory XVI (1765–1846) in 1831. Gregory was twice forced to call in assistance from Austria to quell the rebellion, an action that brought unwelcome outside attention to the internal administration of the Papal States.

Throne and Altar

Gregory was an early proponent of the doctrine that would become papal infallibility, and he favoured a strong church that could enter into an "alliance between Throne and Altar" while maintaining its distinct authority. In 1839 Pope Gregory's papal bull *In Supremo* denounced slavery and the trading of human beings as against the teaching of Christianity. He also supported the ordination of native clergy in South America and Asia and encouraged extensive mission work.

⚲ CATHOLIC NORTH AMERICA

Catholics in the United States began the century as a persecuted minority but soon grew to significance largely as a result of mass immigration and militant American expansion.

c. 1800 John Carroll (1735–1815) of Baltimore is the first and only Catholic bishop in the United States. The Catholic population is estimated at around 50,000.

1809 Educator, social reformer, and peace campaigner Elizabeth Ann Bayley Seton (1774–1821) founds the Sisters of Charity, the first Catholic order for American women.

1845–1850 The Great Blight devastates Ireland's potato crops. The resulting influx of Catholic immigrants to America prompts a rash of anti-Catholic "Nativist" riots.

1846–1848 The American war with Mexico is fuelled by ideas of "manifest destiny"—the popular and largely Protestant belief that the US was divinely ordained to control all of North America. The war inflames anti-Catholic feelings; however, as the USA expands its territories it also absorbs a large Catholic Mexican population.

c. 1860 Roman Catholicism is the largest single Christian denomination with an estimated 3.5 million members.

1899 Pope Leo XIII condemns "Americanism," a liberal and individualistic movement propagated by some US Catholics.

CATHOLIC SOUTH AMERICA

In the nineteenth century, countries under Spanish and Portuguese colonial rule began to assert their independence, renegotiating their relationship to Rome at the same time.

1810–1824 Time of struggle for independence of Spanish American countries. The Catholic Church sides with Spain during these conflicts.

1822 Brazil gains independence from Portugal.

1830 Death of Simón Bolívar, Spanish American national hero who fought against Spain for the liberation of Bolivia, Colombia, Ecuador, Panama, Peru, and Venezuela.

1859–1875 Independent Ecuador governed by the conservative and Catholic Gabriel García Moreno (1821–1875). Shortly after being elected to a third term, he was assassinated outside the Cathedral of Quito.

1889 Brazil declared a republic. Catholic Church disestablished.

KOREA

By the end of the eighteenth century there were several thousand native Korean Catholics, prompting the establishment in 1831 of an apostolic vicariate (a bishop who oversees a region that is not yet a full diocese) and followed by the arrival of Pierre Maubant (1803–1839) from the Paris Missionary Society in 1835. Korean Christians suffered sporadic persecutions throughout the nineteenth century. The fiercest wave of violence (1863–1876) was instigated by Prince Regent Taewongun, leading to the death of more than 2,000 people.

▲ South Korean Catholics attend a Mass for Pope John Paul II at the Myoung-dong Cathedral, 2005 in Seoul, South Korea.   Str/EPA/Shutterstock

The Error of the New

To strengthen the church, Gregory issued numerous encyclicals attempting to stem many of the new ideas animating European culture, ideas that he argued were based on religious error. Revolution and the secular drive to separate church and state were attacked. Movements within the church were also resisted, most notably with the 1834 *Singular nos*, a document attacking the liberalism of the French political theologian Félicité Robert de Lammenais (1782–1854).

Liberal Catholicism

Early liberal Catholics included writers such as Georg Hermes (1775–1831) and H. D. Lacordaire (1801–1860). The school of thought drew much from rationalists like Kant and the theories of Rousseau, emphasising progress in history and embracing political ideals of freedom and humanist equality. Liberalism was also often identified with denial of orthodox

JAPAN

Since 1640, foreigners had been banned from Japan and Christianity suppressed. In 1859 treaties with the French allowed for the return of Christian missionaries. In 1865 thousands of Japanese Catholics were discovered living in small communities that had persisted for two centuries of persecution and without contact with the wider church. An Apostolic Vicariate was established in 1866. Persecution of these Japanese Christians eased in 1873, and toleration was granted in 1890. The next year a Catholic hierarchy was established, although the church continued to be challenged by growing Japanese nationalist and self-reliance movements.

WHITE FATHERS

The Society of Missionaries to Africa was founded in 1868 by Charles-Martial Lavigerie (1825–1892). Known for their distinctive white tunics, the Fathers worked throughout Africa as missionaries, agricultural educators, and anti-slavery campaigners. Many priests were martyred in Uganda during anti-Christian persecutions in 1885–1887.

OLD CATHOLICS

In 1870 some German, Swiss, and Austrian Catholics who refused to accept the doctrine of infallibility seceded from Rome, thus establishing the "Old Catholic" movement.

Christianity, reformulation of traditional doctrines in light of modern ideas, and a critical, sceptical reading of the Bible.

Church Opposition

The church's official resistance to modernism was part of a larger trend within Catholicism at this time. The intellectual innovations and political agitation of the nineteenth century served as a crucible for key Roman Catholic doctrines. Negatively, for example, the church defined itself against socialism and communism (1849); liberalism, secular government, religious toleration, and unrestricted press freedom (1864); and attempts at an Anglican-Catholic reunion (1866).

New Practices for Faith

Positively, Catholicism embraced heightened articles of faith. In 1854 Pope Pius IX issued *Ineffabilis Deus*, declaring that the long-standing general belief in the Immaculate Conception of the Virgin Mary was official church dogma. Pius also extended the Devotion to the Sacred Heart to the universal church in 1856. In 1858 the peasant girl Bernadette Soubirous (1844–1879) reported visions of the Blessed Virgin at Lourdes, with the subsequent pilgrimage receiving official recognition in 1862.

Ultramontanism

In England, France, and Germany, disillusion with bloody revolutions, discredited clergy, and anti-Catholic governments contributed greatly to a movement known as Ultramontanism. Ultramontanes favoured a strong pope and centralisation of power in Rome, rather than amongst diverse regional churches. The movement reached its height under Pope Pius

📖 MODERNISM

A variegated movement within nineteenth-century liberal Catholicism, modernists wanted to align the church's traditional teaching with (then) current understandings of science, philosophy, and sociology. Key leaders included the Frenchmen Alfred Loisy (1857–1940) and Maurice Blondel (1861–1949) and the Englishman George Tyrrell (1861–1909). The movement was condemned as a "synthesis of all heresies" by Pope Pius X in 1907.

📍 LEBANON

The Eastern-Rite Maronite Christians of Lebanon had an association with the Roman Catholic Church and enjoyed close ties with France. When ethnic tensions between the Christians and the Druze (a monotheistic offshoot of Islam) led to violent conflict in 1860, hundreds of churches and villages were destroyed and tens of thousands of Maronites killed, as well as many Druze and Muslim people.

👤 PIUS IX (1792–1878)

The long-serving Pope Pius IX came to power in 1846 with a reputation for sympathetic liberalism. The 1848 revolutions in Rome forced him to flee to Gaeta, after which his opposition to liberal politics hardened considerably. Pius became a force for conservatism, centralising papal authority and establishing many traditional devotional practices in the church. His definition of papal infallibility in 1870 led to much controversy.

Eventually the council affirmed that the pope's decisions were infallible and independent of consent from the church; however, it also made clear that papal infallibility was restricted to those times when the pontiff was acting in virtue of his apostolic authority to pronounce on matters of universal church doctrine. The day following this announcement of spiritual authority, Italian nationalists led by Victor Emmanuel (1820–1878) seized Rome, depriving Pius of all temporal power.

Protestantism

The Protestant world was undergoing similar revolutions as the Catholic world. The political upheavals of the revolutionary spirit sweeping the world provide one important backdrop to the development of Protestant Christianity. Also of importance are the ideological and intellectual movements of the nineteenth century.

Higher Criticism

Protestant scholars such as Hermann Reimarus (1694–1768), Gotthold Lessing (1729–

IX and the First Vatican Council where the doctrine of papal infallibility was declared in 1870.

Papal Infallibility

The question over the meaning and full implications of papal primacy had been wrestled with since the Council of Constance in 1415. At Vatican I, there was significant resistance to the idea both from within the Catholic Church itself and from Protestant and Orthodox theologians.

1781), and Johann Eichhorn (1752–1827) had laid the seeds for the sceptical and liberal theology that would hold sway in most of the theological academies of the nineteenth century. Now, "higher critical" research began in earnest to analyse the literary merits and construction of the Scriptures. These critics disregarded many of the historical claims found in the Old and New Testaments, questioning the designated authorships and modes of production that had long been assumed amongst biblical scholars.

The Tübingen School

Closely related to this examination of the form, date, authorship, and purpose of the biblical texts was the study of the groups who produced the texts. Led by the liberal theologian F. C. Baur (1762–1860), the school at the University of Tübingen adopted a non-supernatural approach to history and the development of religious ideas. According to their theory of historical development—which bore much affinity to the thought of G. W. F. Hegel (1770–1831)—most of the New Testament texts were considered inauthentic, late documents of early Christianity.

The Life of Jesus

One of Baur's students was David Friedrich Strauss (1808–1874). His *Leben Jesu* ("Life of Jesus") appeared in 1835 to much controversy. By applying the theory of mythic development to the Gospels, Strauss denied the historical veracity of any of the supernatural aspects of the life of Jesus Christ. His conclusion, that the essence of Christianity was to be seen in the light of a Hegelian philosophy of human development and that there was an unbridgeable chasm between the "historical Jesus" and the

OXFORD MOVEMENT

One significant response against liberalism in the Church of England was the creation of Anglo-Catholicism. The movement, led by the Oxford clergymen John Keble (1792–1866), Edward Pusey (1800–1882), and John Henry Newman (1801–1890), published its first tract in 1833. The group resisted Reformation theology and encouraged closer relations with Rome. Newman himself converted to Catholicism in 1845 and was made a cardinal in 1877. The beatification of Cardinal Newman was approved by Pope Benedict XVI in 2009.

▲ *Light of the World*, a painting at Keble College, Oxford
Glenn Turner

"Christ of faith," was hugely influential for subsequent liberal Protestant Christian thought and practice.

Dutch Reformed Church

Although Napoleon's yoke had been thrown off in 1815, the Dutch king William I continued the Napoleonic tradition of exercising considerable powers over the church in the Netherlands. Under his influence, liberalism thrived, and the church took a broad approach to matters of dogma. In 1834 a conservative movement inspired in part by the heartfelt religion of Willem Bilderdijk (1756–1831) and Isaak Da Costa (1798–1660) separated, forming the Calvinist "Christian Reformed Church." Further opposition to the modernist school led to another major secession in 1886. This was headed by Abraham Kuyper (1837–1920), the Calvinist theologian, "anti-Revolutionary," and "Christian Democrat" who would go on to exert considerable influence when he became prime minister in 1901.

Danish People's Church

At this time the established Lutheran church in Denmark was largely under the influence of cultural elitists like Bishop Jakob Pier Mynster (1775–1854) and relatively liberal Hegelians such as Hans Larsen Martensen (1808–1884). In reaction to these trends, a revival movement swept the church, led by the poet and preacher N. F. S. Grundtvig (1783–1872). A nationalist theologian, Grundtvig sought to awaken the "Danish spirit" of the people by connecting their Christian present with their pagan, Norse past. Following the bloodless revolution in 1848, the State Church was re-created as the more populist Danish People's Church and a number of *Folkehöjskoler* ("folk high schools") were established.

▲ The nineteenth century saw a renewed interest in the historical details of stories about Jesus, as in this painting *Christ Preaching to the Multitudes* by James Smetham.

Wikimedia Commons

 SØREN AABYE KIERKEGAARD (1813–1855)

Deeply opposed to both the Hegelianism of Martensen and the nationalism of Grundtvig, the Danish writer Kierkegaard sought to "reintroduce Christianity into Christendom" through his philosophical, theological, and polemical works. Relatively ignored in his lifetime, Kierkegaard would later be celebrated as one of the most profound thinkers of the nineteenth century, influencing dialectical theology, psychology, and modern existentialism.

▶ Søren Kierkegaard

Public Domain

Evangelical Action

The scepticism in the universities and seminaries did not tend to undermine the convictions driving English-speaking evangelical Christianity, which reached its highest points of social action and mission in the nineteenth century.

SOUTH AFRICA

The Presbyterian Church of Scotland was especially effective in South Africa. Early African Christian leaders converted by the Scots include the hymnist Ntsikana (?–1821), the professor Tengo Jabavu (?–1921), and Tiyo Soga (?–1871), who translated the Bible and *The Pilgrim's Progress* into Xhosa. A Wesleyan minister, Nehemiah Xoxo Tile (?–1891) founded the first independent tribal Tembu Church in 1884.

▲ Pella Cathedral, Northern Cape Province, South Africa
South African Tourism/Wikimedia Commons, CC BY 2.0

Africa

There had been a Christian presence in Africa since the sixteenth century, most of which centred around Catholic Portuguese outposts in Angola and Mozambique. However, it was not until the mass Protestant missions and the colonial "Scramble for Africa" in the nineteenth century that Christianity firmly took root throughout the continent.

British Missions

British pioneers such as Robert Moffat (1795–1883) worked amongst the Hottentot, Bechuana, and Sechwana peoples in the south, providing translation materials and services that laid the foundation for future missionary endeavours. In 1840 Moffat persuaded the Scottish Presbyterian David Livingstone (1813–1873) to travel to South Africa. Livingstone saw more success as an explorer than as a missionary; nevertheless, reports of his discoveries aroused much interest in England, inspiring many more missionary projects.

Mission and Colonialism

While Christian mission and colonial interests often coincided, a number of missionaries spoke out against the exploitation and abuse of native Africans. Livingstone opposed slavery, as did the Anglican J. W. Colenso (1814–1883) and the Scottish evangelical John Philip (1771–1851) working amongst the Xhosa people of South Africa. With the Great Trek of 1837, Dutch Afrikaan settlers moved away from British rule in the Cape Colony and into the wider territories of South Africa. They brought with them various iterations of the Dutch Reformed Church, most of which sanctioned Afrikaner nationalism, slavery, and apartheid in the years to come.

Nigeria

In the latter half of the century, other African Christians began to organise themselves independently of the original European missions, aided in large part by the "native clergy" policies of the Clapham Sect vicar Henry Venn (1796–1873). British missionaries were first invited to Nigeria in the 1840s at the request of former Yoruba slaves who had converted to Christianity while living in Sierra Leone. The most effective of these missionaries was Samuel Ajayi Crowther (c. 1806–1891), himself a Yoruba who led an all-African Niger mission from 1857 and was the first African to be ordained an Anglican bishop in 1864. Crowther's authority was undermined by white missionaries in 1889, leading to the creation of the Niger Delta Pastorate in 1891 and the United Native African Church in 1892.

Clapham Sect

In England, an informal group of well-connected Anglican evangelicals such as Charles Grant (1746–1823), Henry Thornton (1760–1815), and Granville Sharp (1735–1813) had been meeting since the end of the previous century. Known as the Clapham Sect, the group was responsible for promoting foreign missions, bettering working conditions for the poor, and encouraging literacy through Sunday schools. However, by far the most pressing issue of the day was that of slavery

Abolition of Slavery

The most prominent Clapham Sect member was the parliamentarian William Wilberforce (1759–1833). Largely as a result of Wilberforce's political activity, and bolstered by a popular campaign appealing to Christian morality, the slave trade was made illegal in England in 1807. Shortly before his death in 1833, the Emancipation Act abolished slavery throughout the British Empire.

📍 **WORLDWIDE PROTESTANTISM**

1801 Establishment of the Church Missionary Society (CMS).

1815 Chief Pomare II of Tahiti (?–1824) converts to Christianity.

1822 Wesleyan missionaries active among Maoris in New Zealand.

1825 Abdul Masih (1776–1827) becomes one of the first native Anglican clergymen to be ordained in India.

c. 1830 Native Tahitian missionaries introduce Christianity to Fiji. Tongans introduce Christianity to Samoa.

1865 J. Hudson Taylor (1832–1905) founds the China Inland Mission.

1876 First Protestant missionaries arrive in Korea.

▲ William Wilberforce campaigned for the end to slavery.

HANNAH MORE (1745–1833)

A celebrated English playwright, Hannah More was drawn into the Clapham Sect at the encouragement of the hymnist John Newton. She founded a number of countryside schools and used her writing talents to produce tracts of moral and religions edification for the poor.

📖 **SALVATION ARMY**

The Methodist William Booth (1829–1912) founded the "Christian Mission" to London's East End in 1865, which was renamed "the Salvation Army" in 1878. Booth campaigned tirelessly for the poor and marginalised in urban settings, establishing missions throughout the world.

📖 **EVOLUTION**

Charles Darwin (1809–1882) published *On the Origin of Species* in 1859. His theory of organic development by natural selection came at the same time as critical readings of the Bible were becoming popular, thus dividing Christian opinion. Most churchmen were able to incorporate evolution into the Christian doctrine of creation, while conservative groups (especially in America) would later develop various responses collectively known as "Creationism."

An Evangelical Alliance

Slavery was a crucial component of other national economies, and its abolition remained an issue for many. When the interdenominational Evangelical Alliance was founded in England in 1846, largely as a response to liberalism and Anglo-Catholicism, it was welcomed throughout Europe. However, conflicts over slavery at its first meeting meant that a branch of the Alliance would not be opened in the United States until 1867.

American Awakening

Since 1800, open-air "camp meetings" and other revival events had contributed to a largely Presbyterian, student-led Second Great

 ANTOINETTE LOUISA BROWN (1825–1921)

The first woman to be ordained as a church minister, Antoinette Louisa Brown was appointed to a Congregationalist church in 1853. Olympia Brown (1835–1926) was the first woman to graduate from a theological college, becoming a Unitarian minister in 1863. From 1880, US theological seminaries began to admit women for non-ordained ministries. Nine more Congregationalist women were ordained in 1893.

▶ Antoinette Brown became the first ordained woman minister in 1853.

Public Domain

Awakening in the northern and eastern states. Similar effects were seen by Baptist and Methodist preachers in the West and South, making them the largest Protestant denominations in the US. These revived Christian energies were often channelled into creating new social agencies and voluntary organisations. By the 1830s, multiple Christian societies were in operation, disseminating religious literature, running colleges and Sunday schools, and advancing social reforms.

📍 AFRICAN AMERICAN CHRISTIANITY

Evangelical awakenings and abolitionist movements led to the establishment of a number of independent African American congregations and organisations.

1816 Foundation of the African Methodist Episcopal Bethel Church in Philadelphia with Richard Allen (1760–1831) as bishop.

1821 African Methodist Episcopal Zion Church established in New York by James Varick (1750–1827).

1865–1877 During the Reconstruction period following the Civil War, a number of Northern missionaries travel south to establish churches for former slaves.

c. 1877 Bishop Henry McNeal Turner (1834–1915) and Alexander Crummell (1819–1898) encourage black Christians to return to Africa as missionaries and immigrants.

1895 Formation of National Baptist Convention.

📍 NEW RELIGIOUS MOVEMENTS

The Protestant emphasis on personal interpretation and heartfelt religion led to an explosion of new sects, especially in the United States. Many of these new movements departed significantly from creedal Christianity.

1814 Death of Joanna Southcott, self-styled English apocalyptic prophet who attracted a number of followers.

1827 Joseph Smith (1805–1844) receives the revelation of *The Book of Mormon*, leading to the formation of the polygamous Church of Jesus Christ of Latter-Day Saints, based in Salt Lake City, Utah, since 1847.

1831 First meeting of the biblically literalist and sectarian Plymouth Brethren in England. Prominent Brethren preacher J. N. Darby (1800–1882) sees success in America with his theory of dispensationalism, an apocalyptic scheme of biblical history promoting, amongst other things, a theology of the "rapture," which teaches that all true Christians will be taken up into heaven at the second coming of Christ.

1844 The apocalyptic Seventh-Day Adventists movement persists in New England and Michigan despite its failed prediction that the world would end on October 22.

1875 Mary Baker Eddy (1821–1910) of Boston publishes *Science and Health*, the founding document for the Christian Science movement that denies the ultimate reality of sin, sickness, and evil.

1881 Charles Taze Russell (1852–1916) founds the Jehovah's Witnesses in Pittsburgh, Pennsylvania, claiming that the second coming of Jesus ("the perfect man") had already occurred six years previous.

North and South

By 1830 the agricultural economy of the South was deeply dependent upon slavery at the same time that the abolitionist movement led by people such as William Lloyd Garrison (1805–1879) and Theodore Weld (1803–1895) was gaining momentum in the North. Christians were not in agreement over the right response to slavery, and most of the various Protestant denominations divided along regional lines. Presbyterians split in 1837. Methodists split in 1845, as did Baptists that same year with the creation of the pro-slavery Southern Baptist Convention. The victory of the North in the Civil War (1861–1865) brought abolition, but racial segregation continued in the South, leading to deep ideological and cultural differences between American Christians.

Orthodoxy

In the nineteenth century the different religious groups living in the Ottoman Empire were organised into millets (from *millah*, Arabic for "nation"). Millets were legally protected confessional groups enjoying a certain degree of autonomy. Under this system the patriarch of the Greek Orthodox Church was the highest authority, or ethnarch, exercising much influence over all Orthodox Christians in the empire, including the Bulgarians, Albanians, Romanians, and Serbs. Armenian Christians comprised a separate millet, which also included the Coptic and Syriac Orthodox churches.

Orthodox Nationalisms

In the nineteenth century the ferment of the French Revolution and the rise of nationalist

THE INDUSTRIAL REVOLUTION

The invention of mechanised farm machinery in Britain in the 1700s led to an explosion in mechanical and factory production in the areas of agriculture, manufacturing, textiles, communication, and transportation all around the world, continuing into the nineteenth century and beyond. The Industrial Revolution affected every aspect of daily life for everyone, whether they be rich, poor, landowner, tenant, consumer, or producer. People migrated from the countryside and city populations swelled. The revolution saw the increase of unprecedented riches alongside grinding poverty. For Christianity the effect was as varied as it was profound. The period saw the rise of evangelical revivalism, the consolidation of the conservative establish-

ment, and the rise of the liberal social gospel. Many denominations and churches benefitted materially, supporting factory owners and landlords in the creation of wealth and the raising of living standards. Protestant groups such as the Methodists, the Quakers, and the Salvation Army directed their efforts primarily towards the workers, agitating for labour reform, mission, and the temperance movement. Roman Catholic groups such as the Society of St. Vincent de Paul directed their efforts towards the poor. Pope Leo XIII issued the papal bull "On Capital and Labour" in 1891, and Pope Pius XI issued "On Reconstruction of the Social Order" in 1931.

movements in Europe led to the strong association of millets with national sovereignty for the disparate peoples living under Turkish rule. In addition to agitating for political independence from the Ottomans, the different national churches would achieve autonomy from the Greek Church in this era.

For Greeks living under Ottoman rule, the Hellenist national identity, language, and culture had largely been preserved through association with the Greek Orthodox Church. These strong nationalist feelings led to the first uprising led by Alexandros Ypsilanti (1792–1828) in 1821.

CYPRUS

The autocephalous Cypriot Orthodox Church had been a focal point for Cypriot national identity under Ottoman rule. When Cypriots joined Ypsilanti's Greek revolution, many bishops were executed, including the "New Martyr" Archbishop Kyprianos (1756–1821).

ENCYCLICAL OF THE EASTERN PATRIARCHS

In 1848 Pope Pius IX (1792–1878) asserted Catholic universality with his *Epistle to the Easterns*. In response, Anthimus VI of Constantinople (1790–1878) and the other Orthodox patriarchs issued a public reply. Their *Encyclical* strongly rejected papal supremacy, condemned Catholic missions in Orthodox lands, and reiterated the objection to the *Filioque* clause.

Last of the New Martyrs

In 1821 Gregory V (1746–1821) was patriarch of the Greek Church for the third time. Twice before, the sultan had deposed the ethnarch, and Gregory was known by the Turkish authorities as a supporter of the Greek national cause. To avoid violent reprisals to the church in Constantinople, Gregory attempted to distance himself from Ypsilanti's rebellion. His attempts failed, and Gregory was publicly executed as a revolutionary.

Church of Greece

After Gregory was martyred, his name became a rallying cry for the new independence movement. Eventually, with the aid of the English, French, and Russians, Greece was established as a free state in 1830. Following the political developments, in 1833 the Church of Greece asserted its independence from Constantinople and was recognised as fully autocephalous in 1850.

Church of Bulgaria

The transition to autonomy was rarely easy, as demonstrated by the events in Bulgaria. During the Ottoman period, the Bulgarian Church hierarchy was dominated by Greek churchmen and Greek culture until 1870. The Bulgarian nationalist movement was inspired in large part by earlier activists such as Neofit Bozveli (c. 1785–1848) and led by Ilarion Makariopolski (1812–1875) and Bishop Antim I (1816–1888). The Turks had recognised the Bulgarian Church in 1870 as a separate entity. In 1872 Ilarion and Antim led the call for a unilateral declaration of a Bulgarian Orthodox Church autocephalous from Constantinople.

APRIL UPRISING

The nationalist feelings fostered by the invigorated Bulgarian Church were closely connected to agitation for political sovereignty. In 1876 a nationalist Bulgarian uprising against the Ottomans was severely repressed by Turkish soldiers. The ensuing massacres attracted international attention, turning American and British opinion against the Turks and acting as the catalyst for the Russo-Turkish War (1877–1878), which had as one of its aims the liberation of Balkan Christians and the reinstatement of Orthodox influence in Bulgaria.

 SYRIAN CATHOLICS

The ruling Ottomans recognised the Uniat Syrian Catholic Church as a distinct body from the Syrian Orthodox Church in 1830, with the seat of the patriarchate in Beirut. An influential leading figure was Patriarch Ignatius Ephrem II Rahmani (1848–1929) who, in 1899, was responsible for the rediscovery and publication of the *Testamentum Domini*, an early liturgical text from the fourth century.

SERAFIM OF SAROV (1759–1833)

From 1794 the monk Serafim lived in seclusion. When he opened his doors in 1825 he received a stream of visitors, becoming a popular spiritual adviser (or *staretz*). His discipline, gentleness, and cheerfulness are celebrated throughout Russia.

Against Tribalism

The patriarchate of Constantinople resisted this move and the motives for creating the new church. In 1872 the Holy and Great Orthodox Synod, including the patriarchs of Alexandria and Jerusalem and led by Ecumenical Patriarch Anthimus VI, excommunicated the Bulgarian nationalists on the charge of phyletism. From the Greek *phyla* meaning "race" or "tribe," phyletism describes the heresy of confusing the church with a single nation and employing ethnic principles in church organisation.

Independence and Autonomy

The Bulgarians were not the only ones to organise along nationalistic lines. By identifying phyletism as a modern heresy, the Orthodox Church had named a temptation faced by many of the Balkan states emerging from under Turkish rule. Following the logic of national political sovereignty, many other Orthodox churches also asserted autonomy in the nineteenth century. The Serbian revolutionary period from 1804 to 1833 led to a fully recognised autonomous Serbian Orthodox Church in 1879. In 1859 the independent Romanian state claimed a national church separate from Constantinople, a claim finally recognised by Ecumenical Patriarch Joachim IV (1830–1887) in 1885.

Slavophiles

In Russia in the 1830s, Christian nationalism manifested itself as the anti-Western, pro-Slavic movement known as *slavophilism*. The Orthodox Church was seen by many as the key

FYODOR DOSTOEVSKY (1821–1881)

A Russian novelist, journalist, and Slavophile revolutionary, Dostoevsky is also recognised as a theological thinker. Through novels such as *Notes from the Underworld* (1864) and *Crime and Punishment* (1865), and through the character of the "Grand Inquisitor" in *The Brothers Karamazov* (1880), Dostoevsky helped to articulate an existential Christian response to institutional religion.

▶ The celebrated author Fedor Dostoevsky included much autobiographical material in his novels. His characters wrestled with questions of violence and forgiveness, faith and atheism, and the search for truth. Portrait by Vasily Perov, 1872.   Wikimedia Commons

institution to promote traditional Russian values and culture against "Western" innovations such as socialism, industrialisation, and rationalism.

The Mystical Community

An important Slavophile theologian was Aleksei Khomyakov (1804–1860). A philosopher and reformer, Khomyakov fought to abolish serfdom, believing that the common Russian people had access to truths denied to the materialist, individualist Western Protestants and Catholics. His theological concept of *sobornost*, which relates to the mystical community of Christian fellowship and simple faith, has had a lasting impact on Russian and Greek Orthodox theology.

Russian Serfdom

Serfdom—the feudal system of bonded labour—comprised a major part of Russian life.

By the nineteenth century, agricultural peasants formed the majority population, and there was much social unrest. As a conservative force in society, the Russian Church tended to maintain the status quo; occasionally, however, Orthodox clergy spoke out on the issue. Some priests stressed the duties that Christian landowners had towards their indentured workers. Other clergy, such as Gregory, archbishop of Kaluga (dates unknown), challenged the system itself, arguing in 1858 that Christianity and the slavery of serfs were incompatible. Ultimately, it was fear of political revolution more than religious concerns that led to the great agrarian reforms of Tsar Alexander II (1818–1881) and the emancipation of the serfs in 1861.

Russian Toleration

Another perennial issue was that of toleration for religions and Christian traditions other than Orthodoxy. In 1811–1812 Tsar Alexander I (1777–1825) and Minister of Spiritual Affairs Alexander Golítsyn (1773–1844) introduced some toleration measures, as well as establishing the Russian Bible Society c. 1813. However, the measures brought fierce resistance. Under the influence of the Orthodox monk Photius, Alexander agreed to have Golítsyn ousted from office in 1824. The Russian Bible Society, which published Bibles and books of a non-Orthodox nature, was eventually repressed in 1826. In 1863 further tension between Rome and the Orthodox Church arose over Russian treatment of Polish Catholic rebels.

Procurator Pobedonostsev

Constantine Petrovich Pobedonostsev (1827–1907) became procurator of the Holy Synod in 1880. Under his influence, Orthodox education of priests and laypeople flourished, while persecution of other religious believers, especially Jews, Protestants, and Catholics, became widespread. In 1885 the Holy Synod forbade mixed marriages between Lutherans and Orthodox in Estonia and Latvia. Constantine was probably the model for the character of Alexei Karenin in *Anna Karenina* by Leo Tolstoy.

Doukhobors

Tolstoy (1828–1910) was deeply involved in the struggle for religious tolerance, feeling a special affinity with the pacifist, agrarian Christian Doukhobor movement. When the Doukhobors were forced to leave Russia in 1895, their mass emigration to Canada was financed by proceeds from his novel *Resurrection*.

 LADY WITH A LAMP

The Englishwoman Florence Nightingale (1820–1910) achieved worldwide prominence for her care for the soldiers in the Crimea and her campaign to establish professional nursing. A Christian Universalist who believed that the whole of humanity would be saved and rejected the idea of hell, Nightingale saw her work directly as a divine calling to love and serve all people.

▲ Florence Nightingale

Wikimedia Commons

CRIMEAN WAR (1853–1856)

This major conflict involved Russia, the Ottomans, and most European powers, leading to massive casualties on all sides. One root of the conflict lay in Russia's claim since the previous century to be the protector of the Christians living in the Ottoman Empire, a religious claim with political implications. In 1852, seeking a European alliance, the sultan granted France and the Roman Catholic Church guardianship of the Holy Places in Palestine. Russia's retaliation against the Ottomans soon drew in France, England, and eventually Austria on the side of the Turks, an event seen by the Russian Orthodox Church as the ultimate betrayal within Christendom

VÉRITABLE EXTRAIT DE VIANDE LIEBIG.

Episodes de l'histoire de la Russie.
Abolition du servage par Alexandre II, le 3 Mars 1861.   6.

Voir l'explication au verso.

▲ Tsar Alexander II orders emancipation of serfs throughout Russia, 1861.

Historia/Shutterstock

SACRIFICE AND INVENTION: 1900–2000

Two thousand years after its inception, Christianity remains in vigorous health, expanding worldwide, developing new ideas, and incorporating current cultural developments into its various theologies. Yet the modern era also gives rise to explicitly atheistic, totalitarian, and bloody regimes that pose the greatest challenges to followers of Christ. There are more martyrs in the twentieth century than in any other time in history.

Oppression and Resistance

China

By the end of the nineteenth century, most of China had been opened to Christian missions, with a Protestant population estimated between 40,000 and 75,000, and a Roman Catholic population upwards of 580,000.

THE BOXER REBELLION

The spread of Christianity was linked in the popular imagination with aggressive Western expansionist policies, and in 1900 nationalist feelings led to the Boxer Rebellion. Foreigners were expelled, Catholic and Protestant missionaries were killed, and close to 50,000 Chinese Christians were martyred.

CHINESE RECOVERY

The churches recovered in the period following the Republican revolution led by Sun Yat-sen (1866–1925) in 1911. Churches and educational institutions flourished under the leadership of Protestants like Cheng Ching Yi (1881–1939) and Timothy Tinfang Lew (1891–1947). Twenty-six Chinese Catholic bishops were consecrated in 1926. By 1927 there were an estimated 3 million Christians, four-fifths of whom were Roman Catholic. The other fifth comprised mainline Protestant denominations and several independent evangelical, national-run churches keen to develop independently of foreign influence.

COMMUNIST CHINA

Concurrent with the Chinese Christian revival was the rise of Chinese communism.

Aggressively anti-religious, the communist revolution of 1948 and Chairman Mao's subsequent declaration of the People's Republic of China in 1949 drove the churches underground. By 1952 most foreign Protestant missionaries had fled or been expelled, and in the following decade Roman Catholic priests were forcibly removed. At this time the Chinese Church was brought under control of the government with the creation of the officially sanctioned Three-Self Patriotic Church. Chinese Catholics were forced to sever relations with Rome in 1957. Mao's "Cultural Revolution" of 1966 attempted to purge Chinese culture of much of its past and all of its religions, leading to the deaths of millions of Chinese citizens, including many Christian martyrs. The events of 1966–1967 are considered to be the most systematic attempt ever to eradicate Christianity from a state. However, through the official church, underground movements, and congregations meeting secretly in people's homes, Christianity has survived in China and even thrived in the face of growing discontent with Marxist ideology. In 2005 there were estimated to be more Christians (80 to 100 million) than members of the Chinese Communist Party (70 million).

The Spanish Republic

The Second Spanish Republic replaced the monarchy in 1931, instituting anti-clerical measures. The Catholic Church was once again disestablished, education was secularised, civil marriage and divorce legalised. Accordingly, the church became closely identified with conservative opposition to the radical social and economic reforms of the Republic, with Pope Pius XI (1857–1939) siding with the perpetrators of a military coup in 1936. During the ensuing Civil War

▲ Marching crowds waving red banners and posters of Mao during the 1967 Cultural Revolution

Eye Ubiquitous/Shutterstock

ARMENIAN GENOCIDE

Still officially denied by the Turkish government, the systematic destruction of the Armenian population living in the Ottoman Empire began in 1915 and continued until 1918. The massacres, confiscation of property, and destruction of religious artefacts practically decimated the Armenian Church, the oldest Christian culture in the world.

▲ The bodies of Armenian children who were massacred in Turkey during the First World War

Wikimedia Commons

MEXICO

The Catholic Church was deeply involved in the political and economic affairs of the Mexican State. Following the Revolution in 1910 and the institution of the Constitution in 1917, church privilege was severely curtailed. Harsh anti-clerical measures were stepped up under President Calles in 1924, leading to fines and imprisonment for clergy. The church peacefully resisted for two years; however, popular uprisings against the government eventually led to the period of violence known as the Cristero War, with rebels fighting as "soldiers of Christ" from 1926. After considerable bloodshed of laity and clergy, an uneasy truce between church and state was reached in 1929. Catholicism remains strong in popular Mexican culture, and diplomatic relations between Mexico and the Vatican were restored in 1992.

▲ General Franco, nationalist dictator of Spain

AP/Shutterstock

and the modernising influence of the Second Vatican Council (1962–1965). Since the 1978 Constitution, Spain has no state church, freedom of conscience has been enshrined, and legal restrictions on Protestantism have been relaxed.

Communist Russia

Since 1721 the Russian Church had been ruled by the Holy Synod—all twelve members of which were nominated by the tsar. In 1917 the patriarchate was finally restored following the abdication of Tsar Nicholas II (1868–1918), with Metropolitan Vasil Belavin Tikhon (1866–1925) elected as its head. The same year that the patriarch took office, the Bolshevik Revolution swept the Communists into power and Tikhon was arrested. In 1918 Vladimir Lenin (1870–1924) banned the teaching of Christianity to people under age eighteen and made it illegal for churches to own property. A famine in 1921 led to the Communist confiscation of church land and icons. Orthodox clergy who resisted were killed, imprisoned, or sent into exile. The "League of the Militant Godless" was founded in 1925. Jewish, Muslim, Protestant, Roman Catholic, and all other religious believers living in the Union of Soviet Socialist Republics (USSR) suffered severe persecution.

between Republicans and Nationalists, Spanish clergy faced anti-clerical violence on a scale not yet seen in Western Europe, with hundreds of churches destroyed and over 7,000 priests killed. When the Nationalist general Francisco Franco (1892–1975) finally assumed control in 1939, the church was re-established. The close alliance between the Catholic Church and Franco's dictatorial state persisted relatively unchallenged for the next three decades. Under Franco, the minority Protestant churches in Spain were seen as Republican sympathisers and their activities suppressed. By the time of the dictator's death in 1975, Spanish Catholicism had distanced itself somewhat from his regime, following the social justice message of Pope John XXIII (1881–1963)

▲ A unit of Soviet soldiers march with their rifles in Rod Square, Moscow, on the seventieth anniversary of the Russian Revolution in 1987.   Peter Turnley/Getty Images

GEORGI GAPON (1870–1906)

The Orthodox priest Georgi Gapon campaigned for workers' rights and better conditions for Russian peasants. In 1905 he led a procession to appeal to Nicholas II, but the protesters were stopped and attacked. This incident, known as "Bloody Sunday," was a catalyst for the 1905 Revolution. Father Gapon fell out with the Socialist Revolutionary Party and was executed by them in 1906.

ORTHODOX ACCOMMODATION

During the Soviet era, Orthodoxy survived largely due to a series of accommodationist policies. In return for granting varying degrees of assent or allowing government control, the church was able to persist in truncated form, although persecution was never abolished entirely. These compromise measures were controversial within the church and led to much recrimination and mistrust after the Communist era had passed. In the early 1920s the "Living Church" was established with Soviet blessing. This church, which was used to communicate the government's message, was not generally accepted and was considered schismatic by the wider Orthodox body. Tikhon was released from prison in 1923 after agreeing not to oppose Soviet rule. In 1927 Metropolitan Sergius I (1867–1944) reached a compromise with the ruling powers, but the agreement was not popular with the other bishops. In the late 1940s the Orthodox Church welcomed the state-sponsored incorporation of the Uniat Ukrainian Eastern-Rite Catholic churches, and it supported the suppression of Protestantism and Catholicism. At an ecumenical conference held in Moscow in 1948, the Orthodox clergy took the party line, largely opposing rapprochement with Western Protestant, Catholic, and Anglican churches. Often the Moscow patriarchate was forced to hide the extent of the persecution it was suffering.

THE STALINIST PURGE

Persecution of all Christians reached its height under Josef Stalin (1879–1953) and his Great Purge of 1934–1937. Estimates for the total number of people killed in Stalin's regime range between 15 and 20 million. Christians were often a primary target for persecution.

By 1939 state-sponsored anti-religious propaganda, church closings, murder, and mass exile

◀ Josef Stalin, leader of the Soviet Union. Despite a bloody campaign, he failed to eradicate Christianity from Russia.

Wikimedia Commons

ALBANIA

Persecution of Christians was especially strong under the Communist dictatorship of Enver Hoxha (1908–1985). Orthodox clergy were imprisoned and executed in 1949. That year Archbishop Kristofor Kisi (1881–1948) was removed from office, tortured, and incarcerated. He died in prison in 1948. In 1967 Albania was declared an atheist state. All expressions of religion were outlawed, including street and family names derived from Christian tradition. Hundreds of clergy were killed, including Archbishop Damianos of Tirana in 1973. Following the collapse of Communism, the church was officially re-established in 1991. Restoration continues.

SOLIDARITY

The first non-Communist trade union was established in Poland in 1980 under the leadership of the Catholic Lech Wałęsa (1943–). The Solidarity movement was profoundly influenced by Catholic social teaching and received crucial support from Pope John Paul II. In 1984 Jerzy Popieluszko, a Polish priest, was executed for his public association with the movement. The election of Solidarity candidates in 1989 inaugurated peaceful anti-Communist revolutions throughout the Eastern Bloc and led to the collapse of the Soviet Union.

had driven Christianity largely underground. Yet the faith was not eradicated, and when restrictions were relaxed for patriotic reasons in 1941, following the German invasion, thousands of churches were reopened. It is estimated that in the Soviet Union between 1947 and 1957 roughly 90 million babies were baptised, about the same number as before the Revolution in 1917 and more than were baptised in Britain or any other Western European country during the same time.

RETURN OF RELIGIOUS FREEDOM

Between 1959 and 1964 persecution resumed under Nikita Khrushchev (1894–1971), with Baptists and other evangelicals especially targeted. The suppression of Christian activity continued until the appointment of Mikhail Gorbachev (1931–) as Soviet leader in 1985. A new relationship with the state ensued whereby, in recognition of Christianity's service to society, many Orthodox seminaries and monasteries were re-opened, new Protestant churches were built, and, in 1989, the Uniat Eastern-Rite Church was restored in Ukraine. With the collapse of Communism, between 1990 and 1993, laws restricting religious freedom were repealed. Freedom brought to light long-standing grievances, however, with mutual hostility expressed between Catholic and Protestant groups on the one hand and between those groups and the dominant Orthodox Church on the other. Internally, too, there was competition between the Orthodox Moscow hierarchy and those Orthodox groups living abroad who returned to Russia from exile in 1990.

Nazism

Following its defeat in the First World War, Germany had been forced into signing a humiliating and untenable peace with the Treaty of

▲ Hitler receives the salute of the Columns in Adolf Hitler Plats, during the Reichs Party Congress in Nuremburg, Germany, 1 September 1938.

The Art Archive/Shutterstock

Versailles in 1919. The population was in a state of disaffection, paving the way for the rise of Adolf Hitler (1889–1945). Hitler's Nazi party represented the possibility of making Germany strong again and found in the Jews a scapegoat for the country's ills. The racist ideology of Nazism was built on a history of European anti-Semitism. To this long-standing prejudice, Nazism also brought a nationalist, neo-pagan sentiment, celebrating (and largely inventing) the virtues of pre-Christian Norse culture and religion.

German Christians

Against this pagan "German Faith Movement" could be found the "German Christians." Equally nationalistic, this movement attempted to purge Christianity of the notion of original sin and of all Jewish elements, and they saw in Hitler the latest historical development of the law of God. Supported by theologians like Emanuel Hirsch (c. 1886–1954) and led by Ludwig Müller (1883–1945), the German Christians became the dominant group of the established Lutheran Church in 1933.

KARL BARTH (1886–1968)

The Swiss theologian and pastor served in Germany until forced to leave by the Nazi regime in 1935. Early readings of Kierkegaard and Dostoevsky led Barth to break with theological liberalism, inaugurating instead the method of dialectical theology that emphasises the concrete nature of truth as revealed only by Christ, the Word of God. His fourteen volume *Church Dogmatics* has played a leading role in Protestant thought. It has also influenced Roman Catholic theologians including Pope Pius XII (1876–1958), Hans Urs von Balthasar (1905–1988), and Hans Küng (1928–).

BARMEN DECLARATION

Composed largely by Karl Barth and Dietrich Bonhoeffer at the Synod of Barmen in 1934, the declaration sets out the doctrinal foundation of the Confessing Church against Nazism: "We reject the false doctrine, as though the church could and would have to acknowledge as a source of its proclamation, apart from and besides this one Word of God, still other events and powers, figures and truths, as God's revelation."

Confessing Church

The accession of the German Christians galvanised resistance from theologians and pastors in the Lutheran Church. Led by Martin Niemöller (1892–1984) in 1934, the movement began to set up alternative parishes and administrative

DIETRICH BONHOEFFER (1906–1945)

As a pastor, Bonhoeffer played a key role in the creation of the Confessing Church. As a committed opponent of the Nazi regime, he entered into a plot to assassinate Hitler. For this Bonhoeffer was arrested by the Gestapo in 1943 and executed two years later. Bonhoeffer's influential publications include *The Cost of Discipleship* (1937) and the posthumous *Letters and Papers from Prison* (1951).

structures for those "confessional" churches that rejected the nationalist theology of the German Christians. The Confessing Church served as a focal point for Christian resistance, especially before the outbreak of war in 1939. Many Confessing clergy and laity were conscripted into the army or sent to concentration camps; Niemöller himself served time in Sachsenhausen and Dachau between 1937 and 1945.

THE HOLOCAUST

The Nazi programme to purge the German nation from all "undesirables" began in 1941. It led directly to the murder of an estimated 6 million Jews and another 5 or 6 million victims including gays, communists, the physically disabled, black people, Slavs, Roma, and other ethnic populations. Christian groups were not the primary target of the Holocaust; however, Jehovah's Witnesses, Protestant dissidents, Catholic priests, and other citizens who tried to protect others were deported to the concentration camps.

With the end of the Second World War in 1945, the full extent of the horrors of the Holocaust (known in Hebrew as *Shoah*) became known, instituting a long process of internal examination within Christian circles that continues into the present day. "Post-Holocaust theologians" such as Jürgen Moltmann (1926–), who wrote *The Crucified God* (1972), began to reconsider Christian notions of suffering and the nature of God. Recognition of the long history of Christian anti-Semitism has also prompted some groups to repair relations with Judaism through bodies such as the International Council of Christians and Jews, which was founded in 1947. In 1986 Pope John Paul II (1920–2005) attended prayer at a Roman synagogue—the first ever recorded visit of a pope to a Jewish place of worship. In 1997 the Catholic Church in France offered a "Declaration of Repentance" for its silence during the deportation of French Jews to the camps during the Nazi occupation.

Innovation and Tradition

The twentieth century was the bloodiest time in the history of Christianity, but the era also saw spectacular growth. In this era the population base of Christianity definitively shifted from Europe and North America to Latin America, East Asia, and Africa.

African Missions

From 1900 there was a rapid expansion of Christianity throughout the Congo, Nigeria, Buganda (Uganda), South Africa, and elsewhere. Foreign missions continued apace, including outstanding work from the Anglican bishop Alfred Tucker (1849–1914), the Catholic White Father Archbishop Léon Livinhac (1846–1922), and the German Lutheran Dr. Albert Schweitzer (1875–1965), who was awarded the Noble Peace

ANTI-SEMITISM

Jesus, his disciples, and all his earliest followers were Jewish. However, within a century of its founding, the church was populated mostly by gentile, or non-Jewish, believers. By the fourth century, many Christians tended to treat Jews as a condemned race, supposedly rejected by God because of their rejection of Jesus. Jews in the Christian-dominated Roman Empire and throughout Europe faced expulsion, curtailed rights, and sporadic mass violence, including, notably, in 1096 when the Holy Roman Empire saw a wave of anti-Semitic persecution at the hands of the knights of the First Crusade. For centuries Jews were expelled from their home countries across Europe, including England in 1290, Germany in 1350, Spain in 1492, Portugal in 1496, and the Papal States in 1569. Both the Protestant Reformation and the Catholic Counter-Reformation in the sixteenth century gave rise to anti-Jewish sentiment, segregation, and oppressive laws. Ukrainian and Polish Jews were subject to violent pogroms under Eastern Orthodox and Catholic auspices in the seventeenth century. In 1882 the Orthodox Russian Empire passed laws restricting Jews to certain regions and removing them from their farmlands. In 1903 agents working on behalf of the Russian state forged the *Protocols of the Elders of Zion*, a document purporting to expose the Jewish scheme to take over the world. The *Protocols* were demonstrated to be fraudulent; however, they continue to fuel anti-Semitic conspiracy theories in Russia and beyond.

European violence against Jews reached a crescendo under Adolf Hitler and the Nazis in the 1930s until 1945, when approximately 6 million Jews were systematically exterminated. The attempted genocide has come to be known as the Shoah, or the Holocaust. Nazism is not a Christian ideology; however, many Christians actively supported the Nazis, while most were silent in their acquiescence. A minority of Christians opposed the Nazis and supported the Jews, often suffering internment and execution themselves as a result. The conclusion of World War II saw the immigration of large numbers of European and North American Jews to Palestine after the creation of the State of Israel in 1948. In 1965 Pope John XXIII issued the bull *Nostra aetate*, which altered the anti-Jewish elements of the Good Friday Catholic liturgy and universalised the blame of the crucifixion of Christ to all people. Anti-Semitic theology running throughout traditional Lutheran teaching was formally renounced by the Lutheran Church Synod in Missouri in 1983 and by the Evangelical Lutheran Church in America in 1994. In 2000 Pope John Paul II (1920–2005) visited Israel and deposited this prayer into the Western Wall:

We are deeply saddened
by the behaviour of those
who in the course of history
have caused these children of yours to suffer,
and asking your forgiveness
we wish to commit ourselves
to genuine brotherhood
with the people of the Covenant.

JANANI JAKALIYA LUWUM
(1922–1977)

The Ugandan dictator Idi Amin (1925–2003) came to power in 1971. One of the most outspoken opponents of Amin's brutal regime was the Anglican archbishop Luwum. In 1977 he was publicly accused of treason and arrested. Luwum's bullet-ridden body was discovered before he could go to trial, with some witnesses accusing Idi Amin of personally carrying out the execution. Luwum is commemorated as a martyr by the Anglican Church.

◀ Janani Jakaliya Luwum
AP/Shutterstock

▲ African worshippers raise their hands in praise. The explosion of Pentecostal Christianity in Africa represents one of the most successful cultural movements of the modern era worldwide.   AP/Shutterstock

Prize in 1952. The majority of foreign missionaries at this time were American, with conservative evangelical missions established in Nigeria (1904), Chad (1909), Congo (1918), Upper Volta (1921), and the Ivory Coast (1935).

AFRICAN CHRISTIANITY

Twentieth-century African Christianity is characterised by the growth of national churches, an increase in native clergy, and the rise of African prophetic movements. Charismatic preachers and healers such as Garrick Braid (active in Nigeria from 1909), Isaiah Shembe (Zulu church leader in 1911), Sampson Opong (in Ghana from 1920), and Joseph Babalola (in Sierra Leone in 1928) attracted followers independently of the mainstream foreign denominations. William Wade Harris (c. 1860–1929), founder of the indigenous Harrist Church, was celebrated throughout the Ivory Coast and Ghana for his apocalyptic preaching, resistance to colonialism, and flamboyant opposition to local magicians and priests. Simon Kimbangu (c. 1889–1951) faced opposition from Baptists, Catholics, and the Belgian colonial authorities for his healing ministry in Zaire. Kimbanguism, which incorporates elements of non-Christian African spirituality with charismatic Christianity, is thus strongly associated with national independence. One of the largest native African Christian movements, the Kimbangu Church was admitted to the World Council of Churches in 1969.

The Social Gospel

A number of new forms of Christian thought and practice rose to prominence in the twentieth century.

DESMOND TUTU (1931–)

In 1984 the Anglican priest, educator, and campaigner Desmond Tutu was awarded the Nobel Peace Prize for his work against apartheid in his native South Africa. In 1986 he became the first black African archbishop of Cape Town, and in 1994 President Nelson Mandela appointed him chair of the Truth and Reconciliation Commission to help investigate and heal the abuses of thirty-four years of official segregation in South Africa.

▲ Desmond Tutu

Money Sharma/EPA/Shutterstock

KOREA

1919	Korean Protestants are prominent in the movement for independence from Japan.
1950–1953	During the Korean War many Christians are killed in the North. The South sees an increase in Korean Catholic and other Christian aid activity.
1958	Foundation of the Assemblies of God church that will grow into the Yoido Full Gospel Church, boasting the largest single Christian congregation in the world.

▲ Yoido Full Gospel Church

N/Shutterstock

1984	Pope John Paul II canonises ninety-three Korean martyrs. It marks the first canonisation ceremony to take place outside of the Vatican.
1991	Of Koreans who profess a religion, 34% are Protestant, 10.6% Catholic, and 51.2% are Buddhists.

Largely in reaction against the individualistic and quietistic nature of much North American evangelical Christianity, various Protestant theologies with an emphasis on social justice arose in the years before the First World War. The ground-breaking work of British "Christian Socialists" such as F. D. Maurice (1805–1872) and Charles Kingsley (1819–1875) was joined by that of Americans like Washington Gladden (1836–1918) and Walter Rauschenbusch (1861–1918), whose 1917 *Theology for the Social Gospel* became a template for the movement.

Social gospel practitioners came from a variety of denominations; however, they were generally united by a liberal theological emphasis on the natural goodness of mankind and by their critical views of capitalism's ability to create a just society.

Fundamentalism

This multifaceted conservative movement rose to prominence in America in the 1920s. The name derived from *The Fundamentals*, a series of tracts published between 1910 and 1915 designed to defend "fundamental" Christian truths from liberal theology and higher critical biblical research. Early leading figures included Princeton Presbyterian J. G. Machen (1881–1937). Soon, grievances against the political implications of the social gospel and against the teaching of evolution in schools became associated with the fundamentalist cause, especially following the trial of the Tennessee schoolteacher J. T. Scopes in 1925.

Conservative Evangelicalism

By the 1950s, the fundamentalist movement had acquired a reputation for divisiveness, prompting many American evangelicals to seek alternative associations. Led by the likes of Harold John Ockenga (1905–1985) and Carl F. H. Henry (1913–2003), these new evangelicals retained much of the conservative theological and political ethos of fundamentalism but strove to be more cooperative and intellectually respectable. Seminaries and interdenominational colleges such as the Moody Bible Institute in Chicago and Prairie Bible Institute in Three Hills, Canada, became centres for conservative evangelicalism.

The Great Reversal

The evangelicals of the eighteenth and nineteenth centuries were at the forefront of cultural reform and led campaigns for social justice inspired directly by the ethical implications of biblical texts such as the Sermon on the Mount. Yet the new evangelicals of the twentieth century as a rule tended towards political conservatism, shunning the radical social implications of their namesake predecessors. This aversion to liberalism, an overriding concern with personal salvation (being "born again"), and a close association of conservative Christian culture with patriotic American values led to what the English evangelical leader John Stott (1921–2011) and others have called the "Great Reversal" in evangelical social concern. This development within the dominant branch of

---

BILLY GRAHAM (1918–2018)

A Southern Baptist and native of North Carolina in the USA, Billy Graham rose to international prominence for his evangelistic "crusades," stadium campaigns, and televised addresses. More people around the world have heard him than any other Christian preacher.

▶ Billy Graham   Peter Foley/EPA/Shutterstock

Protestant Christianity has had a significant effect worldwide.

Moral Majority

In America, the latent political nature of evangelical Christianity was mobilised to great effect in the 1970s and 1980s. The televangelist Jerry Falwell (1933–2007) established the Moral Majority movement in 1976. Rather than emphasise social justice, the group's aim was to rally American evangelical support for politically conservative causes. The Moral Majority was a key player in the 1980 and 1984 presidential elections of Ronald Reagan. These successes led to a revived "Christian Right," which proved the electoral base for subsequent Republican presidents. Internal divisions and dissatisfaction with the conservative political agenda in the last decades of the twentieth century somewhat fragmented the Christian Right, leading to the rise of prominent centre or left-wing evangelicals such as Rick Warren (1954–), Tony Campolo (1935–), and Jim Wallis (1948–).

MARTIN LUTHER KING JR. (1929–1968)

King was a Baptist minister and theologian in Alabama when he became involved in organising and participating in boycotts in support of Rosa Parks (1913–2005) and in protest against racial segregation in the southern United States. The 1955 protest catapulted King to national prominence and he became known as a leader in the Civil Rights movement. King was famous for his peaceful approach, which included organised civil disobedience, non-resistance to arrest, and principled nonviolence—tactics drawn explicitly from the example set by Jesus in the New Testament. In 1964 King was awarded the Nobel Peace Prize for his nonviolent work fighting racial injustice. There were multiple attempts on his life, and he was assassinated on April 4, 1968. His official birthday in January was recognised by the USA as a national holiday in 1983.

NARNIA

In 1950 Oxford professor C. S. Lewis (1898–1963) published *The Lion, the Witch and the Wardrobe*, a children's novel set in the fantasyland of Narnia. The book and its sequels were intended as an allegorical introduction to Christian themes. They are widely read and have been translated into over thirty languages.

L'ABRI

French for "shelter," the L'Abri fellowship established study centres designed to provide shelter for honest questions. The network primarily serves scholarly minded evangelical students. The first centre was established by the American authors Francis (1912–1984) and Edith (1914–2013) Schaeffer in Switzerland in 1955, and the fellowship has since expanded to the United States, Canada, the United Kingdom, Germany, Brazil, Sweden, the Netherlands, Australia, and South Korea.

Liberation Theology

In the 1960s and 1970s a Roman Catholic theology was developed largely out of the context of political resistance to US and European foreign policy in Latin America and partly as a theological counter to the conservative evangelicalism that was seen as supporting that policy. "Liberation" theologians and activists objected to the exploitation of the poor that was occurring in the name of industrial development and

---

PENTECOSTALISM AND THE CHARISMATIC RENEWAL

The exercise of the "spiritual gifts," or "charismata," has long been a feature of Christian experience, dating back at least as far as the gift of the Holy Spirit to the disciples at Pentecost in Acts 2 and the community addressed by the apostle Paul in 1 Corinthians 12:8–11. The twentieth century saw a renewed interest in incorporating these gifts into regular church life, leading to some of the most controversial and also vibrant Christian traditions in operation today. It is estimated that Pentecostal and charismatic Christians represent a quarter of all Christians worldwide, with perhaps half of that population living in Latin America.

1901   Emergence of Pentecostalism in Topeka, Kansas, under the leadership of Bible school teacher Charles Parham (1873–1929) and his student Agnes Ozman (1870–1937).

1906   African American Pastor William J. Seymour (1870–1922) presides over the Azusa Street Pentecostal revival in Los Angeles, California.

1908   Azusa Street Pentecostal missionaries active in China.

c. 1910   Italian missionaries establish the first Pentecostal congregations in Brazil. The movement quickly spreads throughout South America, rivalling and often exceeding adherents to Roman Catholicism.

1914   Foundation of the Assemblies of God in America, now the largest affiliation of Pentecostal churches worldwide.

1960   Father Dennis Bennett (1917–1991) is instrumental in bringing charismatic renewal to his Episcopal church in California.

1967   Growth in the charismatic movement amongst Roman Catholic university students.

1974   John Wimber (1934–1997) helps to found the Vineyard Church movement with his "Signs and Wonders" teaching at Fuller Theological Seminary.

Cardinal Léon Joseph Suenens (1904–1996), a leading theologian of the Second Vatican Council, endorses charismatic renewal in the Catholic Church.

1990   Holy Trinity Brompton, a charismatic Anglican Church in London, makes its "Introduction to Christianity" course available to other organisations. The "Alpha Course" has been used by Protestants, Roman Catholics, and Orthodox churches, with an estimated 13 million participants worldwide.

1994   Charismatic revival at a Vineyard church in Toronto, Canada is dubbed the "Toronto Blessing," receiving worldwide attention.

Western capitalism. Encouraged by the atmosphere of progressive theology following the Second Vatican Council (1962–1965), two conferences of Latin American Bishops (1968, 1979) and the writings of the Peruvian Dominican priest Gustavo Gutiérrez (1928–)—especially *A Theology of Liberation* (1974)—helped set the parameters of liberation theology. Taking the view that social structures can be inherently violent and oppressive, the movement emphasised that the church should have a "preference for the poor," that individual salvation can come only with social transformation, and that right belief (orthodoxy) can come only from right action (orthopraxis).

Catholicism and Liberation

In 1984 Cardinal Joseph Ratzinger (1927–), future Pope Benedict XVI (2005–2013), led the Sacred Congregation for the Doctrine of Faith

📖 HEALING

The New Testament is clear that a major component of Jesus's ministry involved healing the sick, and he expected his disciples to do likewise. In one way or another, healing activities have been part of church experience ever since: from the foundation of hospitals, mental health asylums, and counselling and nursing organisation to individual care for neighbours' needs and healing through prayer, worship, and the biblical practice of "laying on of hands." Early in his church career, Augustine of Hippo taught that the time of healing miracles had passed; however, as a mature theologian he recanted this view and later became known for his healing ministry, some of which he writes about in *The City of God.* Churches across medieval Europe maintained the healing efficacy of the prayer of saints. The Orthodox Church and Roman Catholic traditions have many holy sites where pilgrims go for healing, such as Ostrog Monastery in Montenegro, and the Sanctuary of Our Lady of Lourdes in France. The "charismatic renewal" movements associated with Catholic, Anglican, and Protestant churches maintain that the healing miracles of the New Testament continue into the modern era. Pentecostalism, the fastest-growing and most widespread global Christian movement in history, emphasises healing prayer, with Pentecostal preachers attracting many followers as well as detractors. Besides the founder of the first Pentecostal church, William J. Seymour (1870–1922), other key men and women with healing ministries include Maria Woodworth-Etter (1844–1924), Smith Wigglesworth (1859–1947), John G. Lake (1870–1935), Aimee Semple McPherson (1890–1944, founder of the Foursquare Gospel Church), Kathryn Kuhlman (1907–1976), and Randy Clark (1952–), whose healing meetings are accompanied by reports of the miraculous disappearance of metal plates and medical pins in people's bodies as well as the appearance of gold teeth and fillings where before there were none. The methods, practice, and expectation of healing are matters for investigation and controversy; however, all the major denominations have space for healing in their liturgies, and many different traditions agree that the Christian work of healing did not cease with the church of the first apostles.

THE TROUBLES

Also known as the Northern Ireland Conflict, "the Troubles" describes the era of low-level war, terrorist attacks, and skirmishes from the late 1960s. The conflicts had deep historic roots, tracing back to 1609 and the government-backed immigration of Scottish and English Protestant settlers to Ireland, displacing the native Irish Roman Catholic population. Despite the denominational affiliation of many of the participants, the Troubles of the twentieth century are largely understood to be nationalist and sectarian in nature: the fighting was not over theological differences. The locus of the struggle revolved around Loyalists who wanted Northern Ireland to remain part of the United Kingdom, and Republicans who agitated for a united Ireland independent of British rule. More than 3,500 people were killed in the fighting until the Good Friday Agreement, brokered in 1998.

in an examination of liberation theology. The findings endorsed the preference for the poor but objected to the Marxist critique that most liberation theologians used to analyse society. In 1986 the Congregation issued the slightly more favourable *Libertatis Conscientia*, and the following year Pope John Paul II publicly adopted liberation language when addressing concerns for social justice.

▲ Ecumenical Orthodox Patriarch Bartholomew I and Pope Benedict XVI wave from a balcony of the Patriarchate in Istanbul, Turkey, 2006.   Orestis PEPAgiotou/EPA/Shutterstock

CATHOLIC DOCTRINE

1962–1965 Second Vatican Council. Established by Pope John XXIII, this was in many ways a modernising council. Major effects include the proscription of the use of vernacular, rather than Latin, in the liturgy of the Mass; a thawing of relations with Protestants and Orthodox; and a renewed emphasis on issues of peace and justice, especially in the Majority World. Vatican II has continued to cause controversy between "traditionalist" and "progressive" parties within the church.

1965 Pope Paul VI (1897–1978) and Ecumenical Patriarch Athenagoras (1886–1972) agree to retract the mutual excommunications of the Great Schism of 1045.

1968 *Humanae Vitae* reaffirms Catholic opposition to birth control.

1970 Pope Paul VI reaffirms clerical celibacy as the requirement and law of the Catholic Church.

ORDINATION OF WOMEN

Catholic and Orthodox churches do not ordain women, nor do many Protestant denominations. In the twentieth century a number of Anglican and mainstream Protestant churches accepted women as priests and bishops.

1944 Florence Li Tim-Oi (1907–1992) of Hong Kong becomes the first woman Anglican priest.

1956 In the US, the Methodists and Presbyterians ordain their first women ministers.

1977 The General Convention of the American Episcopal Church authorises the ordination of women into the priesthood.

1989 Barbara Clementine Harris (1930–) becomes the first female Suffragen Bishop in Massachusetts. Penelope Jamieson (1942–) is elected Bishop of Dunedin in New Zealand.

1994 The Anglican Church of England begins training women for ministry. By 2007 there are more women than men preparing for ordination.

HOMOSEXUALITY

The Orthodox churches, the Roman Catholic Church, and most evangelical and Pentecostal denominations do not allow for the ordination of practicing homosexual clergy or sanction the blessing of same-sex partnerships. In the twentieth century a number of Protestant churches have opened the way for full inclusion of gays and lesbians, including the United Church of Canada; the Lutheran Churches in America, Germany, and Scandinavia; and many Presbyterian congregations. Within the Anglican Communion, the Church of Canada (in 2002) and the American Episcopal Church (in 2003) have gone ahead with ordination and same-sex blessing, contravening the Lambeth Resolution of 1998, which reaffirmed homosexual practice as incompatible with Scripture. The issue, which takes in matters of healing, discipleship, politics, biblical authority and interpretation, the role of tradition, and matters of church obedience, has led to deep internal divisions. It looks set to dominate the agenda of the Christian church in the twenty-first century.

South American Struggle

Nonetheless, liberation theology has not been endorsed by Rome, with some priests forced to leave the clergy, such as the Brazilian Leonardo Boff (1938–) in 1992. The willingness of some South American priests to engage in armed struggle and support revolutionary parties has not helped their cause within the church. Liberation communities in Brazil and El Salvador engage in political agitation and endorse political parties. The poet and priest Ernesto Cardenal (1925–) actively supported the Sandinista guerrillas, joining the revolution that overthrew the dictator government in 1979. Another priest, Camilo Torres Restropo (1929–1966), was killed by the Colombian government when fighting for the National Liberation Army.

The Ecumenical Movement

A noteworthy development in the history of Christianity is the rise and reach of the

OSCAR ARNULFO ROMERO (1917–1980)

Originally appointed archbishop of San Salvador in 1977 on the strength of his opposition to liberation theology, Romero eventually changed his mind in the face of the corrupt dictatorship ruling El Salvador. He attracted severe opposition from the government and was assassinated while celebrating Mass in 1980.

MOTHER TERESA (1910–1997)

An Albanian Catholic nun and admirer of Francis of Assisi, Teresa founded the Missionaries of Charity in Calcutta, India, in 1950. Her work with the orphaned and dying drew international attention (she was awarded the Nobel Peace Prize in 1979) and inspired a number of similar initiatives throughout India and other countries.

▲ Mother Teresa   David Hartley/Shutterstock

worldwide ecumenical movement in the twentieth century. The ecumenists strove for the unity of all Christians everywhere, regardless of denomination, tradition, or variation of creed. Inspired by the interdenominational evangelical revivals of the eighteenth and nineteenth centuries, the modern movement began in 1910 with the World Missionary Conference in Edinburgh, Scotland. In 1920 the patriarchate of Constantinople issued the first of *The Encyclical Letters by the Patriarchate of Constantinople on Christian Unity and the "Ecumenical Movement"* (completed in 1952). The major statement of doctrine urged full participation in forging closer links with separated Christians. It was not fully accepted by all the autocephalous churches, including Russian Orthodoxy. These bodies were thus absent from the first World Conference on Faith and Order in Lausanne, Switzerland, in 1927.

Worldwide . . .

The World Council of Churches (comprising 147 members) formed in 1948 under the leadership of Dutchman W. A. Visser 't Hooft (1900–1985). The Russians joined with most of the other Orthodox churches in 1961. Following a visit from the Anglican archbishop Geoffrey Fisher (1887–1972) to Pope John XXIII in 1960 (the first such visit since 1397) the Vatican also sent official observers to the Council in 1961, although the Roman Catholic Church has not become a full member. By 1993 there were 322 participating churches of all denominations working together on matters of mission, social justice, and worship.

. . . and Beyond

Two thousand years after its inception as a radical, persecuted sect, Christianity is now a truly

LAUSANNE CONGRESSES ON WORLD EVANGELISATION

In 1974 the American preacher Billy Graham (1918–2018) expressed his desire to "unite all evangelicals in the common task of the total evangelisation of the world." The result was the gathering together of over 2,400 men and women church leaders and missionaries from 150 countries in Lausanne, Switzerland, for the First International Congress on World Evangelisation. The event, chaired by British theologian John Stott (1921–2011), focused on mission to "unreached people groups" and on the need for mission to engage in social justice. This latter point was especially resisted by American evangelicals wary of the "social gospel" associated with theological liberalism and politics that were critical of capitalism. In a follow-up meeting, Stott confronted Graham over this resistance, arguing from the New Testament that missionaries were to care for people's bodies as well as their souls. The result was the Lausanne Covenant and an endorsement of holistic mission that integrates evangelism with social justice.

▲ The Sunday night closing session of The Third Lausanne Congress on World Evangelization at Cape Town 2010

Third Lausanne Congress on World Evangelization in Cape Town, 2010. www.lausanne.org

▼ Billy Graham and others at the First International Congress on World Evangelisation, 1974

international phenomenon, the most populous religion in the world with a wider variation of expressions than any other belief system on the earth. Indeed, it has spread beyond the earth. The first extra-planetary food and drink ever consumed occurred on July 20, 1969, when astronaut Edwin "Buzz" Aldrin (1930–) celebrated Communion on the surface of the moon. While it will never be possible to tell the whole story of Christianity in all its detail, it is without a doubt true to say that the obstinate atheists who so troubled the governors of a past empire have come a long way.

▲ A view of Earth from space   PhotoDisc

GLOSSARY

Anabapism: from the Greek *anabaptizein* (to baptise again). Various strands of radical sixteenth c. Reformers rejected infant baptism in favour of the baptism of adults. These Europeans would have been baptised as babies but were now making a conscious profession of faith. Anabaptist groups tended towards pacifism and the strict separation of church and state. The Anabaptist tradition continues to the present day.

anchorite: a person who takes vows in order to triumph over temptations and pursue a life of contemplation and prayer. Anchorites may be solitary hermits or live in organised monasteries. They typically live in confined, uncomfortable quarters, and practice rigorous discipline. The most famous example was Simeon the Stylite, who lived atop a pillar until his death in 459.

Antichrist: the adversary of Christ and the prince of his enemies. Historically, various Christian groups have denounced opposing rulers and religious leaders as the antichrist. Some traditions identify the name with a principle of evil rather than with a specific person. In the Bible the word only appears in 1 and 2 John in singular and plural forms. The antichrist is also usually identified with the description in 2 Thessalonians 2 and several symbolic characters in the book of Revelation.

Antipope: a person set up as Pope in opposition to the person currently elected to the see or held to be in lawful possession of the office.

apocalyptism: from the Greek *apokalypto* (to reveal). The belief in the future destruction of the world, or at least the present world order. It looks forward to the foundation of a new Heaven and a new Earth and God's triumph over evil. The *Apocalypse* is the name given to the last book in the Bible, also called the book of Revelation.

Apocrypha: early religious writings not included in the canon of Scripture. Roman Catholic and Orthodox Bibles contain Hebrew books not accepted by Protestants as part of the Old Testament canon. The term also applies to early Christian works of doubtful authenticity and theology that were not accepted for inclusion in the New Testament.

apostasy: the abandonment of Christianity, usually public and usually in the face of persecution.

autocephalous: the term usually refers to those Orthodox Churches governed by their own national synods. They are in communion with other Orthodox Churches but are not under the superior authority of another Patriarch or Metropolitan.

baptism: the application of water to the head, or full immersion of the body. The ceremony is a sacrament representing the purification of sin and entry into the community of Christians.

basilica: an early form of church modelled after Roman architecture. The title is now reserved for churches of ceremonial, historical or privileged importance.

bishop: a chief or senior member of the clergy who oversees several congregations in a diocese or bishopric. Some Christian traditions do not have bishops. For Roman Catholicism, Anglicanism, and Orthodoxy, cardinals, archbishops, popes, patriarchs, and metropolitans are all gradations of the office.

bishopric: see: *diocese*

bull: a papal bull is an official document issued by the Pope, relating to matters of high importance to the Church and wider society.

canon: an official list of rules, saints, or Biblical books considered authentic and standard. Within Roman Catholicism and Anglicanism, a Canon is also a senior priest in a church or parish.

cardinal: high ranking Catholic clergy of parishes in Rome who administer the Church and are the Pope's immediate counsellors. The right of electing a new Pope is exclusive to them.

catechumens: people receiving instruction in the principles of the Christian faith with a view to baptism. In the era of Early Christianity, the programme of catechesis could take a number of years.

charismatic: from the Greek *charisma* (gift of Divine grace). The term generally refers to that which in Christianity has to do with gifts given by God to individuals for the good of the Church, such as described in 1 Corinthians 7 and 12. The term has come to describe those Christian movements that emphasize works of the Holy Spirit and the personal religious experience of healing, prophecy, and speaking in tongues.

Christology: that aspect of theology which deals specifically with the work and person of Jesus Christ. It is often associated with Trinitarian formulations and tracing the implications of the Lordship of Jesus for Christian life and thought.

church fathers: the earliest Christian theologians from the second to seventh centuries whose writings were foundational for church doctrine.

coenobite: a member of a religious community who has taken vows. As opposed to hermits who live alone, coenobites may undertake to live in silence or poverty in common with others.

Communion of both kinds: the reception of both bread and wine during the Eucharist. Historically, various church traditions have sometimes reserved one of the elements for the clergy, and given only bread or wine to the congregation.

concordat: a formal agreement between the Pope and the government relating to the regulation and organisation of the Church in a particular State.

curate: from the Latin *cura* (care) the term refers to the member of the clergy who is charged with the care of the people in the parish. In the Anglican Church, the Curate is a junior or assistant priest.

deacon: from the Greek *diakonos* (servant). A deacon is an official in the church. The exact role changes depending on the Christian tradition in which the deacon serves. Some deacons are ordained members of the clergy, while other denominations reserve the title for members of the lay public who assist the leadership and serve the wider community on behalf of the church.

deism: from the Latin *deus* (God), deism is a movement of thought that has its roots in eighteenth-century Rationalism opposed to Christianity. Deists affirm the existence of a supreme being who created the universe, but they deny any personal dimension, supernatural intervention, or divine revelation to this being. Many Enlightenment philosophers were deist, as were key leaders in the French Revolution and most of the American Founding Fathers.

Dialectical Theology: A mode of theology set against both liberal optimism and conservative dogmatism. It emphasises the limits of what humans can know about God by stressing the transcendence of the Divine, our need for revelation, and the inherent tensions and paradoxes of existence. Key figures include Søren Kierkegaard and Karl Barth.

diaspora: the term usually refers to Jewish communities living outside the Holy Land. The label also applies to large populations of other peoples exiled from their traditional homelands.

diocese: from the Greek *dioikēsis* (administration) the term refers to the geographical district or network of churches under the jurisdiction of a bishop.

dissentors: Christian groups and denominations who separate themselves from the Established Church.

docetism: from the Greek *dokeō* (to seem), this is the view that Jesus only appeared to be human. Docetists denied the importance of the body and the doctrine of the Incarnation. As a 'pure spirit,' Jesus had no physical form and thus only seemed to suffer and die. It was condemned as a Gnostic heresy by the early Church Fathers, however the ideas persisted until the medieval era of the Albigensians.

doctors of the church: in Roman Catholicism, the Pope can bestow the title to theologians of outstanding merit, proven historical influence and saintly lives. By 2009, there were thirty-three men and women on the list.

doctrine: a belief or set of beliefs that are considered authoritative by a group or tradition. Within Christianity, doctrines are those fundamental tenets that form the essential body of Christian dogma.

dogma: from the Greek *dokein* (to think). Statements and ideas that are to be accepted or obeyed by all Christians. The Early Christian era designated as revealed truth the teachings of Christ and his apostles. Later traditions expanded the role of the Church in defining and interpreting dogma, however, the distinction is always preserved between the teaching of Christ and the teaching of others.

ecumenical patriarch: the Patriarch of Constantinople and the highest official of the Orthodox Church.

encyclical: originally a circular letter sent to multiple recipients, the term now refers to official Papal documents. Unlike Papal Bulls, which have a general audience, encyclicals are addressed to bishops and archbishops of the Roman Catholic Church.

end times: see: *apocalyptism* and *eschatology*

eschatology: from the Greek *eschatos* (last). This aspect of theology addresses the nature and destiny of creation and the implications of the Kingdom of God preached by Jesus. It considers the matter of death, resurrection, immortality, Divine judgment and salvation, and the future state of the world. It is related to Apocalytism but not synonymous with it.

established church: any church tradition that is recognised as the official church of the state, or given the status of a national institution. There are a variety of State–Church settlements.

ethnarch: the ruler of an ethnic group or kingdom. The Muslim Ottoman Empire established ethnarchs over the minority religious national communities (called *millets*) living under its influence.

Eucharist: from the Greek *eukharistiā* (thanksgiving). The central act of Christian worship. Also called Holy Communion, the Lord's Supper, the Blessed Sacrament, the Divine Liturgy, or Mass according to tradition. The rite celebrates the Last Supper of Jesus with his disciples (Mark 14 and parallels) and is one of Christianity's earliest institutions (see 1 Corinthians 11). The taking of bread and wine in commemoration of Jesus giving his body and blood has been a source of much controversy as to the exact nature of the elements and their meaning. For Orthodoxy and Roman Catholicism, at the point of consecration the bread and wine undergoes a metaphysical transformation (*transubstantion*) and becomes the body and blood of Jesus Christ. For many Anglicans and Lutherans, the event instead signifies the *real* or *spiritual presence* of Jesus with the communicants. Other Protestant groups see it as a memorial event with only symbolic significance. All Christian traditions regard the Eucharist as an important event in the communal life of the Church.

excommunication: the formal exclusion of a person from the communion of the Church. A person so excluded cannot lawfully administer or receive the Eucharist, and any action they carry out on behalf of the Church is rendered invalid.

filioque: a Latin word meaning *from the Son*, the phrase designates the dogmatic Trinitarian formula whereby the Holy Spirit proceeds from both the Father and the Son. It was inserted into the Nicene Creed by the Western Church without consultation with the East and remains a central point of contention between the traditions.

Gallicansim: the term refers to the doctrines and practices of church and court that claimed certain privileges and freedoms for the French Church in relation to Roman authority. The movement has its intellectual roots in the teaching at the University of Sorbonne in the thirteenth century.

Gnosticism: from the Greek *gnosis* (knowledge). The term does not refer to a specific religion or system, but rather to the family of heretical beliefs emanating from pre-Christian pagan, Jewish, and early Christian sects that placed a high value on obtaining secret knowledge about creation and the spiritual realm. Gnostics looked to the release of the pure soul from the prison of physical matter and usually claimed that the world was created by a demon (or *Demiurge*) who should be distinguished from the true God. Gnostics denied the bodily incarnation, crucifixion and resurrection of Jesus Christ. Many of the apocryphal books rejected from the New Testament canon such as the *Gospel of Thomas* and the *Gospel of Mary Magdalene* were Gnostic in origin.

heresy: the formal denial and maintained opposition to any defined doctrine of the Christian faith.

homoousion: a Greek technical phrase meaning 'of one substance.' First used at the Council of Nicaea (325) in order to describe the relation of the Son to the Father. This Trinitarian formulation was deliberately intended to exclude the followers of Arius.

icons: flat pictures, usually painted on wood and often incorporating gold leaf or other precious material. The images represent Saints, the Blessed Virgin Mary, or the Lord Jesus Christ and they play a central part in the public and private devotion of many Christians, especially in the Orthodox traditions.

Immaculate Conception of the Virgin Mary: In Roman Catholicism the dogma that from the first moment of conception, Mary the mother of Jesus was kept free from Original Sin.

incarnation: the Christian doctrine that in the person of Jesus Christ, the Divine took on human flesh. Christ is both fully God and fully man. The doctrine was formally defined at the Council of Chalcedon in 451 but its roots trace back to the earliest Christian beliefs about Jesus, such as found in Galatians 4, Matthew 11 and John 1.

indulgences: the traditional practice of remitting the penalty for sins by drawing on the merits of Christ and the saints. In the Middle Ages this took the form of granting indulgences to those who took part in crusades, or selling certificates of remission issued by the Church.

Lay investiture: the practice of a King (or other non-ordained ruler) appointing Bishops and other key Church officials, granting them the symbols of their authority and sponsoring their time in office.

liturgy: in the Orthodox Church, the Liturgy primarily refers to the rite of the Eucharist. More generally within the Christian traditions, liturgies are prescribed forms of public worship in contrast with private and informal practices.

mass: see: *Eucharist*

Mennonites: originally followers of the Dutch Anabaptist Reformer Menno Simons, the movement is known for its non-violence and simplicity of life.

metropolitan: in Orthodoxy, this is the title for the bishop who exercises provincial jurisdiction, enjoying a rank just below the Patriarch. In Roman Catholicism the Metropolitan is the bishop with provincial powers who oversees suffragan (or assistant) bishops.

millets: see: *ethnarch*

mysticism: the practice of seeking immediate knowledge of the Divine through personal meditation, religious experiences, and spiritual disciplines such as fasting and asceticism.

nonconformists: British Protestant dissenters who refused to conform to the doctrines and authority of the established Church of England.

ordinand: a person who is preparing for admittance into the ministry of the church as a priest or minister.

original sin: in Christian theology the phrase describes the state of corruption or tendency towards evil innate in all people, a state inherited as a consequence of the sinfulness of the first humans. The idea is articulated by the Apostle Paul in Romans 5 and was accepted in some form by most of the early Church fathers. Later key figures in the formulation of the doctrine include Augustine of Hippo.

parish: subdivision of a diocese. A geographical area under the care of a priest or minister.

parousia: from the Greek *parousiā* ('presence' or 'arrival'). The eschatological doctrine of the return, or second coming, of Christ to judge the living and the dead and to inaugurate a new age.

paschal: from the Hebrew *Pesach* (Passover). The word is used to describe anything to do with the Christian celebration of Easter. Christ is often referred to as the Paschal Lamb in reference to the lamb sacrificed during the Jewish Passover.

patriarch: the title given to the bishops of the five main sees of early Christendom: Alexandria, Antioch, Jerusalem, Rome, and Constantinople. More recently, it is also given to the head of the autocephalous Orthodox Churches.

penance: a sacrament of the Orthodox, Roman Catholic, and some other Churches. A formal system of confession, repentance and reparation for sins committed, usually administered by a religious authority. In the Middle Ages, acts of public penance were occasionally demanded of Kings and rulers who had been excommunicated by the Pope.

pope: from the Latin *papa* and the Greek *pappās*' (Father), in the west the title is now reserved exclusively for the Bishop of Rome, the leader of the Roman Catholic Church. The Orthodox and Coptic Churches use the title for the Patriarch of Alexandria. During the early years of the church it referred to any bishop.

presbyter: the earliest organisation of church leadership was that of a board of presbyters, or elders (see Acts 14). Early Church Presbyters oversaw the teaching and administration of local congregations, ranking below bishops. Later traditions retained the office as a senior minister. *Presbyterianism* describes those denominational structures that have no bishops or appointed leaders, but instead are governed by elders popularly elected to their posts.

purgatory: in Roman Catholic teaching, the souls of people who have died in a state of grace yet who still have need of further purification enter a condition or time of spiritual purging before attaining the final state of blessedness. Prayers for the dead can aid the soul's purification, as can indulgences and acts of penance carried out by the living. Orthodoxy holds to prayers for the dead and a time of purification but is less explicit about the details of purgatory. The doctrine was a main target of the Reformer's attack and is rejected by all Protestant traditions.

quietism: any religious or political philosophy that emphasises passivity and non-resistance to government aggression, or more generally encourages withdrawal from social engagement.

rapture: the literal transportation (or rapture) of believers into heaven at the Second Coming of Christ. Variations of the belief are prevalent amongst some Protestant groups. The idea mainly derives from eighteenth c. Puritan theology and there is no early church tradition of the doctrine. Many Protestant denominations, and the Anglican, Roman Catholic, and Orthodox Churches do not accept it.

sacraments: Christian rites believed to be a means or a visible form of grace. The Orthodox, Roman Catholic and some Protestant Churches hold to the seven rites of Baptism, Confirmation, Eucharist, Penance, Anointing the Sick, Ordination, and Marriage. Anglicanism distinguishes Baptism and Eucharist (which were ordained by Jesus) from the other five. Other Protestant traditions hold only to Baptism and Communion.

second coming: see: *parousia*

schism: the serious and formal breach of union within one Church tradition.

see: the official seat of residence of a bishop.

simony: the purchase or sale of spiritual things. The term especially applies to the practice of paying to be ordained or to attain a position in the Church. The word derives from the story of Simon Magus in Acts 8.

syncretism: the combining of two different religious systems. The practice of presenting Christianity using the rites and concepts of other religions became especially controversial following Roman Catholic missions to Southeast Asia in the sixteenth and seventeenth centuries.

theocracy: 'Government by God.' Politically, the term refers to governments that directly regulate civil laws according to religious principles. A Christian theocracy was attempted in Calvin's Geneva in the sixteenth century.

tonsure: the shaving of all or part of the head as a mark of religious observance and renunciation of worldly values. Traditionally it was practiced by all Roman Catholic monks and clerics. Some modern Catholic orders retain variations of the practice, as do Orthodox clerics.

traditors: the name given to North African Christians who surrendered their Scriptures during the persecution of Emperor Diocletian at the beginning of the fourth century.

transubstantiation: see: *eucharist*

trial by ordeal: a method of determining a person's guilt or innocence by requiring the accused to undertake painful or dangerous tasks. If the person escaped harm or death this was usually taken as Divine proof of their innocence. The technique was often employed against women accused of witchcraft.

vicar: from the Latin *vicarious* ('substitute' or 'representative'). In the Anglican tradition the priest of a parish church is often called a vicar. In Roman Catholicism, vicars are high-ranking priests who act for another priest. Vicar Generals are officials who represent a bishop.

Kierkegaard

Stephen Backhouse

Discover a new understanding of Kierkegaard's thought and his life, a story filled with romance, betrayal, humor, and riots.

Kierkegaard, like Einstein and Freud, is one of those geniuses whose ideas permeate the culture and shape our world even when relatively few people have read their works. That lack of familiarity with the real Kierkegaard is about to change.

This lucid new biography by scholar Stephen Backhouse presents the genius as well as the acutely sensitive man behind the brilliant books. Scholarly and accessible, *Kierkegaard: A Single Life* introduces his many guises—the thinker, the lover, the recluse, the writer, the controversialist—in prose so compelling it reads like a novel.

One chapter examines Kierkegaard's influence on our greatest cultural icons—Kafka, Barth, Bonhoeffer, Camus, and Martin Luther King Jr., to name only a few. A useful appendix presents an overview of each of Kierkegaard's works, for the scholar and lay reader alike.

Kierkegaard: A DVD Study

Stephen Backhouse

Gain a new understanding of Kierkegaard's thought and life, a story filled with romance, betrayal, humor, and riots, in *Kierkegaard: A DVD Study* and the accompanying book, *Kierkegaard: A Single Life*.

Søren Kierkegaard indeed lived an extraordinary life. He never saw the fruits of his work in his life —it would be almost one hundred years after his death that others would unleash his words onto the wider world. Yet the Danish philosopher, theologian, social critic, and writer is now widely recognized as one of the world's most profound writers and thinkers, and his influence on philosophy, literature, and on secular and religious life and thought is incalculable. Philosophers and theologians influenced by Kierkegaard include Karl Barth, Emil Brunner, Albert Camus, Jean-Paul Sartre, Thomas Merton, Dietrich Bonhoeffer, Kafka, Martin Luther King Jr., and numerous others.

In these video lectures, author and professor Stephen Backhouse highlights the interesting and controversial aspects of Kierkegaard's life, recounting a story that few today know, and provides brief, straightforward overviews of his key works.

Zondervan Essential Atlas of the Bible

Carl G. Rasmussen

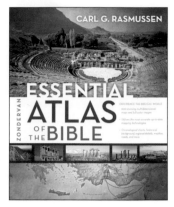

Discover everything you need to know about the lands where Jesus walked, Moses traveled, and Paul preached. Packed with multidimensional maps, photos, and charts, the *Zondervan Essential Atlas of the Bible* is designed to help you better understand the history and places of the Bible and its world. This full-color atlas is concise but thorough, perfect for Bible students, travelers to the Holy Land, or any reader of the Bible curious to find out more about commonly mentioned places in the Old and New Testaments.

The *Zondervan Essential Atlas of the Bible* features:

- Nearly 200 stunning multidimensional and three-dimensional maps and full-color images
- Accurate and up-to-date mapping technologies
- Innovative chronological charts and maps covering historical backgrounds, regions, weather, and roads

With this easy-to-understand atlas, you'll find Bible study more engaging and comprehensible, and you'll learn the essential facts about the fascinating lands of the Bible.

The Essential Bible Companion

John H. Walton, Mark L. Strauss, Ted Cooper Jr.

The Essential Bible Companion gives you what it promises: the essentials. The most vital, absolutely indispensable information you need for reading and understanding God's Word. This unique, easy-to-use reference guide gives you clear, crisp insights into the Bible book by book. From Genesis to Revelation, each book of the Bible has its key details laid out for you clearly and engagingly in a colorful two-page spread that includes:

- Background information
- Timelines
- Important biblical characters

Striking a balance between too little and too much information—between the brief introductions provided in a Bible and the potentially overwhelming detail of a standard reference handbook—this well-designed, extremely helpful volume condenses the most important information into a highly visual, easy-to-understand format.